A GIFT FOR

....

FROM

....

DATE

....

T0274059

TRUSTING
GOD
with Today

CHARLES F.
STANLEY

THOMAS NELSON
Since 1798

Published in Nashville, Tennessee, by Thomas Nelson. Thomas Nelson is a registered trademark of HarperCollins Christian Publishing, Inc.

Thomas Nelson titles may be purchased in bulk for educational, business, fund-raising, or sales promotional use. For information, please email SpecialMarkets@ThomasNelson.com.

Unless otherwise noted, Scripture quotations are from the New American Standard Bible® (NASB). Copyright © 1960, 1962, 1963, 1968, 1971, 1972, 1973, 1975, 1977, 1995 by The Lockman Foundation. Used by permission. www.Lockman.org

Scripture quotations marked csb are from the Christian Standard Bible®. Copyright © 2017 by Holman Bible Publishers. Used by permission. Christian Standard Bible® and CSB® are federally registered trademarks of Holman Bible Publishers.

Scripture quotations marked esv are from the ESV® Bible (The Holy Bible, English Standard Version®). Copyright © 2001 by Crossway, a publishing ministry of Good News Publishers. Used by permission. All rights reserved.

Scripture quotations marked gnt are from the Good News Translation in Today's English Version—Second Edition. Copyright © 1992 by American Bible Society. Used by permission.

Scripture quotations marked niv are from the Holy Bible, New International Version®, NIV®. Copyright © 1973, 1978, 1984, 2011 by Biblica, Inc.® Used by permission of Zondervan. All rights reserved worldwide. www.zondervan.com. The "NIV" and "New International Version" are trademarks registered in the United States Patent and Trademark Office by Biblica, Inc.®

Scripture quotations marked nkjv are from the New King James Version®. Copyright © 1982 by Thomas Nelson. Used by permission. All rights reserved.

Scripture quotations marked nlt are from the Holy Bible, New Living Translation. Copyright © 1996, 2004, 2015 by Tyndale House Foundation. Used by permission of Tyndale House Ministries, Carol Stream, Illinois 60188. All rights reserved.

Scripture quotations marked tlb are from The Living Bible. Copyright © 1971. Used by permission of Tyndale House Publishers, a Division of Tyndale House Ministries, Carol Stream, Illinois 60188. All rights reserved.

Any internet addresses, phone numbers, or company or product information printed in this book are offered as a resource and are not intended in any way to be or to imply an endorsement by Thomas Nelson, nor does Thomas Nelson vouch for the existence, content, or services of these sites, phone numbers, companies, or products beyond the life of this book.

The quote from Augustine on the January 16 entry is from Augustine, *The Confessions of Augustine*, ed. John Gibb and William Montgomery (Cambridge: Cambridge University Press, 1908), 2.

ISBN 978-1-4002-3790-6 (HC)
ISBN 978-1-4002-3802-6 (audiobook)
ISBN 978-1-4002-3800-2 (eBook)

Printed in India

24 25 26 27 28 REP 10 9 8 7 6 5

TRUSTING
GOD
with Today

JANUARY

Not Knowing in the Going

*By faith Abraham, when he was called, obeyed by
going out . . . not knowing where he was going.*

HEBREWS 11:8

The beginning of a new year is like the start of a journey to an unfamiliar land. We may think we know some of the details about where we are headed, but how it will all turn out is shrouded in mystery. Abraham had such an excursion when God called him out of his home country to go to the land of promise. There were numerous unknowns for Abraham, including where he was going, how he would provide food and water for his family and flocks, how God would fulfill the promises, and what difficulties would arise.

You may feel as if your life has just as many uncertainties as Abraham's. You may have so many hopes, burdens, or challenges that your mind reels with questions. Remember, in all those unknowns, the Lord continually teaches you to rely on Him, just as He did His faithful servant. And just as He was with Abraham, He will be with you and work in completely unexpected ways. Your challenge is to let go of control, trust God today, and allow Him to lead step-by-step.

*Jesus, this year belongs to You. Help me to know You and
trust You more every day. Amen.*

Trust His Plan

*In Your book were all written the days
that were ordained for me, when as
yet there was not one of them.*

PSALM 139:16

B efore you were ever born, God already had a plan for your life. He saw you—the real you, fearfully and wonderfully made, with all the traits and imperfections that make you a unique creation. Of course, there may be things about how God created you that you wish were different. But you do not have to understand everything that the Lord has said; you must simply believe that when He says He has a plan for you, He does.

You may trust that fact *in part*, but you may also have doubts because of what has occurred in your past—times when you messed up or when the Lord acted in a manner that you didn't expect. Remember, Jesus always brings redemption. Not only does He forgive you when you repent of your sins, but He also redeems the difficulties of your life and brings good from them.

Christ created you for a purpose—one that He brings about as you obey Him. Trust how He leads you. Let Him guide your life because He assuredly has the best plan.

Jesus, I do not understand all You're doing, but I will trust You. Thank You for Your awesome plan. Amen.

Who Is Guiding You?

"I am the way, and the truth, and the life."

JOHN 14:6

W ho is guiding your life? Consider that question and be honest with yourself. You may think, *I'm a Christian, so I guess Jesus is.* But perhaps you know that is not necessarily true. Just because you've been saved doesn't mean Christ is directing your life. Indeed, there are many things that may be driving you. The need for acceptance, control, worth, respect, possessions, security, tradition, and even survival can shape how you respond to situations. So it is essential for you to recognize if one of those internal needs is compelling you, because they can never get you to where you really long to go.

You either let the Lord Jesus guide you, or you're going in the wrong direction. Allowing Christ to lead is a deliberate decision you must make for yourself—you must *choose* to submit to His instruction, even when it appears contrary to human reason. But following Jesus is *always* the right choice. He is the One who consistently leads you in the best way possible, in this life and in view of the life to come.

Jesus, I want You to lead. Search me and reveal what needs and attitudes control me, then teach me how to follow You wholeheartedly. Amen.

The Path Out

Even though I walk through the valley of the shadow of death, I fear no evil, for You are with me.

PSALM 23:4

Tumultuous times in your life can cause a great deal of anxiety and disheartenment. Your mind may struggle to make sense of it all, and you may even overthink the issues until you're utterly obsessed and confounded by them. Perhaps you are constantly praying—but your supplications are characterized by dread rather than with faith that God is at work through all of it. Maybe you've become so overwhelmed with fear that you no longer trust the One who is truly in control of all things.

God makes many wonderful promises throughout Scripture, but in none of them does He guarantee life will be easy. What He does say, however, is if you will "in all your ways acknowledge Him . . . He will make your paths straight" (Proverbs 3:6). So what you have to decide is what you want life to be. Do you want to remain in the fearful mire? Or will you choose to embrace the hope of what God can do in and through your life by obeying Him? The choice is yours. Follow Jesus out of the valley.

Jesus, I choose to believe and follow You. Thank You for being with me and giving me hope. Amen.

Overcoming Hurdles

I have directed you in the way of wisdom. . . .
When you walk, your steps will not be impeded.

PROVERBS 4:11–12

H ave you ever considered that God has allowed the obstacles in your life for a purpose? This is not to imply that the Lord has *caused* trouble for you or has set you up to fail. Rather, He *permits* hurdles on your path as an opportunity for you to trust Him more. He wants you to see that He has the full picture, and He will get you where He wants you to be despite challenges along the way. After all, there are no hindrances that are a match for the wisdom and power of God.

Therefore, in order to overcome those barriers, you must look to the Lord, who sets the path for you. He will either remove the obstacles, show you how to go through them, or empower you to surmount them.

So do not be discouraged. Often, the people who face the greatest barriers in life outdistance those who are unchallenged. They do so by clinging to the Father, walking in the center of His purpose, and trusting Him to triumph. Take heart and trust God. It's not only the most exciting way to live; it's the only way to live.

Jesus, these challenges are no match for You. I trust You to lead me. Amen.

Accepting What's Given

*"A man can receive nothing unless it
has been given him from heaven."*
JOHN 3:27

One day, while John the Baptist was ministering to a crowd, his disciples went to him and reported, "The one you identified as the Messiah, is also baptizing people. And everybody is going to him instead of coming to us" (John 3:26 NLT). Humanly speaking, this could have made John feel threatened—it certainly caused his disciples some concern. Instead, however, he recognized God's plan coming to fruition.

John provides us with a good example of how to respond when we are confronted with circumstances that produce jealousy or envy within us. *Jealousy* is a feeling of possessiveness that can cause us to fear someone taking our place, our relationships, our position, or our belongings. Likewise, *envy* refers to a feeling of displeasure at someone else's good fortune—we wonder, *Why them and not us?*

Remember that everything that comes to us must first pass through God's loving and instructive hand—and that includes both blessings and adversity. So whenever you sense jealousy or envy rising up in you, it is time to talk to God, remember how good He has been to you, and ask Him to help you understand His will.

Jesus, You know what tempts me to fret. Thank You for Your goodness to me and what has come from Your hand. Amen.

Character Worth Trusting

"Do not fear them, for the LORD your
God is the one fighting for you."

DEUTERONOMY 3:22

When things are going our way, trusting God is easy. But when overwhelming battles, painful trials, unmet needs, or lost hopes assail us, we may be tempted to ask, *Can we still trust Him?* We may question why a caring Father would allow sorrow and difficulty to touch His children's lives. We may even doubt whether He is willing to do anything about our circumstances.

But God assured His people, "Call upon Me in the day of trouble; I shall rescue you" (Psalm 50:15). Can we truly rely on Him to do that? At such times, it is necessary to recognize God's character—to understand that He is not only *able* but also *willing* to fulfill every promise in Scripture. Even when we cannot comprehend *why* the Lord would allow certain situations to occur, knowing His ways can help us trust that He will *always* act in a manner that brings about eternal blessings for His children. Also, believing in His character and love makes it possible to continue obeying Him, which means we position ourselves to endure and triumph in the face of the challenges in our lives. So today, don't despair. Know Him and keep trusting.

Jesus, help me to know You better so I can trust You more.
Amen.

Trust His Love

Do not reject the discipline of the LORD . . .
for whom the LORD loves He reproves.

PROVERBS 3:11–12

G od is perfect in His love and always does what is best for us. The Enemy, who works to undermine our trust in the Father, often takes advantage of adversity by calling God's motives into question. He whispers, "If the Lord really loved you, He would not have allowed this to happen." He wants us to associate the sting of spiritual discipline with a lack of divine caring.

However, the exact opposite is true, as today's verse explains. While natural thinking says peace and happiness are tokens of God's love, the Bible says difficulty and discipline are also evidence of our membership in His family. The reason is clear: God cares for us so much that He will not allow us to stay as we are. Instead, He wants to transform us into the likeness of His Son.

God loves us unconditionally and righteously. Every action He performs or permits in our lives is an expression of His love. Although we may not understand His reason for allowing certain hardships, our difficulties in no way indicate He is anything but a good God and worthy of our trust.

Jesus, in full trust, I yield to You. Teach me to walk in
obedience. Amen.

Returning the Love

"If anyone loves Me, he will keep My word."
JOHN 14:23

When you experience the love of God surrounding you and enveloping your whole being, your natural response will most likely be to show Him love in return. Gratitude, adoration, respect, affection, and tenderness are all feelings that can well up within you, causing you to celebrate your relationship with Him.

You may worship Him—giving praise to the Lord and exalting Him. You may pray, study His Word, or encourage other believers. Yet, as vital as all these activities are, God calls you one step further as you express your love to Him—He calls you to a life of obedience.

Jesus established this connection between love and obedience while He was teaching His disciples, but the principle is true for you as well. What you do with God's Word and whether or not you submit to His commands reveals a great deal about how you feel about Him. Obedience shows that you love Him; disobedience reveals you don't trust Him. So what is your life saying to Jesus today? Tell Him you love Him wholeheartedly by turning every area of Your life over to Him.

Jesus, I want to love You with my whole being. Reveal my disobedience so I can repent, give You my whole heart, and love You in return. Amen.

Trust His Wisdom

The LORD gives wisdom; from His mouth
come knowledge and understanding.

PROVERBS 2:6

You can always trust God because He is infinite in wisdom. The Lord never has need of counsel about the wisest path to take. In His unlimited knowledge, He always knows what is in your best interest and acts accordingly. Regardless of what your circumstances look like, God knows how to turn them for your good.

Of course, sometimes we may look at our difficulties and think, *Lord, I know You are infinitely wise, but I think You've missed something.* But in our limited understanding, we simply cannot see things from God's perspective. We may have all the information that is humanly possible to gather, but the Lord is aware of everything influencing the situation as well as all the potential consequences for you and others. He alone comprehends the totality of every decision. And because He is infinitely wise, He simply cannot make a mistake. This is why it is so important for you to stay in continual fellowship with Him.

You may not know what to do today, but God does—perfectly. Seek Him through His Word and pay attention to what He is teaching you. He is faithful and just to lead you in the way you should go.

Jesus, I trust Your infinite wisdom. Lead me, Lord. Amen.

When We Don't Know

*In paths they do not know I will guide
them. I will make darkness into light before
them and rugged places into plains.*

ISAIAH 42:16

Yesterday we read that the Lord is trustworthy because He is infinite in wisdom. The problem for us is that while God completely understands every situation we experience, He is under no obligation to inform us of the rationale for His actions or decisions—and that can be frustrating.

For example, God did not make clear why He left Joseph in prison for thirteen years before elevating him to the position of prime minister (Genesis 39–41). Nor did He explain why the Israelites had to live more than four centuries in Egyptian bondage before He miraculously rescued them (Exodus 12:41).

While we may never fully know God's reasons, lack of such information is often the very thing that leads to our feelings of frustration, anxiety, and doubt. However, this is the place of faith—we must believe He will reward us as we seek Him (Hebrews 11:6), understanding that we have no legitimate cause for doubting Him. He is the infinite, all-wise God who loves us and always knows the best path to take in our lives. Our responsibility is to acknowledge Him as such, even as He leads us step-by-step.

Jesus, I obey You fully, knowing that You will lead me with wisdom. Amen.

God Is in Control

The LORD has established His throne in the heavens, and His sovereignty rules over all.

PSALM 103:19

When you are out of control in your circumstances, you may feel helpless or hopeless. However, you can always find confidence in the fact that God is sovereign and has absolute authority over everything in creation. That includes your situation today.

Think about it—if even one tiny event in the universe happened outside God's power and control, we could no longer trust Him because we wouldn't be certain that He could work in every situation for our best interest. But we can have faith in Him because He has perfect, complete influence over every last detail of our lives.

Of course, you may be tempted to believe that concepts such as luck, fate, and chance play a role because trusting God can seem difficult when tragedy strikes or your basic needs are not being met. But remember that the Father is perfect in His love, infinite in His wisdom, and utterly sovereign, so there's really no such thing as luck, fate, or chance in a believer's life. No, everything that is allowed to touch your life is for a purpose—God's purpose. So do not fret or despair. Trust the Lord and watch for His mighty hand to help you.

Jesus, You are God. Lead me in Your perfect, sovereign power. Amen.

Believe

"Do you believe that I am able to do this?"

MATTHEW 9:28

What you believe about God is central to who you are—it will shape your life, your relationship with Him, and your interactions with others. If you don't trust that the Lord is sovereign, that He considers you to be worthy and lovable, and that He knows the best path for your life, then you will never have the faith to follow where He wants to lead you. You will inherently distrust His will for your life, which means you will never position yourself to receive all the joy and blessings He desires to pour out on you. This is why it is crucial that you embrace the truth about God and become firmly committed to knowing Him with all your heart, soul, mind, and strength. Because when you do, it will birth within you a deeper trust in Him that will enable Him to lead you to His blessings.

So consider: Do you truly believe in your loving, wise, sovereign Father? Are you in His Word and in prayer daily to deepen and strengthen your beliefs? Are you obeying everything God has instructed you to do? Don't miss a moment that could be spent enjoying the blessings He has promised you.

Jesus, teach me to trust You more and obey You. Amen.

Examine Within

Examine me, O LORD, and try me;
test my mind and my heart.

PSALM 26:2

God is both *able* to meet your needs and *willing* to do so. So the fact that you have some unsolved challenges may leave you wondering what is going on. Understand that the Lord always lives up to His promises and wants to help you, so it is always a wise practice to ask, *What may I be doing that could be keeping God from resolving this issue in my life?*

This question is not to cause you false guilt or frustration. Rather, it is meant to prompt you to seek the Lord and allow Him to examine your life, agreeing with whatever He shows you. After all, there's no outside force that can stand in the way when God chooses to act on your behalf. If there is a hindrance, it may be attitudes or habits you're clinging to that are blocking His blessings. Perhaps He has given an instruction you've failed to follow, or His timetable is simply different from yours. It could even be that the Father is training you for greater responsibilities through the time of waiting.

So examine your heart and trust Him to reveal what you need to know whenever you face challenges and times of uncertainty.

Jesus, examine and lead me so that I may always walk in
step with You. Amen.

His Encompassing Presence

You set me in Your presence forever.

PSALM 41:12

It's interesting to note that when the Lord referred to Himself in a conversation with Moses, He said, *"My presence* shall go with you, and I will give you rest"* (Exodus 33:14 NIV, emphasis added). He wanted Moses to know he wouldn't be alone. Indeed, for the Hebrews of old, and for us as believers today, it is the very presence of God that marks us as His own. Indwelt by the Holy Spirit, all of our life is lived encompassed by Him. We live, eat, work, pray, weep, and rejoice in the presence of our Lord and Savior Jesus Christ. And He is loving, gentle, holy, instructive, renewing, and redeeming to us.

Therefore, we are "called into fellowship" (1 Corinthians 1:9), and we as believers can enjoy intimate, sweet communion with the Savior regardless of where we are or what is happening. He is our ever-present help who encourages, blesses, and sustains us in our journey of faith.

So if you are feeling alone or helpless today, I pray that you come to the face-to-face reality of the Father's personal love and care for you. God is not only for you but *with* you always. And His presence will make all the difference.

Jesus, thank You for Your awesome, abiding presence with me. Amen.

Made to Fellowship

The LORD God called to the man.

GENESIS 3:9

In the beginning, Adam and Eve lived in paradise. It was a place that was perfect, though not because of the surroundings or their life together, as beautiful as it all was. What made their lives so wonderful was the communion they shared with the Creator. They experienced the presence of God. The Father talked with them, and they spoke freely with Him. There was no guilt, shame, or pretense. It was heaven on earth while their intimacy with the Father continued.

But one day, after their world-shattering disobedience, it all ended. Sin brought death into the world, but it also did far worse; it corrupted their relationship with God. The unbroken fellowship with the Creator was lost—leaving a devastating emptiness. It is this intimacy with the Father that Jesus came to restore.

You were made to live in the presence of God. Augustine once said, "Our hearts are restless till they find their rest in Thee." Do you feel a disquiet that nothing can satisfy? That longing is for fellowship with the Father. He calls to you today, just as He called to Adam and Eve in the beginning. Go to Him and enjoy His presence.

Jesus, thank You for restoring our relationship. I need You and want to dwell in perfect union with You. Amen.

The Basis of Approval

*"God is opposed to the proud, but
gives grace to the humble."*

JAMES 4:6

As believers, we can feel very lowly and unworthy when we realize the depth of our sinfulness. We may even fear that God won't want us anymore. But do you realize that Jesus' harshest words were reserved for the people who considered themselves the most perfectly religious—the Pharisees? They were the teachers and guardians of the Jewish faith, but their prideful, legalistic approach had turned God's loving covenant relationship into a twisted maze of impersonal rituals. In other words, they were arrogantly and wrongly self-righteous.

Though the Pharisees assumed God's approval, Christ's admonishment revealed the reality: "Woe to you, scribes and Pharisees, hypocrites! For you . . . outwardly appear righteous to men, but inwardly you are full of hypocrisy and lawlessness" (Matthew 23:27–28).

You see, God prefers when you realize that you don't have it all together and then seek His help. When you think you are holy through your own efforts, you are minimizing what Christ did for you on the cross. But when you acknowledge how much you need Jesus' mercy, compassion, guidance, wisdom, and power—that's when you are rightly positioned to be all He created you to be.

*Jesus, thank You for accepting me as I am. You are my
righteousness and hope. May I honor You always. Amen.*

Self-Righteousness

*He saved us, not on the basis of deeds which we have
done in righteousness, but according to His mercy.*

TITUS 3:5

D o you harbor any self-righteousness? If so, you may be limiting the full extent of God's loving presence in your life. Thankfully, there are warning signs that can help you detect traces of pride before it ensnares you.

For instance, self-righteous believers may demonstrate *an air of superiority.* They inherently consider themselves better than others—that God has gifted them with more spiritual maturity, talent, or discernment than their brothers and sisters in Christ. Because of this, they can be *critical and judgmental.* Whatever degree of success another person may enjoy, they are quick to point out the flaws. They also look slavishly to their *own personal performance,* thinking their behavior somehow earns them points with God. They forget that it was Jesus' sacrifice on the cross that makes us—and keeps us—pleasing to Him.

Are any of these traits true of you? Ask the Holy Spirit to search you and point out any areas in your life where self-righteous behavior may have taken hold. Turn humbly to your forgiving Father, return to childlike dependence on Him, and thank Him for the righteousness that He gives you freely through faith in Christ.

*Jesus, I acknowledge all my righteousness comes from You. I
follow You in humility and gratefulness. Amen.*

At an Impasse

The righteous cry, and the LORD hears and
delivers them out of all their troubles.

PSALM 34:17

A re you facing a seemingly insurmountable challenge today? Throughout Scripture, whenever the faithful were confronted with an impasse, they would cry out to the Lord—and He would always answer. For example, many of the psalms are the recorded prayers of David imploring the Lord to intervene in his circumstances. The Hebrews beseeched God to save them from the oppressive Egyptians (Exodus 3:9). King Jehoshaphat entreated God for help when three powerful armies surrounded Jerusalem (2 Chronicles 20). In every instance, God heard their cries and gave His people victory.

It takes humility and vulnerability to vocalize such an urgent appeal from the soul—imploring God's assistance and acknowledging your inadequacy. It also requires righteousness before Him. That doesn't mean you have to be perfect; it simply means you've received Christ as your Savior and have been credited with His holiness. You've also accepted Him as your Lord, with authority over you. As a child of God, you have the inalienable right to bear your soul and count on Him for help. So do not fear the challenges. Cry out to Him and trust that He knows best how to save you.

Jesus, I cry out to You today. Deliver me in Your wisdom
and power. Amen.

He Stands for You

"The LORD your God who goes before you
will Himself fight on your behalf."

DEUTERONOMY 1:30

I learned one of my most valuable lessons on prayer when I took a mission trip to a rather remote country, even though a crucial meeting would take place at home in my absence. As I traveled, I found myself constantly worrying about the outcome. This was before cell phones, so I couldn't get updates and was very distracted. Although there was an eight-hour time difference, I decided to pray at the precise time the meeting was held. As I talked to the Lord late into the evening, God spoke clearly to my anxious spirit: "Who would you rather attend the meeting, you or Me?" I laughed out loud as God quickly put an end to my fretting.

This is a principle that is essential for you to grasp. When you pray, you are inviting God to become involved in your circumstances and actively placing the results into His sovereign, capable, willing hands. So today, is there a situation that is out of your control? Are you anxious because you cannot plead your case or change your situation? Remember, the Lord can. He is the One who stands in your place and defends you. Trust Him to be and do what you cannot.

Jesus, thank You that these circumstances are in Your strong,
capable, and wise hands. Amen.

Your Part

The slacker craves, yet has nothing,
but the diligent is fully satisfied.

PROVERBS 13:4 CSB

At times, people will say, "I've got a problem, but I know God will fix it." Perhaps they expect the Lord to override their will, emotions, and thought processes—something He does not do except in the most extreme cases where His eternal plans and purposes are involved. Unfortunately, a do-nothing attitude usually results in a nothing-done state. We are never to expect God to do everything for us and require nothing of us.

This is not to say we run out and do as we please. Rather, in everything, we are to seek the Father and be obedient to Him. An older farmer gave this advice to a young farmer: "Ask God to show you what He wants you to grow and when to plant. Then sow the best seed you can buy. Ask Him to nurture the seeds, then cultivate the ground, pull the weeds, and fertilize the crops as they mature. Ask the Lord to yield a great harvest, then go out and gather it when it is ripe. Finally, ask Him to show you how to market your produce, then do as He says. Don't try to do God's part. And don't expect Him to do yours."

Jesus, show me what to do so that I may always honor You. Amen.

You've Got It

*All praise to God . . . who has blessed us
with every spiritual blessing in the heavenly
realms because we are united with Christ.*

EPHESIANS 1:3 NLT

Have you ever considered everything you've received through your faith in Jesus? Most of us haven't—we vastly underestimate all Christ has given us. We are like the man who decides to go on a cruise. He makes his reservation and buys his tickets. He packs his bags, and, when the day comes, he boards the ship. He goes to the first dinner and takes a look at the long, sumptuous buffet table. Then he sits down, opens a little sack, and pulls out a few crackers and a jar of peanut butter. He doesn't comprehend that all his meals on the ship are covered by the price of his ticket.

This example may sound silly until you realize that you have instant access to the God of all creation, and yet you may still fret about issues that are well within His provision to you. You were given all the blessings of heaven in Christ, and there's never a time when you're cut off from His presence or supply. So don't remain in an anxious or needy state. Thank the Father that He has already given all you require.

Jesus, forgive me for underestimating Your blessings. Thank You for taking care of me. Amen.

Listen

"Incline your ear and come to Me.
Listen, that you may live."

ISAIAH 55:3

M y challenge to you today is: *Listen to what God has to say to you.* You may wonder if the Lord still speaks, and I can assure you He does. He communicates to your soul as you seek Him through prayerful times in Scripture. Just quiet your heart and mind and be still before Him. If you are busy and preoccupied, you'll have a difficult time hearing the soft and gentle voice of the Savior. So get your anxious thoughts out of the way by writing them down and then laying your burdens in His hands. Afterward you will be ready to center your attention on Him and what He has to say to you through the Word.

Approach your time in Scripture as hearing the very voice of God and focus on what He is saying to you personally. Ask, "What would You have me to do or understand, Lord?" He wants you to know Him and desires to reveal Himself to you. So keep listening and be patient. Soon enough, He will teach you how to recognize the sound of His voice. And you will be surprised at all He will show you (Jeremiah 33:3).

Jesus, show me Your ways and teach me to hear You
speaking to me through Your Word. Lead me into rich
fellowship with You. Amen.

In the Storm

He made the disciples get into the boat
and go ahead of Him to the other side.

MATTHEW 14:22

After Jesus miraculously fed five thousand people from a few loaves and fishes, He sent the disciples on a journey that would ultimately take them into a storm. The implication in the passage is that they didn't want to go, but Jesus insisted. Soon enough, the winds and waves began to batter their ship.

At best, the disciples might have thought they were going to be off course or late in their arrival. At worst, they may have feared death. But Jesus knew they needed to learn the important lesson that He is not only the Sovereign over the wind and sea but also the omnipotent Lord of their lives.

The same is true for you. Jesus has a plan for bringing you through the storms you are experiencing. He also has a specific timetable. His purposes are perfect, even when you don't understand them or they impinge on your personal goals. But be assured that Jesus is with you in the tempests, regardless of their nature or origin, and that He has a divine plan for getting you through. And just as the disciples arrived exactly where they needed to be right when they were supposed to be there, so will you.

Jesus, teach me to trust You completely in this storm. Amen.

He's Moving You

"Take courage, it is I; do not be afraid."
MATTHEW 14:27

Is Jesus Sovereign over all things or only some? Is He the almighty God of time, situations, the material universe, and all circumstances—or not? These are questions you must answer for yourself. What you believe shapes how you respond to the challenges that arise. The truth is that if you have made Jesus the Lord of your life, and He is the rightful all-powerful, all-wise King of kings over all creation, then why would you ever fear? There will never be a trial you face over which Jesus does not have absolute control. And because He loves you sacrificially, you can be certain that He will make all things work together for your good, in His timing and according to His chosen methods as you trust Him.

Therefore, instead of fretting because of your trials, acknowledge that the Lord works through the winds of adversity in your life to move you to the place where He intends for you to go. Yes, you can make plans, and are wise to do so, but remain prayerful and flexible—you'll find His purposes for you are beyond what you can imagine.

Jesus, You are God. Even though I feel vulnerable, I know You are in control, and I can always have faith in You. Amen.

Remade

The vessel that he was making of clay
was spoiled in the hand of the potter; so
he remade it into another vessel.

JEREMIAH 18:4

T here are situations in life that appear to break us. We feel the pain—whether physical, emotional, financial, or relational—and it can drain our energy, confuse our minds, and dishearten us completely. At such times, refuse to become discouraged by strengthening yourself with reminders of the Lord's purpose and presence. You may be wondering how I can suggest such a thing, but understand that whenever God allows us to be broken, it is because He is remaking us into the people He truly created us to be.

Like clay in the hands of the potter, you may feel like you are being twisted and turned in such ways that you don't know down from up anymore. God is kneading out all the things that can destroy you, which is why it is such a painful process. So do not despair, do not give up, and don't stop trusting Jesus' presence with you through all of it. Remain steadfast and take comfort that He is at work in your life. He is healing you, restoring you, making you whole, and fashioning you into something useful and glorious.

Jesus, my life is so confusing and painful, but I know I am
in Your hands. Remake me into Your vessel. Amen.

Sharing Christ's Love

"This I command you, that you love one another."
JOHN 15:17

It doesn't take a survey or a study to figure out that the world is starved for genuine love. For those who do not know the love of God, the empty space in their hearts gnaws at them continually, regardless of whether they consciously acknowledge the void. Many try to fill that space with a host of distractions or addictions, while others seek attention or whatever affection they can find for the moment.

Therefore, when it comes to sharing God's perfect, unconditional love with others, there is no shortage of takers. That is why you must take your role as Christ's representative seriously and deal with others kindly. You have a Savior and Friend who not only sees past your faults but sacrificed Himself to purchase your salvation. He attends to your needs, gives you a new identity, and provides for you. In difficult circumstances and times of confusion, you know He will never leave you or forsake you. You've benefited greatly from the love Jesus has poured out on you; now, share it with others who are hurting. Don't reject them because of their sin—instead, lead them to the Savior who redeems them from it. The mission field is wide open. Be an example of Christ's love.

Jesus, make me an instrument of Your love to everyone I meet. Amen.

Time to Meditate

*I will meditate on Your precepts
and regard Your ways.*

PSALM 119:15

Many believers think that meditation is only for ministers or
other spiritual leaders. They don't see how it benefits their
lives in a secular world where strife and competition reign. After
all, life can be complicated, noisy, unwaveringly busy, and overwhelming. Yet it is in the midst of such constant turmoil that we
as Christians must focus on Scripture so that we can distinguish
God's voice from the clamor around us.

You see, meditation is different from a cursory reading of
Scripture. We absorb the truth into our very being by asking questions such as, *What did this teach me about God's character and
purposes? What did this mean to the people to whom it was originally
written? How do I apply this to my life? Is there anything I need to
change?*

The Father gave us the practice of meditation so that we might
better relate to Him. When we are alone with the Lord and quiet
before Him, we are better able to listen. It may be for five minutes;
it may be for thirty minutes; it may be for an hour. The important
thing is that we experience God's presence and deliberately seek His
direction and purpose for our lives.

*Jesus, help me to meditate on Your Word and lead me in the
way I should go. Amen.*

Remember His Wonders

Remember His wonders which He has done, His
marvels and the judgments uttered by His mouth.

PSALM 105:5

F ocusing on our difficulties intensifies and enlarges them. But
when we center our attention on God, our problems are put
into their proper perspective and no longer overwhelm us. This is
why it is so important to meditate on all the Lord has done for us
and others in the past and to actively watch for His hand in all of
our dealings.

As we do, we can see the patterns of how He works in our lives,
we can better distinguish how He is moving, and we can discern
His comfort and guidance. We see His greatness, His grace, and
His goodness. He is Yahweh Elohim, the Lord our God, who is
everlasting, infinite in power and wisdom, and absolute in faithfulness. The problems that look like gigantic mountains of trouble and
heartache shrink to nothing when compared to the magnificence
of His sovereignty. The One who created the heavens and the earth
and rules over all creation can do all things. And in the light of all
He is and all He has done, we realize nothing is impossible for us.
Our burdens dissipate in His presence.

Jesus, You are so good to me! I will remember all You have
done and praise Your name. Nothing is too difficult for You.
Amen.

Amid Busyness

My times are in Your hand.
PSALM 31:15

I realize you may be very busy today. We all have times when the pressures of life close in on us and we feel as if we have no margin. The problem is that when we tell God we don't have time for Him, we are really saying we don't have time for life, joy, peace, direction, growth, or achievement because He is the source of all those things. If we are not looking to Him to guide and empower us during our most hectic times, we are inherently missing out on the One who can lead us to success in them.

So set aside time to think about the Lord, listen to Him, and allow Him to examine, heal, and instruct your spirit. When you do, He will equip and empower you to carry out your duties, making you sharper and swifter than you would have been without Him. It is amazing what God can do in your troubled heart in a short period of time. I'm convinced that people who have learned to meditate on the Lord are able to run farther and faster on their feet while remaining calm in their spirits. Wouldn't that be helpful with all you have to do today?

Jesus, empower me to serve You well today, in the power of the Holy Spirit, to Your glory. Amen.

31

Finding Focus

"Blessed is the man who listens
to me, watching daily."

PROVERBS 8:34

S cripture encourages us to take deliberate steps each day to
bring our hearts, minds, and bodies under control so that we
can spend time listening to the Lord and find wisdom. This is life
to us—how we best position ourselves to enjoy the presence and
blessings of God.

However, as we begin to meditate, we may be easily sidetracked
by the issues that press in on us or the noise around us. We find
we must labor mentally just to focus on Him. If being distracted
sometimes is a problem for you, turn to a psalm and say, "Lord, I
have a hard time keeping my mind on You. Help me to immerse
myself in this psalm and center my attention on You fully."

Keep reading Scripture until your spirit begins to worship Him
or He speaks to you. If He puts another passage on your heart, turn
there and meditate on what He is revealing. There can be nothing
better, more productive, or more rewarding in your life than to
become lost in great thoughts about your all-sufficient, loving God.
So listen to Him daily and watch for how He is moving you, for
certainly you will be blessed.

....

Jesus, I do get distracted. Please help me focus on You so I
may worship and learn from You. Amen.

FEBRUARY

Unrecognized Blessings

I will cause showers to come down in their
season; they will be showers of blessing.
EZEKIEL 34:26

D o you realize all the ways God can and does bless you? They are as numerous and diverse as the days of your life. He meets your needs, communicates with you, frees you from fear and anxiety, leads you victoriously through adversity, and has an important plan for you. And you can embrace each of these blessings fully and, in doing so, discover the extraordinary life He has purposed for you.

Perhaps as you read today's verse, you are not feeling particularly blessed. Your life isn't easy, and maybe you wonder when God will show you some compassion. But understand that as a person under Christ's covenant, you are already spiritually blessed in abundance. Yes, there may be times when other types of blessings flow lavishly as well. But those come as you obey Him and learn to see that "every good thing given and every perfect gift is from above, coming down from the Father" (James 1:17). Therefore, thank God for all the ways He is helping you and providing for you. Because it is with gratefulness that you position yourself to see His mighty hand work in astounding ways.

Jesus, bring all Your blessings to my mind so that I may
rightly praise You for them. Amen.

A Blessing to Others

Instruct them to do good, to be rich in good
works, to be generous and ready to share.

1 TIMOTHY 6:18

Why does God bless you? Yes, it is because He wants you to see that He loves you and every good thing comes from His hand (James 1:17). However, God also blesses you so you can be a blessing to others.

You see, as Christ sits at the right hand of the Father in heaven, He sees all the needs in the world. He chooses to fill some of those needs through you so you can be His faithful witness and experience the joy of serving Him. You are His representative in this world—a living example of His goodness. Your hands are the hands He works through. The Lord Jesus speaks to and serves others through the Holy Spirit who dwells in you. That doesn't mean you must meet every need; rather, it signifies that as you seek Him, He shows you where He wants to work through you to help others.

The happiest people I know give generously and have a servant's spirit. Will you allow Him to work through you? Serve Him and experience His joy.

Yes, Jesus, I will be Your faithful witness in the world. Help
me see the needs You desire to fill through me. Amen.

God First

"You shall not worship any other god, for the
LORD, whose name is Jealous, is a jealous God."

EXODUS 34:14

S everal times throughout the Old Testament, the Lord refers to Himself as being jealous for your love and attention. This does not mean that God is petty or selfish or that He wants to keep you all for Himself, as people may wish to do. Instead, God's jealousy signifies that He does not want you to give the chief attention and adoration of your heart to anyone else. God does not desire anything—including your career, goals, relationships, or dreams—to have more influence in your life than He does. He wants you to look to Him first and foremost for all your provision, worth, security, and well-being. When you experience challenges or needs, He wants to be the first One you turn to for counsel, comfort, and solutions.

So, consider: Are you turning to God first when you require help, or is He your last resort? God loves you and designed you to find total fulfillment in a relationship with Him. No other person or thing can satisfy the inner longing He placed within you. So turn to Him first and find what your heart yearns to find.

Jesus, root out anything that comes before You, so You're
always first in my life. Amen.

God Is Good

The Lord *is good; His lovingkindness
is everlasting.*

PSALM 100:5

What comes to mind when you think of God's nature? Whenever I ask, people usually respond with words like *holy, all-powerful,* or *eternal,* but very rarely do they say *good.* Indeed, many people think of the Lord as demanding, distant, and unfeeling. This may be for many reasons, of course. But ultimately, when they hear or read that God is faithful, merciful, forgiving, or loving, they think, *To others, but not to me.*

Is this the case for you? Do you have an easier time imagining other people being kind to you than the Father? Then it is time to confront what you believe about His character. Scripture is clear that what God has planned for you is for your welfare (Jeremiah 29:11) and that He works everything for your benefit (Romans 8:28). What He provides for you is not only ample but is of the finest quality. You may doubt this because of your circumstances. But the Lord sees your whole life from beginning to end, and into eternity, and He always leads in the manner best for you.

God is good—to *you.* Stop doubting and believe in His love for you.

....

*Jesus, help me to trust in Your goodness and loving-kindness
in every area of my life—even when I don't understand
what You are doing. Amen.*

Stand Firm

He took his stand . . . and the LORD
brought about a great victory.

2 SAMUEL 23:12

S hammah was one of David's mighty men, his robust group of thirty warriors who fought alongside David and whose heroics were legendary. But even within this group of mighty soldiers, Shammah was considered one of the elite. This was because "one time the Philistines gathered at Lehi and attacked the Israelites in a field full of lentils. The Israelite army fled, but Shammah held his ground in the middle of the field and beat back the Philistines. So the LORD brought about a great victory" (2 Samuel 23:11–12 NLT). Despite everyone else giving up, Shammah stood firm. And God honored his faith.

There are times in your life when you'll want to give up, but the Lord will call you to take a stand like Shammah. While others around you refuse to deal with the issue or abandon the situation altogether, you will be challenged to remain firm and honor Christ regardless of the fear. Do it. Obey God and leave the consequences to Him. And keep your eyes on Him rather than on the circumstances. He will bring about a great triumph for you as well.

Jesus, I know I never stand alone because You are with me.
Show me how to proceed with wisdom and faith. Amen.

Gather Together

Let us not neglect our meeting together . . .
but encourage one another.

HEBREWS 10:25 NLT

S ometimes this life can be very lonely and uncertain, whether
because of circumstances outside of our control or due to our
own choices. However, as a believer, you do not have to survive the
journey of faith by yourself. Indeed, no Christian has ever been
called to go it alone, apart from the ministry of other believers. We
are instructed to gather together for mutual instruction, encouragement, edification, and ministry to those who have not yet placed
their faith in Christ. As we study Scripture, listen to the Word, and
pray and worship together, we find strength and hope.

Now, I understand that at times, our church experiences may
not be altogether positive. In fact, they can be downright wound-
ing. The Enemy will go to great lengths to cause dissension and
damage our relationships. Do not let him win. God has so designed
us that not only do we need Him desperately, but we also need
one another. Therefore, if you have distanced yourself from a local
body, ask the Lord to lead you to a church where you can find the
godly encouragement, support, and instruction you need.

Jesus, forgive me for the times when I am reluctant to
become involved. In Your wisdom, place me in a local
church where You are gloriously present. Amen.

When We Don't Understand

*He will sift out everything without
solid foundations so that only
unshakable things will be left.*

HEBREWS 12:27 TLB

We live in a fallen world, so there are circumstances we may experience that will not be God's perfect will for us. Indeed, there are tragedies we will witness that are beyond human explanation and that shake us to the core. However, the Lord may allow us to face them through His permissive will for some significant purpose. In His omniscience, the Father knows what is ultimately best, including the long-term consequences of calamities that seem completely devoid of any good. We should not doubt God or abandon our beliefs when we lack understanding. Instead, we should latch on to what we know is true and not let go—and that is the goodness of God.

We must trust Jesus. That can be difficult, but understand that your life matters to God to a degree beyond which you can fathom. He cares for you, and He wants to teach you through what He is doing. So when you face inexplicable circumstances, remind yourself that God always has your best interest in mind. No matter what befalls you, your all-loving, all-wise, all-powerful heavenly Father has you in the cradle of His hand.

....

*Jesus, I want to believe You. Help my unbelief, teach me,
and heal my heart. Amen.*

Refuge in the Shadow

In the shadow of Your wings I will take
refuge until destruction passes by.

PSALM 57:1

Every day, we face battles far beyond our capabilities. We are no match for the spiritual and earthly forces that trouble us. Certainly, this was the case for David as he fled from the jealous King Saul into the wilderness. Yet in the midst of his terrible circumstances, alone and pursued by a dangerous enemy into a thorny and rocky region burning with heat, David found a place of enormous relief, comfort, and safety—the shadow of God's wings.

Like David, you will face situations where all you can do is take refuge until destruction passes by. And as David did, you can find your place of greatest protection and consolation in the nearness of your Savior. The person who lives in the shadow of His wings clings to the Lord, trusts His safekeeping, and finds rest for the soul.

Therefore, if you are in a battle that is out of your control, realize it is not yours to fight. Focus on God, obey Him, and trust His defenses. He will cover you with His impenetrable protection and lift you up to victory at the right moment.

Jesus, I find my comfort, safety, relief, and rest in You. Cover me until destruction passes by and glorify Yourself in this situation. Amen.

True Power

*Yours, O LORD, is the greatness, the power, the
glory, the victory, and the majesty. Everything
in the heavens and on earth is yours.*

1 CHRONICLES 29:11 NLT

Power has always been an important commodity. Nations, corporations, and individuals compete for it with ferocity. They invest incredible effort and resources to attain power for reasons that haven't changed—authority, prestige, wealth, influence, and security. Ultimately, however, supremacy and control belong exclusively to God. The Lord gives strength and bestows might. He alone exercises sovereignty over all humanity.

Thankfully, the Father is willing to give those of us who know and worship Him influence and strength. This is good news for you if you are feeling powerless, disrespected, insignificant, or particularly weak today. Perhaps someone striving for power has trampled over you or has taken something important from you. This can leave anyone feeling fearful and worthless. But understand that your life is not subject to the whims of others—it is in the able hands of the Lord your God. Look to Him, count on Him, and trust Him with your life. Absolutely no one can change His good and acceptable purposes for you—plans that will ultimately bring you great joy and fulfillment.

....

*Jesus, I need to believe You still see and fight for me. Thank
You, Lord, that true power is in Your hands alone. Amen.*

Strength for the Weak

God has chosen the weak things of the world
to shame the things which are strong.
1 CORINTHIANS 1:27

If you are feeling particularly helpless today, good. God delights in imparting His all-sufficient power to those who meet the one paradoxical requirement—weakness. If you have reached a place of exhaustion and emptiness, then look to the heavens and let the Lord breathe His power into your spirit. And take courage. Those who are brokenhearted and at the very end of their own resources are merely a heart's cry away from the renewing surge of Christ's sustaining power.

You may wonder why the ungodly prosper, while you've tried to remain faithful and are suffering. Remember that the Lord has His reasons and will show His hand in due time. But also understand that the power of God is not for clout but for service, not for self-gratification but to glorify Christ. So the Father gives His all-surpassing might to the humble, not for the advancement of personal interests and agendas but to honor His name. He strengthens us so that we might demonstrate to others that He is sufficient and is, indeed, the Lord. Therefore, if you're weary and troubled, keep trusting Him—you are the very person whom the Savior stands ready to empower and through whom He will exhibit His glory.

Jesus, You are my only hope. Strengthen me to honor You.
Amen.

Blessed in Brokenness

We who live are constantly being delivered over
to death for Jesus' sake, so that the life of Jesus
also may be manifested in our mortal flesh.

2 CORINTHIANS 4:11

*B*roken and *blessed*—two words that simply don't seem to go together. We all know what it means to be broken—to feel as if our entire world has fallen apart. We all have times in our lives when we don't want to raise our heads off the pillow and when we're certain the tears will never stop flowing. We feel a void that cannot be filled, the pain of an injustice that will never be made right, a sorrow that cannot be comforted, a wound for which there seems no balm.

Nothing feels blessed about being broken. In fact, certain circumstances in life hurt so intensely that we may believe we'll never heal. But greater usefulness, deeper intimacy with Christ, and a new understanding of His presence, purposes, and character can come in the wake of your suffering. So don't avoid the pain—accept it and experience it fully. Wrestle with God over why He allowed the trial and what He's teaching you—because when you cooperate with God as He does His transformational work in you, His blessing will always follow your brokenness.

Jesus, I trust You to lead me in my brokenness. Teach me,
my Savior. Amen.

Call to Him in Truth

The LORD is near to all who call upon Him,
to all who call upon Him in truth.

PSALM 145:18

There are times in life when you may feel as if God is not listening to you. Although He says, "Call to Me and I will answer you" (Jeremiah 33:3), for some reason He seems far away. You may think the relational fissure originates with Him, but the truth is, the distance always comes from us. When the Father shows you what to do and you refuse to address it, you set up barriers between you. You lie to yourself—and to Him—by saying that He is not serious about that area in your life and you've got it handled. But when you continue in known sin patterns and refuse to acknowledge their corrosive influence, you will have a difficult time enjoying the nearness of God.

The remedy is honesty. Acknowledge your sin, turn away from it, and walk in the path God has shown you. You may not conquer that problem area of your life instantly—sometimes the places we hide from God run deep and are very painful. But by always saying yes to Him and trusting Him to lead, you set the course for intimacy that will help you overcome every obstacle.

Jesus, I open my heart completely and am ready to agree
with whatever You tell me. Amen.

Humbly Seek

These are the ones I look on with favor:
those who are humble and contrite in
spirit, and who tremble at my word.

ISAIAH 66:2 NIV

Y ou are having a quiet time today, so that means you're trying to draw near to Jesus. That is a very good thing. But consider, are you approaching His throne of grace with a humble spirit? Are you seeking the Lord to know Him and learn His path for you? Or are you doing so with an agenda—with a list of requests or a plan of your own that you want Him to bless?

Seeking the Lord with a humble spirit means that you have a right view of God's authority in your life, which is essential for cultivating a sense of His abiding presence. You recognize the Father's sovereign power over people and circumstances and acknowledge that He has a better road map for your life than you do. If your desire is to tell Him what to do, then take a step back and reconsider your intentions. You have access to the God of all creation—the One who sees all, is all-powerful, and is all-wise. Listen to and obey Him. He knows best. And He has all that concerns you in the palm of His hand.

Jesus, I draw near in humility. You are God. Lead me in
Your perfect path. Amen.

Loving Others

God is love, and the one who abides in love
abides in God, and God abides in him.

1 JOHN 4:16

Y ou were created to love and be loved. Your purpose for existing goes beyond your job, family, and the tasks you accomplish each day. Rather, you were formed by God to have a fulfilling, personal relationship with Him and to share His love with others. In this world filled with conflict, anger, pain, and complicated social problems, this mission is both important and powerful.

In fact, when Jesus was asked about the greatest commandment, He replied, "'You shall love the LORD your God with all your heart, and with all your soul, and with all your mind.' This is the great and foremost commandment. The second is like it, 'You shall love your neighbor as yourself'" (Matthew 22:37–39). Jesus' answer is clear: the point of our existence as believers is love.

However, understand that you are not the source of this love. It is as you know the Lord and walk with Him that He transforms you, you experience His love, and you can care for others with wisdom and compassion. The source of love is God Himself, and He is the One who empowers you to represent Him to others.

Jesus, help me to know and love You more. Pour Your love
through me to others. Amen.

Difficult Love

"By this all men will know that you are My
disciples, if you have love for one another."
JOHN 13:35

J esus knows it will be difficult for you to care for everyone—
that there will be people you run into who are challenging to
love. This may be for any number of reasons, including how you
were raised, different personality types, mistreatment by others, or
emotional wounds that have not yet healed.

However, always remember that although your abilities may be
limited, God's capacity to love is boundless. This is why when Jesus
sent out the Twelve on their first ministry excursion, He instructed,
"Freely you received, freely give" (Matthew 10:8). The ability to
care for others in the manner they need comes from rightly relating
to God and embracing how deeply He treasures, provides for, heals,
and accepts you.

You can freely love, generously give, unreservedly forgive, and
be unencumbered in your service because you are the recipient of
unconditional, limitless love from the Father. Open yourself to
Him fully and you won't be able to keep His awesome love from
spilling over into the lives of others.

Jesus, thank You for loving me so freely and unconditionally.
Teach me to receive Your love so I may show it to others.
Amen.

The Way to God's Best

"Not as I will, but as You will."

MATTHEW 26:39

When I ask, "Do you really want God's best for your life?" most people immediately say, "Yes, of course!" But when I follow with, "Are you willing to let the Father do anything necessary to bring you to total surrender so that He is free to accomplish all that He wants to do for you and all He wants to make out of you?" people are less sure.

To have God's very best, we must be willing to submit our all to Him. Our obedience to Him will be difficult and painful at times, but it will bring about our growth. This is because maturing in the Christian life is a process—one that includes setbacks, failures, hard lessons, and even brokenness. As our old ways of functioning stop working or are dismantled, we turn to God's ways. In this manner, we advance spiritually, and our minds and emotions are renewed.

The Father is fashioning us into the likeness of His Son, Jesus—changing what we desire because part of being like Christ is being ready to submit fully to His purposes. Are you willing? I hope you are because truly that is the path to finding what you were created for and experiencing life at its very best.

Jesus, whatever it takes, make me like You. Amen.

His Personal Spirit

"He will give you another Helper, that
He may be with you forever."

JOHN 14:16

Mystery often surrounds the person of the Holy Spirit—our understanding is often muddled about who He is and what He does. However, it is not possible to make progress in the Christian life apart from His presence. This is because the Holy Spirit is God's personal representative here on earth, and His role is to be our Helper and Comforter. In Greek, this word is *parakletos*, and it suggests that He gives us aid much like a legal counselor or advocate would. He comes alongside us, giving us strength and encouraging support. However, if we do not recognize His presence, authority, and power, we can mistakenly believe and act like we are in this life alone.

Jesus knows how important His presence is with us. Therefore, the Lord in His great compassion and wisdom sent His Holy Spirit to teach, guide, and help us. He instructs us in the truth and is our personal advocate before the throne of God. This is our peace and strength regardless of the circumstances—whatever we face, Christ faces it with us personally through the indwelling presence of His Holy Spirit.

Jesus, thank You for the enduring presence, wisdom, comfort,
and power of Your indwelling Holy Spirit with me. Amen.

Empowered by the Spirit

His divine power has granted to us everything
pertaining to life and godliness.

2 PETER 1:3

Y ou have everything you need for the Christian life through the indwelling presence of the Holy Spirit. Consider the fact that Jesus was conceived (Luke 1:35), anointed for ministry (Mark 1:9–15), and raised from the dead (Romans 1:4) all by the power of the Holy Spirit. If the living God specifically pointed out His Spirit's essential role in the earthly mission of Christ (and they are One), then how indispensable and empowering is His presence in your life as a believer? And how much could He do through you?

Understand that the God who saves you has given you His own life in the presence of the Holy Spirit to make you all He created you to be. The Holy Spirit leads you to be born again, teaches you to be a member of His family, and empowers you to live a consistently productive spiritual life. He produces Christlikeness within you and enables you to experience the supernatural, triumphant life of Christ in your practical world of relationships, obligations, conflicts, and challenges. So be encouraged. Through the Holy Spirit, the Lord God is intimately involved with every detail of your existence, taking care of you and leading you to the victorious Christian life.

Jesus, thank You for all that's possible through the presence of Your Holy Spirit. Amen.

Always There

*The LORD is always with me. I will not
be shaken, for he is right beside me.*

PSALM 16:8 NLT

So often, we ask the wrong questions of the Lord. We say, "Where are You, God? Why don't You show up? Can't You see how I am struggling—the pain I'm in?" The Lord's answer, of course, is, "I'm right here with you. I know exactly what's going on." Instead, our questions to the Lord should be, "What is hindering me from seeing You? What would you have me do and learn? Help me to see You and to experience Your presence."

Jesus is always with you through the indwelling presence of His Holy Spirit. The fullness of His almighty, all-wise being is always present and active in your life—every minute of every hour of every day. He will never be more your Savior, Healer, Mighty Warrior, or Deliverer than He is at this moment. He is the same yesterday, today, and forever. So no matter how exhausted, battered, bruised, devastated, or even dead you may feel inside as the result of your struggles, realize that Jesus has not abandoned you but is working in you and for you. He is raising you up into the newness of the abundant life. So don't give up. Keep seeking Him.

*Jesus, thank You for being with me in all I experience.
Amen.*

Go to Him

Blessed be God, who has not turned away my
prayer nor His lovingkindness from me.

PSALM 66:20

God wants *you*—that's what He is most interested in when you pray. He isn't concerned when you don't have elegant words or a persuasive presentation of your needs. Likewise, the Father already knows all the ways you've looked to others for help and found them wanting or have tried your own resources and have discovered them to be insufficient. He sees the wounds you've caused yourself by not turning to Him first. You do not have to hide any of it—He's aware of it all and still loves you unconditionally. So confess it all and unburden your soul.

Of course, because of those failures, you may not feel worthy of His presence. But what matters most to Him is that you return to His arms. So go to Him freely. Recognize who He is—really think about Him and worship. Acknowledge that only He has the right answer for you and the best answer to any question you may have. Don't compartmentalize or prevent Him from directing a certain arca of your life because of fear, embarrassment, or pride. Go to Him with the respect and earnest sincerity due to your Lord God and Creator. He will never turn you away.

Jesus, I need You. Thank You for loving and accepting me.
Amen.

Satisfied by the Source

You open Your hand and satisfy the
desire of every living thing.

PSALM 145:16

When we talk about having our needs met, we often look to everyone and everything except God. We seek answers from a host of places—some helpful, others harmful to our spirits. But the ultimate Source for providing all we require is the Father. He works through a variety of methods and instruments, but ultimately, He is the Author and Originator of all that we need, both in the outer material, natural, and physical realm and in the inner emotional, mental, and spiritual realm.

Many of the ways the Lord helps us can be found in His Word, which teaches us the right and wrong ways of finding meaning and contentment. But the best news about God's methods for meeting our needs is that there are no negative side effects. We are not left with residual feelings of anxiety, guilt, frustration, or embarrassment. Rather, when we look to the Lord as our Provider, He responds in a way that leaves us with deep inner peace, satisfaction, and a sense of fulfillment. Therefore, examine whether you're looking to anything other than God for your needs and turn back to Him to answer the longings of your soul.

Jesus, other things never satisfy, but You fill my life to
overflowing. Thank You, my loving Provider. Amen.

Illuminating the Darkness

The LORD my God illumines my darkness.

PSALM 18:28

D o you perceive a dark unknowing in some areas of your life? There is something supernatural and powerful about having God shed *His* light on your questions. Paul prayed that we might be given a "spirit of wisdom and revelation in the knowledge of Him" so that "the eyes of [our] understanding [would be] enlightened" (Ephesians 1:17–18 NKJV). We cannot rightly see ourselves, the situations we're in, or even the Lord Himself without His revelatory participation.

The Father helps us to see things from a very different perspective—His. And when we observe life from His viewpoint, the issues that worry us lose their grip. He turns the trials that weaken us into strength. The ways we perceive ourselves, others, our tasks, and our problems all change because we understand what He is accomplishing. We become aware of His activity in the unseen, the hidden details and forces at work, and we discover solutions we could never have imagined on our own. And through it all, He is working on our inner beings—refreshing, instructing, molding, transforming, and energizing our minds and spirits.

So spend time in His presence and allow His light to shine on your darkness. You'll be surprised at all He shows you.

....

Jesus, shine Your light on my life and teach me Your perspective. Amen.

What's Wrong?

*"No servant can serve two masters . . . he will
be devoted to one and despise the other."*

LUKE 16:13

I s it wrong to like quality things or to purchase the best you can
afford? Is it problematic to desire a spouse and children? Is it
against God's will for you to want to succeed in your work? No!
What is wrong is when we believe we can't live without these things
or when we allow them to replace our relationship with God.

When we set our eyes on accomplishing our goals, we nearly
always lose sight of the Lord's purposes for us. Only when we make
our relationship with Jesus our number-one priority can He bring
us into a position where we can achieve and receive what will truly
satisfy us.

If there's anything in your life that you think you just can't live
without, that should be a warning sign to reevaluate your relationship with God and to take another look at your priorities. The
Father knows what you need and what's best for you. So stop trying
to define your future and turn to God. He will satisfy your longings with perfect fulfillment and will give you far more than you
could ever imagine, arrange, manipulate, or create on your own.

*Jesus, set me free from whatever consumes my attention so
You will always come first. Amen.*

Gifted

As each one has received a special gift,
employ it in serving one another as good
stewards of the manifold grace of God.

1 PETER 4:10

E ach person has a longing to be special—to be exceptional in some area of life. For believers, that yearning is satisfied through discovering and developing our spiritual gifts. Thankfully, God wants us to use our gifting, so He makes it fairly simple to determine what He has empowered us to do.

For example, if you like and are good at helping others, service is probably your motivational gift. If you enjoy study and investigation, teaching is more likely your calling. If others consistently benefit from your counsel and correction, the Father has probably endowed you with the powerful ministry of exhortation. Likewise, the Lord will work through other believers to help you know where you best fit in the body of Christ. They will verify your giftedness by seeking it out.

Exercising your spiritual gift is the key to a lifetime of rewarding service in God's kingdom. Therefore, ask the Father to reveal your spiritual gift. Examine your likes and dislikes and seek the input of others. Above all, remember that your gift is given and determined by the Spirit and is to be used to glorify Jesus.

Jesus, please reveal my spiritual gift to me so I may serve You effectively. Amen.

Face the Giants

The LORD delivered them into the hand
of Israel, so that they defeated them.

JOSHUA 11:8

T ackling the strife in our lives is such a wearisome task that we may often prefer to take the easier route of retreat and escape. We grow tired of fighting the same old battles that always leave us worn out and disheartened, so we choose to avoid them. And they continue to assail us.

Certainly, this was the case for Israel. When spies reported that the land of Canaan was full of giants, the people refused to face them and take the land God had promised them. As a result, they wandered the wilderness for forty more years.

Don't be like them. Instead, be like Joshua and Caleb, who trusted that the Lord would give them victory throughout the land of promise. And He did. Like Joshua and Caleb, you may face overwhelming obstacles—whether spiritual, physical, financial, or relational—but you must look at them through the eyes of faith. Focus on the power of God rather than the size of your adversary. Yes, giants are big. They are mightier than you are, but the Lord is always greater still. So face them in the wisdom and strength of your Savior, and He will lead you to triumph over them.

Jesus, help me face the giants of my life in Your strength and with Your wisdom. Amen.

With Jesus

*As they observed the confidence of Peter and
John . . . they were amazed, and began to
recognize them as having been with Jesus.*

ACTS 4:13

F illed with the Holy Spirit, Peter and John had been ministering
powerfully, proclaiming Christ's death and resurrection. God
was obviously at work through them because thousands of souls
had been saved and added to the fledgling group of Christians.
However, this made the Jewish religious rulers uneasy, so they
arrested Peter and John and questioned them about their work.

Perhaps you can imagine Peter and John—two rough, uneducated fishermen—standing before a room full of highly educated
and influential religious leaders. They had plenty of room to feel
inadequate. Yet they testified about Jesus forcefully, and the Lord
shone through them. They left the council amazed at the power
of their message. And it was all because they had been with Jesus.

The principle we see here still holds true today. When we make
time alone with Christ a priority, it affects every single facet of our
lives. Indeed, it is the fellowship we have with Jesus—meditating on
His Word and seeking His face   that establishes our fruitfulness
and influence in the kingdom. There is nothing that empowers us
or lifts us up more than spending time with Him.

*Jesus, show me Your ways and teach me so that others may
see I've been with You. Amen.*

Confront It

"This day the LORD will deliver
you up into my hands."
1 SAMUEL 17:46

A re you fearful of something today? If so, understand that it is crucial for you to confront that fear by obeying whatever positive step of faith the Lord instructs you to take. An example of this is seen in the account of David and Goliath. Once David knew the Lord's plan, he *ran* toward Goliath despite his trepidations. He proceeded in faith, remembering how God had delivered him from a bear and a lion. He darted forth in confidence, knowing the Father had given him the ability to run fast and use a slingshot well. Finally, he advanced in wisdom, declaring the Lord would provide the victory.

As you look back over your life, there's no doubt you can recount many instances in which God has been with you through fearful circumstances. Like He did with David, God has delivered you before, has given you the abilities needed to confront your challenges, and has promised to give you wisdom. So whenever you experience a frightening situation, do not retreat; rather, deal with it calmly, in a direct and prayerful manner. Advance, trusting God as you go. Surely, He will show you in no uncertain terms that He is far greater than whatever it was that caused you anxiety.

Jesus, I'm fearful, but I will go forth boldly, trusting You all
the way. Amen.

Joined to the Vine

"I am the vine, you are the branches; he who
abides in Me and I in him, he bears much fruit,
for apart from Me you can do nothing."

JOHN 15:5

Would you like to be more like Jesus, but it just seems too difficult? Do you find yourself falling short? Don't despair—you're not supposed to be godly in your own strength. Being Christlike is a fruit that comes from God Himself.

There's a reason that peach trees bear peaches, not apples; why pear trees bear pears, not bananas; and why branches cut off from the vine wither away. It's because life is given through the vine, with the sap that flows into the branches determining the identity of the fruit. In much the same manner, God's life within you produces the Christlike character you long for. As you spend time with Him and acknowledge Him as Lord, His "divine sap"—the Holy Spirit— produces the spiritual qualities that reflect His character in you.

This means that you are empowered to be and do all God created you to because He does it all through you. However, you must live in continual union with the Vine, Jesus. So stop struggling. Abide in Christ and allow the Holy Spirit to reproduce His char acter in you.

....

Jesus, help me to abide in You so that Your life, character,
and fruit may be produced in me. Amen.

Bearing Fruit

"As the branch cannot bear fruit of itself
unless it abides in the vine, so neither
can you unless you abide in Me."
JOHN 15:4

What kinds of sounds do you hear in a grape arbor or other fruit orchard? You can probably enjoy birds chirping, the wind rustling through leaves, and other outdoor refrains. What you don't hear is the noise of the vines groaning or trees straining. The plants are not laboring to produce their fruit—it comes out of their branches naturally as a part of the growing process. The vine does not have to struggle to produce grapes. When the branches attached to it are healthy and have all the water and nutrients they need, the grapes come forth in abundance.

The same is true for you. The secret to producing fruit as a believer is as natural for you as it is for a grapevine—you stay joined to the Vine, focusing all of your energy and attention on abiding in Christ. The fruit of your life is a direct reflection of the quality of your relationship with Jesus. So worship Him, praise Him, meditate on His words, seek solitude in Him, obey Him, and let yourself be absorbed into His purposes. Then rejoice in how He works through you.

Jesus, thank You for doing Your work through me. Keep me close, my Savior, as I abide in You. Amen.

MARCH

All Your Needs

My God will supply all your needs according
to His riches in glory in Christ Jesus.
PHILIPPIANS 4:19

Today, you may be fretting about challenges in your life. You feel helpless because you fall so short of meeting what is required, and you wonder how you will overcome this hurdle. But consider this: Do you believe there is any need you could have that is outside God's ability to meet it?

Of course, perhaps it is not the Lord but yourself that you doubt. I have heard people say, "I have a need in my life, but God has already been so good to me." In essence, these people believe they've used up the portion of blessings the Lord has allotted to them. Their current necessities lie just beyond God's storeroom of supply. Maybe they feel unworthy of His help, or they fear being selfish or greedy, and therefore, they expect God to turn down their urgent pleas for help.

Is that you today? Understand that when Paul wrote that God would supply *all* your needs, he meant precisely that—*all.* Not a percentage of or a fraction of. *All.* Of course, He does so in His timing and in His way, but He is more than willing to help you. Turn to Him.

....

Jesus, I need Your help. Do what only You can in this
situation. Amen.

Loving Enemies

*The one who does not love his brother whom he
has seen, cannot love God whom he has not seen.*

1 JOHN 4:20

If you live long enough, you're bound to face conflict. At some point, you'll encounter people who may seem intent on making your life miserable, whether it's a family member or a coworker with whom you seem to be at constant odds. Dealing with those individuals can be one of the most challenging experiences of your life. But it can also be rewarding if you allow the Father to teach you. The Lord works for your good even through the most difficult people in your life.

So how do you handle the conflicts? Scottish-born pastor of Moody Bible Church, Alan Redpath, wisely said, "If you begin with God, your enemies grow small. If you begin with the enemy, you may never reach God." As with any other challenge, starting with the Lord gives you His perspective, wisdom, power, and love for every person you encounter. He teaches you to walk in His plan. Therefore, focus on Jesus and He will give you the ability to "love your enemies and pray for those who persecute you" (Matthew 5:44), so you can be His representative to others.

*Jesus, I need Your wisdom, strength, and love in my
relationships. Help me to walk in Your purposes for them.
Amen.*

Trusting God in the Conflict

*The Lord is my strength and my shield; my
heart trusts in Him, and I am helped.*

PSALM 28:7

When people wrong us, we can be in danger of dwelling incessantly on what they've done, which can lead to bitterness. Angry thoughts can bombard us because of the injustice, vulnerability, and pain we feel. But rather than giving in to resentment, we must refocus our thoughts on God and His purpose for allowing the conflict.

Focusing on the Lord will help you rely on His ability to deal wisely and justly with your antagonists. You don't have to be afraid of being a victim of someone else's power plays or deception. Instead, you can be confident that your reputation, success, and security rest firmly in the hands of your sovereign God. Yes, people may hurt you and even set you back. But you don't have to fear or retaliate. You can forgive as Christ commands, and the Father will protect you, vindicate you in due time, and give you insight into why people respond as they do.

The Lord is greater than all your enemies combined, and the power of the risen Christ can sustain and guide you through whatever rough encounters you face. So honor Him because He will certainly help you.

*Jesus, You are my Defender. I trust You to help me and
redeem this situation. Amen.*

Go to Him First

The salvation of the righteous is from the
Lord; He is their strength in time of trouble.

PSALM 37:39

P raise God—He knows our frame. When we are weakest, He is strongest. Our painful pleas come before Him, and He inclines toward us. He gives us the mercy and grace we need to bear up under the load and release us from our burdens.

Unfortunately, we often wait until we're at the end of our ropes to seek God's supernatural assistance. We try our own ways until we make such a mess that the only remaining option is for the Lord Almighty to act on our behalf—unless He intervenes, we have no hope. Why doesn't He help us before then? Lest we think our flawed methods work, He waits for us to approach Him fully submitted to His power and wisdom. That's when He reveals Himself as our great and awesome God—so that we would have no doubt that He was the One who delivered us.

The point is that you should never wait to cry out to the Lord. Go to Him immediately, whatever challenge should arise. And go for *His* solutions, not to ask Him to bless yours. He will change your situation in ways you could never have engineered and bless you for seeking Him first.

Jesus, thank You for being my Deliverer. I trust Your
wisdom and power to save me. Amen.

Good Purposes

"You meant evil against me, but God meant it for good . . . to preserve many people alive."

GENESIS 50:20

There is an essential principle that can help us endure in our faith, and that is understanding that God Himself ultimately allows everything that happens to us. This is a difficult notion to accept, particularly in setbacks and painful trials, but it provides us with a perspective that always leads to triumph.

Consider Joseph, who was sold into slavery as a teenager by his jealous brothers. He spent years in servitude in Potiphar's house and was then wrongly accused and imprisoned in an Egyptian jail. However, Joseph remained faithful all those years because He saw God at work, positioning him for greater service through all the betrayal and injustice. Sure enough, after more than a decade of suffering, the Lord miraculously delivered Joseph and made him second in command in the most powerful nation on earth.

Such is the awesome ability of our Savior—He works through the fallenness of this world to accomplish His purposes for us. So regardless of what happens—no matter how unfair or painful— remember God has allowed it for a good and holy purpose. Then, like Joseph, wait in expectant hope for Him to reveal His excellent plan to you.

Jesus, I am so grateful You have a good and holy purpose in all I endure. Amen.

Who He Really Is

Let us press on to know the Lord.

HOSEA 6:3

When I was a child, my concept of God was that He was a stern judge sitting up in heaven just waiting for me to make a mistake so He could punish me. I tried hard to please Him, and much of the time, I didn't think I did a very good job. I lived in fear that the Lord would chastise me in a terrible way.

But now I know the truth, and when I think about my loving heavenly Father now, my thoughts are the exact opposite. I see Him as my Sustainer, Protector, Provider, and the Preserver of my life. I have confidence that He will forgive me when I sin and that I am eternally secure in my salvation. I also trust that His desire is always for my eternal good.

How did my perception change? First, I tested everything I thought about the Father with Scripture and discovered who God really is. Then I made the decision to believe Him. You can too. Trust in the Savior who loves you, provides for you, cares for you, is always available to you, and is in control of your life. As you do, you'll grow to adore Him too.

Jesus, I want to know who You really are. Lead me in Your truth. Amen.

Don't Worry

"Do not be worried about your life."
MATTHEW 6:25

Anxiety is a problem we all face at one time or another. It produces in us a distracted, uncertain feeling of, *What next?* It is a sense that the rug has been pulled out from under us and we have no idea if and how hard we'll fall.

For many people, worry has become a way of life. They live in a state of uncertainty and constant fear. If that describes you, I encourage you to remember what Jesus taught during the Sermon on the Mount. He said, "Do not worry" (Matthew 6:34). This is not a suggestion; it is a command. You may say, "But I can't help feeling anxious; I've always been a worrier!" I've heard that from many people throughout the years. My response is always, "Yes, you can."

There's nothing about a circumstance that automatically creates anxiety. Rather, fear occurs because of the way you perceive a problem. But the ability to choose is part of God's gift to every human being. You can decide how you feel, what you think about, and how you will respond. You can decide not to worry. So resolve to trust the Lord rather than focusing on your circumstances.

Jesus, I want to be a person of bold, confident faith rather than a worrier. I set my eyes on You. Amen.

Dispel the Panic

In panic I cried out . . . But you heard my cry
for mercy and answered my call for help.

PSALM 31:22 NLT

Have you ever had a panic attack—a time when anxiety spun you completely out of control? Perhaps your heart began to race, you started to sweat profusely, and you felt as if you were falling apart. I've had such an experience. It was due to the incredible pressure, conflict, and extreme fatigue I was facing. I felt as though I was coming apart at the seams. In my desperate hour, I cried out to God—like a little boy calling for his daddy after a bad dream. His presence surrounded and sustained me through that difficult season.

How about you? How do you respond when fear overwhelms you? People often turn to drugs, alcohol, or other means that promise momentary escape. However, they will never satisfy or heal like crying out to God will. When you call to the Father with a sincere heart, He reveals His presence, drives away your anxiety, makes sense of your circumstances, and gives you genuine peace. So look to Him and allow Him to hold you tightly in His everlasting arms and comfort you. The closer you cling to Him, the less reason you'll have to fear.

Jesus, hold me and help me. Surround me with Your
calming presence. Amen.

When Anxiety Strikes

"Do not be afraid any longer, only believe."

MARK 5:36

Are you anxious today? What can you do when fears arise, and you have no idea how to handle your problems? First, ask God to give you His peace and answers. Be willing to let go of your perception of your troubles and allow the Lord to deal with them in His wisdom and power. This isn't something you'll do just once; rather, recommit your concerns to Him each time they come to mind. Ask the Father to help you focus your thoughts and energy on what He wants you to do.

Also, settle this issue in your mind once and for all: Is God your loving heavenly Father at all times—always seeking your eternal best—or not? This is crucial because the key to overcoming anxiety is to get your thinking about Him right. The Lord is sovereign, which means He has absolute control over every aspect of creation. He is all-powerful, all-knowing, and ever-present. He knows how to produce wholeness out of your present brokenness, how to heal what is sick, and how to bring reconciliation and love out of estrangement and hate. Furthermore, He loves you with an unconditional, unfathomable, immeasurable love. You can trust Him. Choose to believe Him, and watch your anxiety disappear.

Jesus, You are in control and know what to do. I will trust You. Amen.

Friendship

Those who refresh others will
themselves be refreshed.

PROVERBS 11:25 NLT

A friend's encouraging word that directs our hearts to God can be one of the most powerful demonstrations of His provision and care. Throughout Scripture, the Lord worked through many strong relationships to accomplish His work. Moses had the support of Aaron and Joshua. David had Jonathan's friendship and the protection of his mighty men. Jesus had the companionship of His twelve disciples and numerous followers.

Although this world tends to isolate and divide us, God created us to be in fellowship with Him and others. Indeed, Jesus said that we would have a unique experience of His presence when we gather together (Matthew 18:20). An authentic, godly Christian friend can share encouragement that is filled with the power and wisdom of the Lord.

If you tend to isolate yourself from others and want a fresh experience of God's presence, try something different today. Think of someone you can help in a tangible way and be a friend to them. Be alert for ways you can develop godly relationships with other believers. You'll find incredible blessings in return.

....

Jesus, I thank You for the gift of friendship. Help me to be a
friend to others. Amen.

Be a Friend

*Jonathan went to find David and encouraged
him to stay strong in his faith in God.*

1 SAMUEL 23:16 NLT

We all know how meaningful it is to have a caring friend. A friend who calls on a lonely night, who brings a meal when we are sick, and who prays with us when we are discouraged is an indispensable instrument of the Lord's encouragement.

David understood the powerful encouragement the Lord could give through friendship. Constantly on the run from King Saul, driven into the wilderness, David found the consolation and strength he needed in Jonathan, his beloved friend. Jonathan left the comfort of his royal residence to make sure David stayed strong in the Lord. That's what genuine friends do—they don't mind being inconvenienced if it means supporting us in a time of need. They stick with us when the going gets rough. Sadly, if we are always inwardly focused and preoccupied with our own needs, we will seldom find the rich rewards that friendship brings.

Therefore, today consider, what kind of friend are you? Recognize that at times, God's most meaningful ministry through you will be accomplished through your relationships with others— how you support, love, and care for them. So make an effort to be the best friend you can be.

....

*Jesus, teach me to be the kind of excellent friend You are to
me. Amen.*

Supplying Our Needs

"Your heavenly Father knows that
you need all these things."
MATTHEW 6:32

You may believe that the unmet needs you have in your life betray a lack of care on the Lord's part. However, just the opposite is true. God will allow challenges in your life so that you will turn to Him and grow in your relationship with Him. If you never lack for anything, you might believe that you are completely self-sufficient and do not require His presence, which could cause you to ignore Him. This is why any deficit in our lives is an opportunity for us to rely on the Father more. It is how we mature in our faith, which makes us even more effective servants of God and witnesses of His grace.

Yet also be assured that you will never have a need that is too great for the Lord to meet or have a challenge that takes Him by surprise. Everything you require has already been given by your heavenly Father and made available to you through Christ. You may not have received it yet, but you can trust His plan to provide for you.

Today, thank the Lord for the opportunities that help you to realize how deeply you need Him, and trust Him to provide what you require.

Jesus, I will take this opportunity to trust You more. Thank You for drawing me near. Amen.

Know Him

"I will give them a heart to know Me,
for I am the LORD; and they will be My
people, and I will be their God."

JEREMIAH 24:7

A re you content with where you are with the Lord? Are you spending enough time with Jesus to genuinely know Him? I have discovered over the years that most people haven't made the effort to truly get to know God. Not really. Not deeply. Not in an intimate way that allows them to experience His holy, compassionate character and grasp His eternal love.

The reasons for this are as diverse as the people who call on His name: fear of His judgment, erroneous beliefs, a lack of support, laziness, and so forth. But invariably, once a person truly gets to know the Lord, they discover that spending time with Him is delightful, fulfilling, and ministers to the spirit like nothing else can. They do not want anything to interfere with that relationship. They only want what He does.

Friend, your heart is aching for just this kind of profound, intimate relationship with Jesus—one in which you're all in. So spend time with Him today and seek to experience Him as deeply as you can. Because it is in knowing Him that every longing of your heart is satisfied.

Jesus, I want to know You. Reveal Yourself to me. Amen.

Worth Much More

*"Look at the birds of the air, that they do not
sow, nor reap nor gather into barns, and
yet your heavenly Father feeds them. Are
you not worth much more than they?"*

MATTHEW 6:26

Have you lost sight of your value to God? If you have low self-esteem, you may not deem yourself worthy of His care. Yet you have immeasurable value to Him. And He's not only *able* to meet your needs, but He is also *willing* to do so.

Of course, I've had people say to me, "God doesn't notice when my car breaks down." Yes, He does. "The Father isn't interested in whether I can pay my bills or not." Yes, He is. "The Lord doesn't care about my broken heart and shattered dreams." Oh child, yes. He absolutely does.

God is intimately involved in every detail of your life, and His plan is to provide for you. There may be several reasons why you see yourself as being unworthy of His love, but have you forgotten His gift of salvation? Jesus sacrificed *Himself* for you! That's how much He cares—and how valuable you are to Him. Nothing the Lord could ever do could be a greater display of His love than that. He considers you to be absolutely worthy of loving, nurturing, and blessing.

*Jesus, thank You for making me worthy and loving me
unconditionally. Amen.*

Joy Regardless

Though the olive crop fails and the fields produce
no food . . . I will be joyful in God my Savior.

HABAKKUK 3:17–18 NIV

Sometimes we may catch a glimpse of difficult times coming on the horizon. For the prophet Habakkuk, it was the brutal conquest of his country, Judah, by the Babylonians. Habakkuk foresaw how grim the hostile invasion would be. Eventually, everything would be destroyed, the agrarian economy would be decimated, and the people would be carried off to captivity.

Yet, at that crucial moment, when the anxiety could have overwhelmed him, Habakkuk stated his unwavering faith in God. He affirmed that the sovereign Lord, who rules over all people and nations, is the hope of his life. God Himself was Habakkuk's joy.

Such should be our response as well. In good times and bad, God is working out His purposes, and nothing is outside His power. Therefore, there isn't anything that can thwart His ultimate plans for us—plans that are good. Challenging seasons are never an excuse for discouragement; rather, they're an opportunity to see Jesus work in our circumstances and trust Him for the outcome. He gives us strength for the journey, prepares us for greater service, and sees us through. And we can always find our joy in Him.

Jesus, I'll find my joy in You regardless of what happens.
Amen.

First Step to Freedom

Keep your servant from deliberate
sins! Don't let them control me.

PSALM 19:13 NLT

People usually don't seek freedom from their bondage until they are truly miserable in it. This is because they tend to view the pleasures or sense of empowerment they receive from sin as alleviating their despair rather than causing it. For this reason, our sinful behaviors—whether physical, financial, relational, or spiritual—can dominate us for many years. It's not until we realize the extent to which they control and wound us that we cry out for release. Thankfully, it's never too late to be delivered.

Recognizing our helplessness is our first step on the road to freedom. Sadly, too many of us do not fully receive the liberty Christ purchased for us because we cling to the feeling of control. We want to do things our way. But in that, we find ourselves unable to conquer our fears, heal our relationships, or overcome the obstacles before us.

Perhaps you view helplessness as weakness—as an admission that you're inadequate to solve your problems. But in God's eyes, your feelings of powerlessness are the birth pangs of a miracle. So let go of control and let Him show you how to find relief from all that imprisons you.

Jesus, reveal to me what I'm in bondage to and set me free
from it through Your truth. Amen.

Abundantly Beyond

*God's weakness is stronger than the
greatest of human strength.*

1 CORINTHIANS 1:25 NLT

Through the years I have seen that it's often the most gifted, self-confident people who have the worst difficulty yielding to God. Those who are satisfied with what they have rarely look to the Lord to empower them. Usually, unless something bad happens, they don't recognize the need to. On the contrary, they'll say, "God, you can have these lesser parts of my life, but this one area—I'm good at this. I reserve this for myself. I've got this." They don't—they can't—know what they're missing because they don't feel that they lack anything.

This is not to say we should despise or ignore our accomplishments, talents, or skills. The problem is not in having them but in relying on them. When we trust in ourselves, we are limited by what we can do—which is never enough. However, when we surrender to Jesus and allow Him to work through us, He does "far more abundantly beyond all that we ask or think" (Ephesians 3:20).

You will never lose when you surrender your all to God. And whatever you submit to Him, He returns to you in great abundance. So rely on Him and find true joy, success, and fulfillment.

....

*Jesus, I surrender all to You—work through me, my Savior.
Amen.*

Nothing Off-Limits

Why do you boast as if you had not received it?

1 CORINTHIANS 4:7

W hat area of your life are you withholding from God today? The places that we keep off-limits to Him are the very ones He focuses on so that every aspect of our imagined independence is brought into submission to Him. His loving desire for us is total dependence on Him and acknowledgment of Him. After all, He's the One who gives us all good things, and as believers, it's essential that we recognize the authority He has in our lives. Additionally, when we act independently from Him—going outside His plans to satisfy our needs or desires—we put ourselves in danger.

But understand, in addressing your presumed self-sufficiency, God doesn't destroy your spirit. You won't lose your zest for living or your personality when you surrender to Christ—on the contrary, it is when you stray from His path that sin drains you of your very life, joy, and identity. He brings your will into alignment with His so that when He speaks, you put up no argument, make no rationalization, offer no excuses, and assign no blame. Instead, you immediately obey the leading of the Holy Spirit because you know without a shadow of a doubt that the result will be great blessing.

Jesus, everything I have is from You. I submit all I am to You. Amen.

Your Work

*Jesus told them, "This is the only work God
wants from you: Believe in the one he has sent."*

JOHN 6:29 NLT

Being a Christian isn't a matter of *doing*—going to church, singing hymns, praying, giving, reading Scripture, or sharing God's Word, although those are all good things that help build our faith. Likewise, being a believer is not about what we *don't* do—smoking, drinking, swearing, sleeping around—though it is wise to avoid those activities.

Rather, being a Christian is about being in a relationship with Jesus. The work to be done is His—the Savior is responsible for transforming you and making you more like Himself. He is your Author and Completer, the One who disciples you so that you can grow in godliness and walk according to His plan. You cannot change your sinful nature, but the Lord uses the situations in your life to move you to a point where you acknowledge, "I can't do this by myself." Then He enables you to overcome them in His power.

Only God's Holy Spirit can change your human heart. So do not beat yourself up, despair, or retreat. Instead, let go of your illusion of self-sufficiency and accept that the One who saved you is the One who teaches you to walk with Him. Then obey Him.

*Jesus, I believe You. Help me to know and serve You
wholeheartedly. Amen.*

Unexpected Help

"The one who showed mercy toward him."

LUKE 10:37

There are people in your life God has specifically put there to be a help and blessing to you, but they may not be the ones you expect. For example, Jesus told a story about a Jewish man who took a journey to Jericho from Jerusalem. While on the road, the man was beaten, robbed, and left for dead. Two religious leaders passed by without offering him assistance. However, a man from Samaria—a region and people despised by the Jews—not only noticed him and stopped but also assisted him and took him to a safe shelter in Jericho, where he paid for the injured man's lodging and further medical help.

We often expect certain people to help us, such as family, friends, and the ministry staff we know. However, when they don't come through for us, we can feel heartbroken and even betrayed. Yet Jesus often sends you comfort in the form of a Good Samaritan—someone who may be very different from you, with whom you may not agree, but who ministers to you in a profound manner. Do not be quick to dismiss that person. Instead, appreciate the individual as the hands and feet of Jesus at work, and show kindness in return.

Jesus, help me to love and appreciate the helpers You send to me, and show me how to be a blessing to them as well. Amen.

Not Disappointed

*There is no fear in love; but
perfect love casts out fear.*

1 JOHN 4:18

For many years I was afraid of disappointing God by not
performing up to His high standards, but I now know that
those were unfounded fears. How did I come to this conclusion? I
realized that a deity who can be disappointed is one who loves con-
ditionally, accepting us when we behave well and casting us aside
when we don't. That's not the God described in Scripture, who
consistently shows us that He is unconditional in His love for us.

What this means is that at times, you are going to disobey
the Lord—either willfully or unknowingly—and reap His consequences as a means of chastisement. But you will never *disappoint*
Him. He always loves you with an infinite, overwhelming, merciful, gracious, passionate love. Of course, when you fail, you may
feel inadequate and unworthy of His assistance, but He still helps
you. He may whisper to your heart, "I can help you do better than
that. I created you for better." But even as He says that, He is holding you close and valuing you beyond measure. God will never
withdraw His presence from you.

*Jesus, thank You for loving unconditionally and accepting
me wholeheartedly. I'm so grateful I can always count on
You. Amen.*

Today and Tomorrow

"Do not worry about tomorrow; for tomorrow will care for itself. Each day has enough trouble of its own."

MATTHEW 6:34

Many people face anxiety because they are completely focused on the future—perhaps there is something good they are waiting for, such as getting the right job, having a particular relationship, or receiving a long-awaited opportunity. In actuality, their full hope is invested in tomorrow because they are so desperate to escape the difficulties of today.

But the God who is in control of tomorrow is also the Lord of today. Yes, He sees your situation—your burdens, fears, sorrows, and frustrations. He understands your desire to escape the pressures. However, He also knows that the trials of today will prepare you for the blessings of tomorrow you truly long for.

The job, relationship, or opportunity you hope will rescue you may end up making your problems even worse. But the Lord is the One who can truly deliver you. He provides peace that passes understanding and a path to victory for everything you face. So instead of seeking a future path of escape, go to Him right now. Confront your troubles in His strength today and He will give you true, unshakable hope for tomorrow.

Jesus, I trust You for today. Show me how I may honor You right now and every day. Amen.

Read It with Feeling

"We are merely human beings—just like you!"

ACTS 14:15 NLT

The problem with studying any familiar passage is that we rarely slow ourselves down long enough to really process what the individuals in those accounts must have felt. Why should we? We know what happens in the end. God wins.

Unfortunately, this familiarity with the Scriptures often robs us of its richness and applicability to our own lives. For example, we don't often consider the fear David must have felt when he faced Goliath because we know from the outset that he comes out the victor. Likewise, we miss the frustration, regret, isolation, and physical strain Moses must have experienced as he fled from Egypt into the unforgiving wilderness. After all, he goes down in history as a hero.

But as you approach God's Word, remember that the people didn't know what the end of their story would be, just like you don't today. If you read what happens but neglect to consider what they must have experienced and felt, you lose some of the richest insights of the story. They were fallible people like us, full of questions, doubts, fears, and challenges. So do your best to put yourself in their sandals, and then imagine what it was like for them to see God come through.

....

Jesus, thank You for working through people like me and for encouraging me through their testimonies. Amen.

He Knows Your Pain

When Jesus therefore saw her weeping . . . He
was deeply moved in spirit and was troubled.

JOHN 11:33

M ary and Martha had asked Jesus to come quickly to heal
Lazarus, but the Lord delayed in going. By the time Christ
got there, Lazarus had been in the tomb four days. We wouldn't
blame Mary and Martha for giving in to the hollow, helpless feeling
that accompanies death, or asking, "Why didn't He help us? How
could He stay away when He knew what we were suffering?"

Perhaps these are some of the questions you have asked as
you've cried out to God. But Jesus always knows exactly what is
going on. We must realize that some things are so important to
Him that it's worth interrupting the happiness and health of His
children to accomplish them.

But understand this: Jesus is not emotionally isolated from
the pain you're suffering. Regardless of what He may be in the
process of accomplishing, or how noble His purposes may be, He
remains intimately in touch with what you're feeling. Jesus wept
over Lazarus, and He weeps with you as well. And if, like Mary
and Martha, you continue to trust in Him, you'll see His glory and
understand His loving care through all He allows.

Jesus, thank You for seeing my heartbreak and always having
a good purpose in all I experience. Amen.

Eternal Purposes

*"I am glad for your sakes that I was not
there, so that you may believe."*

JOHN 11:15

What did Jesus have in mind by delaying His return to Bethany, thus allowing Lazarus to succumb to death? What was so important that He was willing for Mary and Martha to experience the agony of watching their brother die? The answer to that question gives us a great deal of insight into the character of God.

From the very beginning, Jesus' objective was not to cause Lazarus, Mary, or Martha pain or emotional anguish. On the contrary, Christ's goals were to bring glory to God and to help others to believe in the eternal life He was providing. To Him, this opportunity to publicly display the power of God and teach others about His coming crucifixion and resurrection was worth it.

Remember this when you suffer. There are difficult circumstances you will experience for the express reason of revealing the Lord's glory and plan of salvation to those watching you. Your temporary anguish may be difficult, but the suffering of a soul eternally separated from God is unfathomable. Take heart knowing that the difference the Savior can make through your humble obedience can be eternal—and that's always worthwhile.

*Jesus, in every situation, shine Your truth and glory through
me, that others may know You as Savior. Amen.*

Just Do It

Jesus said, "Remove the stone."
JOHN 11:39

Lazarus had been in the tomb for four days when Jesus gave the strange command to remove the stone that blocked the entrance to his grave. It was a lot of work—and for what? Yet Jesus assured them that if they believed, they would see God's glory in their situation.

Just imagine if Mary and Martha had refused. They would have suffered for nothing and missed an astounding miracle. You may think, *They would never have denied Jesus.* But how often do we suffer and then shut God out, refusing to move the obstacles that block the way to our deepest hurts? We see no immediate good in our situations and may even believe God has abandoned us. So when He comes and tells us what to do to see His glory, we refuse Him and ask, "What's the use?"

Friend, remove the stone. Things may not make sense to you. You may be hurt. You may think, *If I do what He asks, it will stink.* But do not decline anything the Lord shows you to do. When Martha obeyed, Lazarus emerged alive from the tomb. And when you do as God says, what comes forth will bring joy to your soul and help you see how anything is possible with Jesus.

Jesus, I believe You. Help me obey You when it doesn't make sense. Amen.

A Powerful Witness

*This confirms that what I told
you about Christ is true.*

1 CORINTHIANS 1:6 NLT

You may wonder, *Would God allow me—His child—to hurt for the sake of reaching an unsaved person?* But isn't that what Jesus did for you? He endured the cross that you might be saved. So He will work through you during times of difficulty because nothing gets the attention of an unbeliever like a saint who is suffering successfully.

For example, I read of a pastor who discovered his baby would be born with Down syndrome. He was tempted to be disheartened, but then he read Exodus 4:11, where God said to Moses, "Who has made man's mouth? Or who makes him mute or deaf, or seeing or blind? Is it not I, the LORD?" So this young pastor declared to his wife, "The Lord has *blessed us* with a child with Down syndrome." They accepted the situation in faith and, when the baby was born, they shared their joy with everyone. News of their response spread throughout the hospital. The Sunday following the child's birth, thirty nurses went to hear this pastor preach and ended up trusting Jesus as their Savior.

Never underestimate how powerfully your godly attitude to a difficult situation may affect others. Instead, whatever happens, trust Jesus and allow Him to work.

Jesus, may many come to know You as Savior through my struggles. Amen.

Accepting Adversity

We rejoice in our sufferings.

ROMANS 5:3 ESV

The reason many of us struggle so intensely with adversity is that we have yet to adopt God's perspective and priorities. But as you read about the lives of people in Scripture, you will notice that their stories do not end with, "And they lived happily ever after." Often, their stories seem to end just the opposite. Moses died in the desert just a few miles from the promised land. According to tradition, Paul was beheaded by Nero. Many of the disciples were martyred.

Are we to conclude from these examples that God has no interest in His children being happy? No! We are told that heaven will be a place of great rejoicing and that contentment is possible here on earth (Hebrews 13:5). But the Father wants far more for us than a life that is problem-free. Indeed, it's a mistake to think that a problem-free life means we'll be happy. Rather, what He wants for us is much more meaningful and lasting—a relationship with Him that sustains us, spiritual maturity that gives us understanding, a purpose that motivates us, and a vibrant view of eternity with Him in heaven that gives us hope. And that's often what adversity gives us.

·····

Jesus, thank You for all You do through my trials. Help me to learn, Lord. Amen.

God Wants You

He first loved us.

1 JOHN 4:19

We all like to feel wanted. Think about how you've felt whenever someone offered you a job, picked you for a team, or invited you to a particular event. That feeling of being chosen is vital to a proper sense of well-being. One of the most remarkable aspects of the Christian faith is that *God is actively pursuing you.* He has proceeded decisively throughout history to reveal Himself and to demonstrate His love for you.

In a world dominated by the struggle for preeminence and power, divisiveness, alienation, loneliness, rejection, and discouragement are potent predators of the soul. But the entire narrative of Scripture, spanning thousands of years and multiple continents, is the enthralling story of God's relentless pursuit of a relationship with you. And you can celebrate as you see Him as the great lover of your soul.

So if you are feeling down about yourself today, remember that no sin can drive Him away and no failure can thwart His plan for you. Others may ignore or reject you, but your Savior has accepted you for eternity, adopted you permanently into His family, and given you all you need for life and godliness. He wants you—always.

Jesus, thank You for making me worthy by setting Your love on me. Amen.

God's Love

Keep yourselves in the love of God.

JUDE 1:21

The word *love* has so many connotations and has been so often misused that many people have become jaded with it. But the term Scripture uses for the Father's unmatched care—*agape*—is distinct from those that describe common human affection. Therefore, it is crucial to differentiate what we mean by the "love of God," so we can understand the awesome gift we have been given.

Agape love is the unfathomably perfect, completely unselfish, profoundly forgiving, unconditionally sacrificial love that our Savior has shown to us. The most generous or benevolent act a human being could ever perform could never compare with the magnitude of the Father's eternal, unshakable love for you. God's love for you never ends. Like His character, His love remains the same yesterday, today, and forever (Hebrews 13:8).

So what does Jude mean in today's verse? How do you keep yourself in God's love? Always remember that no matter what happens, the Father still loves you unconditionally. Do not allow the Enemy to convince you that you've lost God's acceptance and care because of the trials you face. Instead of fretting over your circumstances, love God back by staying close to Him and obeying Him (John 14:15).

> *Jesus, thank You for Your perfect love. I will follow wherever You lead. Amen.*

God Supplies

*"Because of the groaning of the needy,
now I will arise," says the LORD; "I will set
him in the safety for which he longs."*

PSALM 12:5

The human body is an amazing creation. For example, when a person runs for a long distance, blood flow to the lower extremities increases to supply the muscles. When an infection attacks a certain part of the body, antibodies scramble to the site of the contagion.

The principle that God teaches us through the body is that supply moves to the point of need—and there's a close parallel in the spiritual life. The Lord's help flows to those who admit their inadequacy. Self-reliant people, who may deny their need for divine intervention, are often blinded to their poverty of soul and spirit because of their self-sufficiency. But those who open their broken spirits and contrite hearts to the Lord are filled.

Your need, whatever it may be today, is the signal for God's great and all-encompassing provision. And it isn't just for the obvious place of lack but for all the emotion, energy, and woundedness associated with it. So stop denying it. You don't have to pretend to be strong and invincible. Open your heart to Jesus. Admit you need Him. And watch as He shows you that He is indeed God.

Jesus, thank You for answering my need and ministering to my heart. Amen.

APRIL

Strategic Revelation

*As high priest at that time he was led to prophesy
that Jesus would die for the entire nation.*

JOHN 11:51 NLT

Reading through the Gospel of John, you may catch a strange passage. After Lazarus was raised from the dead, the religious leaders gathered to address how to deal with Jesus. They were afraid Jesus' enormous following would provoke the Romans to destroy Israel to prevent an insurrection.

However, the high priest Caiaphas saw an opportunity to win favor with Rome. He noted, "It's better for you that one man should die for the people than for the whole nation to be destroyed" (John 11:50 NLT). In other words, they would sacrifice Christ to show Rome that Israel wasn't interested in rebelling. But the most shocking part is that Caiaphas said it because *God Himself* had shown him that Jesus would die for the nation.

Of course, we know that Caiaphas heard what he wanted to and completely mistook what the Lord had revealed. But the point is that God will sometimes lead your opponents to do His will, even if they do it for the wrong reason. Ultimately, the Lord's plan of salvation succeeded—not just for Israel but for the whole world. God accomplishes His purposes for you as well. What others mean for evil, He can use for good—always.

....

Jesus, I am so grateful You are always in control. Amen.

Greater Foes

*"Hosanna! Blessed is He who comes
in the name of the Lord."*

MARK 11:9

When Jesus made His triumphal entry into Jerusalem the week before His crucifixion, the people shouted, "Hosanna," which in English roughly means, "We beseech You to save us!" But save them from what? Of course, we know the people were asking for deliverance from Roman oppression. So it must have confused them that Jesus didn't ride in on a warhorse ready to conquer but on a humble foal to be the Suffering Servant. This is because Jesus saw the greater threat to our souls—sin, which would cause an eternity of suffering separated from the Father in hell.

We often do the same thing as the people in Jerusalem—we cry out for God to save us from temporary pain when there are far more destructive forces at work in us. Thankfully, our heavenly Father is always on the offensive toward our greatest foes and is triumphant over them. He not only sets us free from the problems we're aware of but from the unseen adversaries that truly cripple us.

So whenever you're perplexed about what the Lord is doing, remember that He has a unique perspective about your most pressing needs and never ignores any of the challenges you face. Trust Him to choose the right battles.

*Jesus, thank You for saving me in every way—especially
when I'm not aware of the danger. Amen.*

An Example of Service

*"I gave you an example that you also
should do as I did to you."*

JOHN 13:15

P eter was a natural leader, and he had an established view of
what the role required. However, the events of Christ's last
week on earth changed Peter's perspective concerning earthly
authority. Certainly, watching the Savior wrap a towel around His
waist and wash the disciples' feet had to be shocking and impactful.
In fact, when Christ approached Peter with the basin of water, the
disciple recoiled. But Jesus was firm, saying, "If I do not wash you,
you have no part with Me" (John 13:8).

Jesus was teaching how humanity would be accepted by God
and what serving the Lord would mean. We now know that He
first cleanses—saves—us so that we may know Him. But second,
He demonstrated how to represent Him to others through ministry. It takes humility to allow God to work through you in His way
and power in order to serve others. But as Jesus said to the disciples,
"If anyone wants to be first, he shall be last of all and servant of all"
(Mark 9:35). The only way you will develop a servant's spirit is to
put God first, others second, and yourself last. Do as He's modeled
and serve in the manner He commands.

Jesus, teach me to serve others as You would. Amen.

Enduring the Trial

"These things I have spoken to you so that
you may be kept from stumbling."

JOHN 16:1

J esus was aware of the suffering ahead and how His crucifixion
would affect His disciples. He warned them, "You will weep
and lament, but . . . your grief will be turned into joy" (John 16:20).
Christ's plan for redemption didn't include rescuing His followers
from the immediate trouble of their circumstances. The test of faith
would be great, but necessary, as they would become His representatives throughout the world.

Soon after Jesus said these words, He bore the agony of the
cross and was a living example of how to withstand tribulation.
Because He was anchored in the Father's plan, not in the things of
the world, Christ endured. He was not shaken when false accusations were hurled at Him, nor was He cowed by the earthly pain.
He went to the cross, fulfilled His mission, and was gloriously
resurrected.

Jesus made it clear that we'll all face adversity as believers. But
we can do so victoriously when we remember His word to us: "Take
courage; I have overcome the world" (John 16:33). So don't fret
if you suffer today. Like Jesus, tell the Father, "Not My will, but
Yours be done" (Luke 22:42), and expect Him to conquer in your
situation and bring you joy.

Jesus, not my will, but Yours. Glorify Yourself in me. Amen.

Stand in the Spirit

If you are reviled for the name of Christ,
you are blessed, because the Spirit of
glory and of God rests on you.

1 PETER 4:14

The night of the Lord's last supper, Peter told Jesus, "Lord, with You I am ready to go both to prison and to death!" (Luke 22:33). It was a courageous declaration. A short time later, however, as Jesus struggled in prayer in the garden of Gethsemane, Peter could not stay awake long enough to intercede for the One he called Master. His resolve was further weakened after Jesus' arrest, when Peter denied Jesus three times.

When the time came for him to stand for the Lord, Peter folded. What happened? It simply wasn't within his ability to withstand an attack of the Enemy. He relied on his own limited strength and failed.

However, the good news is that in the book of Acts, Peter was completely transformed because God's Spirit was alive within him—empowering him to stand firm. In other words, he could hold on to God because the Lord held on to him. The power you have in Christ is all you need to endure in the fiercest battles, the deepest sorrows, and the longest waits. What Peter could not do on his own, he did mightily in the Holy Spirit, and you can too.

Jesus, strengthen me by Your Spirit to stand firm for You.
Amen.

In the Plan

"All this has taken place to fulfill the
Scriptures of the prophets." Then all
the disciples left Him and fled.

MATTHEW 26:56

Like the disciples when Jesus was arrested, you may be in a situation that appears completely overwhelming. Do not despair—God is in control. When Pilate asked Jesus, "Do You not know that I have authority to release You, and I have authority to crucify You?" Christ answered him, "You would have no authority over Me, unless it had been given you from above" (John 19:10–11). Earlier, Jesus reassured His disciples that not even a common sparrow—worth only half a penny—could fall to the ground apart from the Father's will (Matthew 10:29). Whether the circumstance is large or small, God is in absolute control.

We must realize that nothing can touch us except what the Father allows. Sometimes that includes hardship, which leaves us wondering, *How can this possibly be good?* Yet many people who have gone through tremendous trials can say, "I despised the difficulty while I was going through it. But on this side of it, I can see why He allowed it." God has His purposes and with perfect timing will bring blessing from our tribulations. That was certainly the case for Christ's crucifixion, which purchased our salvation.

My Savior, I trust You. May Your will be fulfilled in my
life. Amen.

The Ultimate Demonstration

God demonstrates His own love toward us, in that
while we were yet sinners, Christ died for us.

ROMANS 5:8

You can depend on God's character because it is His very nature to love (1 John 4:8). He is both merciful and holy, which means He could never mistreat one of His children. He will always do what is beneficial and caring in our lives—even when we don't understand what He is doing.

Of course, there is no greater proof of God's profound love than the cross. All of us were in dire need of forgiveness and rescue from the penalty of sin, but we could not save ourselves—our debt could be satisfied only by the payment of a perfect life (Deuteronomy 17:1). The heavenly Father made our salvation possible by sending His Son, Jesus, to die on the cross as our substitute, which is indisputable evidence of His sacrificial, infinite love.

God's love is also revealed in the covenant expressing His intention to make us His children (Jeremiah 31:33). Once we trust Jesus Christ as our personal Savior, we are members of God's family and our perfect heavenly Father guides us as His children.

We can trust God because He gave everything for us. Therefore, give yourself freely to Him.

Jesus, thank You for loving me so sacrificially. Help me to live my life for You. Amen.

Remember What He Can Do

*"Go quickly and tell His disciples that
He has risen from the dead."*

MATTHEW 28:7

God has given us resurrection power to overcome any seeming defeat. But that's so easy to forget, isn't it? After all, the disciples had witnessed the resurrection of Lazarus shortly before Jesus was crucified, and they still fell apart when they saw Him on the cross. However, imagine how much easier the three days between the crucifixion and resurrection would have been if instead of wondering, *What are we going to do now?* they had simply asked each other, "What does God want us to learn through this?" Perhaps they would have remembered Jesus' words when Lazarus came out of the tomb: "I am the resurrection and the life . . . If you believe, you will see the glory of God" (John 11:25, 40). Or maybe they would have recalled when He told them that He would be raised on the third day (Matthew 16:21).

There are so many things you'll learn and so much comfort you'll receive if you'll just trust God, obey His instruction, and wait for Him to work—especially when things are at their worst. Keep your heart open and teachable whenever you face disappointments, and fix your focus steadfastly on Jesus. Because in His economy, resurrection follows crucifixion.

*Jesus, help me always to remember how You can bring good
from every situation. Amen.*

Resurrection Transformation

"Why do you seek the living One among the dead?"

LUKE 24:5

Jesus is alive. Let that fact sink deep into your soul.

He had no more heartbeat, no pulse. But the battle was not over. Three days later, by His supernatural power, He arose. He lives! Indeed, Matthew 27:51–53 talks about the incredibly colossal force of the crucifixion and resurrection: "The veil of the temple was torn in two from top to bottom; and the earth shook and the rocks were split. The tombs were opened, and many bodies of the saints who had fallen asleep were raised; and coming out of the tombs after His resurrection they entered the holy city and appeared to many." With Jesus' victory, heaven and earth were eternally shaken and transformed to the core—and even the dead came out of their graves to testify. The way to God is open, and the empty tomb proves it.

But has the power of resurrection shaken *you* to the core? Do you serve a dead religion? Or have you really considered what it means that you have a living Savior—one who can enliven the grave places in your life? Don't continue to endure a weak, meaningless existence when the very power of the resurrection is available to you. Look to Jesus and live.

....

Jesus, help me to know and understand the power of Your resurrection. Amen.

The Victorious Life

Thanks be to God, who gives us the victory
through our Lord Jesus Christ.

1 CORINTHIANS 15:57

his is the essence of the abundant life Jesus gives you: you can endure and overcome any situation because you are joined inseparably to the Lord Jesus Christ, who has victoriously conquered the forces of sin and death. Paul wrote that he wanted to know the Savior in "the power of His resurrection" (Philippians 3:10). He longed to experience the indwelling, supernatural might of Christ day by day—the kind that fears no foe or obstacle because the Lord God has been proven triumphant over them all through the empty tomb. Nothing is too difficult for Him.

For you, that is a reality through your indivisible union with the risen Jesus. Your life can be victorious as well. But understand that you overcome not by willpower or positive thinking but by submission to and reliance on the triumphant Spirit of God in you.

So claim it—victory is yours! It may not arrive instantly, but it takes hold as you walk with Jesus, obey Him, and trust in His wisdom and power. The Christian life will be abundant as you shift your focus from self-effort to the all-conquering resurrection might of Christ Jesus, within whom is your hope and your path to the greatest triumph.

Jesus, in You is my victory always. Amen.

In His Power

"You are clothed with power from on high."

LUKE 24:49

D o you believe Christ was merely a good man who gave us an example of how to live? Or do you believe that Jesus is God incarnate and that His sacrifice on the cross achieved supernatural, eternal victories over sin and death, opening the way for you to know Him? This belief about Christ makes all the difference in your life.

When you receive Jesus as your Savior and Lord, He indwells you with His Holy Spirit and empowers you to know Him, trust Him, and serve Him. Unfortunately, many people see Jesus as merely a moral example rather than the living God who works through them to carry out His will. So they try to be good and to please Him in their own strength and wisdom. It is no wonder they eventually grow tired and discouraged.

That was never Christ's plan. He wants to pour His power, wisdom, and strength through you so others can see Him in you and believe in Him. So what do you really believe about Jesus? Place your faith in Him to do more than you could ask or imagine.

Jesus, I want to know the power of the resurrection. Teach me to walk in Your Spirit, wisdom, and strength. Amen.

A Single Seed

"Unless a grain of wheat falls into the earth and dies, it remains alone; but if it dies, it bears much fruit."

JOHN 12:24

A single seed will remain in its solitary state until it is dropped into the earth and covered with soil. The seed must be buried—positioned to die with the purpose of reproducing life. Before long, the seed's outer shell breaks open, and a little green sprout begins to push its way up through the soil until it breaks through into the sunshine. It grows into a stalk of wheat, producing dozens of grains that could propagate into plants of their own. From one grain, there could eventually be millions of acres of wheat.

In today's verse, Jesus described what would happen to Him through His crucifixion and resurrection. Before He could purchase salvation and His resurrection life could work through us, Jesus had to die. So He willingly gave His life as a sacrifice. But Jesus also taught that this principle applies to us—as long as we remain unyielded to Him, we cannot bear eternal fruit that lasts and multiplies. Therefore, we must take up our crosses daily, dying to ourselves and living according to His purposes. When we do so, He works through us, doing the miraculous and saving others.

Jesus, I die to myself and surrender to You. Work through me. Amen.

In Dying, Live

"He who loves his life loses it, and he who hates his life in this world will keep it to life eternal."

JOHN 12:25

Some trials feel like death to us, and we wonder, *Where is God?* Understand that He's been with you from the first hint of pain and continues to be with you as He does this refining work in you. But before you can live as fully as the Father created you to, you must first die to your desire to control your circumstances. You must be prepared to let go of your self-will—your dreams, ambitions, and goals—and allow the Lord to make you into a vessel useful for *His* purposes.

We see this principle in all God's works. Grain must be ground into flour for us to have bread. Olives must be pressed to make oil. And of course, we have salvation because Jesus allowed Himself to be crushed by the weight of our sins.

It is painful when our self-will dies, but as a result, we find fully productive and useful lives. So ask God to reveal to you what He's doing and to help you see this breaking process in light of His great design for you. Only then can you truly know life to the fullest and find your purpose realized completely.

Jesus, I belong to You. Breathe Your resurrection life in me. Amen.

A New Role

*"You will receive power when the Holy Spirit has
come upon you; and you shall be My witnesses."*

ACTS 1:8

Before Jesus' ascension, the disciples eagerly asked the resurrected Savior about His intentions for their persecuted nation: "Lord, is it at this time You are restoring the kingdom to Israel?" (Acts 1:6). Jesus never answered their query, informing them instead of the imminent, personal ministry of the Holy Spirit and their new role as His followers.

Don't miss the importance of this. Although we all have piercing questions we would like answered, we are never to be overly occupied with them. The nation God had established as His own was enslaved. The disciples' desire to see Israel freed was good and godly. However, Jesus was establishing a new citizenship for His eternal realm. And in order to be partakers in His holy kingdom, what the apostles needed—and what we need as well—were the power and presence of the Holy Spirit.

There is something so much bigger that God is doing in the world, and He actively wants you to be part of it. He gives you the divine enabling to know and follow Jesus in order to accomplish the eternal goals He sets. Therefore, let go of the lesser things. Trust Him, obey Him, and let Him work through you.

*Jesus, I trust and obey You for the sake of Your kingdom.
Amen.*

Praying for Others

Pray at all times in the Spirit . . .
and petition for all the saints.

EPHESIANS 6:18

W hen you're praying for yourself, you can usually express what you want and how you feel. But when you intercede for someone else, it's much more difficult to articulate requests for them. After all, you may not be familiar with their personal needs and desires. Yet God designed prayer as the primary way we support our brothers and sisters in Christ. Of course, He doesn't need your participation in order to work on their behalf, but He chooses to involve you so you can experience the joy of seeing His answers in the lives of those around you.

So where do you begin? Start with a heart of love and a desire to see the Lord transform the person's life as He pleases. Next, try to put yourself in their shoes and identify with their needs so you can pray effectively. Most important, be willing to be an active participant in God's answer if that's what He calls you to do. As you pray for the people the Lord brings to your attention, you'll experience the motivating joy of being His hands and feet, you will see His work in their lives, and you'll be filled with wonder as His blessings unfold mightily.

Jesus, teach me to pray for others and make me a blessing to Your people. Amen.

True Faith

*Believe that God exists and that he
rewards those who sincerely seek him.*
HEBREWS 11:6 NLT

Faith isn't just for spiritual heroes of great renown. It's not a mysterious condition that the super-godly enjoy or a contrived mindset that admits only positive thinking. Put simply, faith is trust that God is who He says He is and that He'll do what He promises in His Word.

For example, Moses didn't stand before the pharaoh of Egypt on behalf of the people of Israel because he believed he would perform well for the Lord. Rather, he confronted Pharaoh because he trusted God to give him the ability to accomplish what he'd been called to do. Indeed, when you read the stories of Old Testament saints, you discover that many were powerless, poor, inadequate, or unskilled when the Lord laid His hand on their lives. But they became His instruments to do mighty works as they expressed confidence in His holy character. In other words, they were weak people who served the almighty God. The emphasis was always on Him.

That's who you can be too. Faith is the ability to lean on God with all you face. Trust that He exists and that He wants to bless you. Then obey whatever He tells you to do.

*Jesus, I believe You exist and that You're always good to me.
Help me to honor You. Amen.*

Empowered in Prayer

These all with one mind were continually devoting themselves to prayer.

ACTS 1:14

Jesus' disciples saw Him work many miracles during the three years He mentored them. So it is no surprise that they asked Him to give them the key to His phenomenal power and wisdom. "Lord, teach us to pray," they requested (Luke 11:1). They had watched how Jesus spent time with the Father and had seen that it was central to the astonishing things He accomplished. So after Jesus had been crucified and resurrected, they retreated to do what He had taught them: pray.

What Jesus taught them was a pattern for all of us as believers. At the heart of Christ's instructions was the pivotal phrase, "Your kingdom come. Your will be done, on earth as it is in heaven" (Matthew 6:10). That is the core of genuine prayer: seeking and submitting to the will of God in every circumstance. It helped that small group of disciples take the gospel to the world after Jesus' resurrection—through it, the Lord gave them the message, strategy, and endurance to prevail despite persecution. Prayer will help you endure and succeed in whatever your circumstance is today as well. Let your time with the Father steer you into His will and give you the power to triumph in His name.

Jesus, teach me to pray so that I can serve You with passion, purpose, and power. Amen.

Beyond Imagination

"Follow Me, and I will make you fishers of men."

MATTHEW 4:19

While the disciples labored with their nets at the Sea of Galilee, they most likely had no idea of all the things that Jesus had in store for them. However, they acknowledged Christ's authority and felt compelled to obey Him because "immediately they left their nets and followed Him" when He called (Matthew 4:20).

Although it's likely that Peter and Andrew had learned about Yahweh throughout their lives, they probably never dreamed He'd choose them for His most important mission. Indeed, walking with the incarnate God was beyond what they could have imagined. They couldn't possibly have anticipated the blessings and trials of the future or how the Savior would work through them to take the gospel to the world. But Jesus did so because Peter and Andrew obeyed Him.

This is a pattern God replicates in your life. As you mature in Christ, you may struggle to put His instructions into practice. But remember that the Lord has a future planned for you that requires you to take the steps of obedience that He sets before you. Just as He transformed Peter and Andrew from fishermen into world-changers, He wants to do the same for you as well. And what He'll accomplish through you will certainly be beyond imagination.

Jesus, I will obey You. Work through me, Lord. Amen.

Not Easy, but Worthwhile

*I consider that the sufferings of this present
time are not worthy to be compared with
the glory that is to be revealed to us.*

ROMANS 8:18

At times, the adversity you face will be so long-lasting, painful, and profound that your response to any type of encouragement may be, "That's easy for you to say." How could anyone possibly know the depth of the despair you feel? Devotions, sermons, and books about trials tend to oversimplify when it comes to the subject of suffering, and I realize that what you face may be truly heart-wrenching. But that doesn't change the fact that God wants to work through the adversity to advance your spiritual growth.

We know the Lord could erase all difficulty from our lives with just a word—and someday He may do so for you. However, Scripture tells us that when He chooses not to it's because more important than our ease, comfort, and pleasure is our transformation into Christ's likeness. The Lord is in the process of teaching us about Himself: His faithfulness, goodness, compassion, and holiness. He is also breaking down all the places in us where we have erroneously set ourselves up as god instead of Him. It is painful. But the process is essential if we are to mature in the Lord and represent Him to others.

Jesus, I submit to You. Do as You see best in me. Amen.

He Remembers

God remembered Noah.

GENESIS 8:1

Waiting for the water to recede must have felt interminable to Noah. Sure, God had saved him and his family from the flood, and they were grateful. But how long would they be trapped in the ark with a cargo hold full of restless animals?

Much to their relief, the Lord remained faithful to His promise and eventually placed Noah and his crew on dry ground. However, we may feel somewhat unnerved when we read, "God *remembered* Noah." Had the Lord forgotten him? No. Our omniscient Redeemer forgets nothing—especially when it comes to His people.

The human authors of Scripture used the term *remember* to describe God's activity after it *seems* His involvement had lapsed. Surviving the difficult days when it *appears* that our cries for help have been ignored can be challenging for our faith. We feel forgotten—especially when circumstances go from bad to worse.

But always remember: although God is silent, He is never still—He's always at work in your life to bring about His purpose and plan. You can count on Him, regardless of the situation. He does not forget or ignore you, and He never abandons you. So do not despair. Take heart and wait for His deliverance. Soon enough, He will open the door.

Jesus, thank You for the reminder that You are always at work, even when I don't see it. Amen.

His Goals and Methods

"Has the LORD as much delight in burnt offerings
and sacrifices as in obeying the voice of the LORD?"
1 SAMUEL 15:22

S aul wanted to be a good, godly king who ruled fairly and followed God's ways. However, his motives weren't always pure.
At one point, the Lord told him to utterly destroy the Amalekites
in battle. They had ruthlessly persecuted Israel after the Exodus,
and God never forgot the evil they committed against His people.
So Saul complied with the Lord's command and headed into battle.
However, once the dust settled, he decided to spare the Amalekite
king, his strongest fighting men, and the best of his sheep and
oxen. Saul tried in vain to convince the prophet Samuel that he
had obeyed God by saving the best of the spoils as a sacrifice. But
it was not obedience that motivated Saul; it was pride, and that cost
him his throne.

Partial obedience is not obedience; it is disobedience, and there
is never an excuse for it. Whatever goal the Lord has placed before
you, He has a method in mind for you to follow in achieving it. Ask
Him to give you His wisdom so that you may accomplish the goal
perfectly, completely, and—most important—obediently.

Lord Jesus, show me what to do so that I may faithfully
honor You in both Your goals and Your methods. Amen.

Embrace the Pauses

*Cease striving and know that I
am God; I will be exalted.*

PSALM 46:10

I am an achievement-oriented person; I like to see projects begun and completed—and I often have several of them going at the same time. I enjoy moving forward. Because of my go-go-go personality and lifestyle, nothing is more frustrating to me than getting sick or experiencing some kind of setback because I feel like I'm wasting time.

Perhaps you have trouble with illnesses and impediments to your productivity as well. Maybe you're like me and think, *I just don't have time for this.* It could even be that you believe everything will fall apart if you're not actively managing it all.

But the truth is, ultimately, God is in charge. And He allows sicknesses and setbacks to remind us to look to Him. We may begin to ask, "Lord, what are You saying to me? What do You want me to learn? What about my lifestyle needs to be changed or eliminated?" But often, we don't ask these questions until we're flat on our backs. It is during these seasons that God will teach us some of the most exciting things we've ever learned.

Jesus, thank You that these pauses are Your way of refocusing my attention on You. Amen.

Good Answers

*I hope in You, O LORD; You will
answer, O Lord my God.*

PSALM 38:15

Whenever you request something from God, you can confidently expect one of three answers from Him—yes, no, or wait. You can also know for certain that His response is informed by His love and wisdom—He has the best in mind for you. This may be particularly difficult to accept when He says no to something you desire. However, do not despair. God has not rejected you; rather, He is working through your external circumstances to shape and direct you.

The way to keep yourself in the position for His perfect plan to be accomplished in you is to think about the following questions. First, *Have I yielded every area of my life to God, or does my request represent a corner of resistance within me?* At times, what we ask of Him are ways we've constructed to avoid either His will or His authority. If so, repent and surrender everything to Him immediately.

Second, we ask, *Am I obeying God in what He has already shown me to do?* The Lord will direct you step-by-step. At times, His "no" is because you are refusing to obey in some area He has already revealed to you. So do as He says and always trust His answers.

Jesus, I accept Your response and how You direct me. Amen.

Restoration to Ministry

"Do you love Me? . . . Tend My sheep."

JOHN 21:17

Each of us at one time or another has done something to cast a shadow over our relationship with the Lord, and we've felt terrible about it. Peter certainly did. We can imagine that after denying Jesus before the crucifixion and then witnessing the resurrection, Peter must have felt incredibly unworthy.

However, it is noteworthy that one of the last appearances Jesus made to His disciples was along the Sea of Galilee, where Peter had returned to his former occupation of fishing. After a meal of grilled fish, Jesus took Peter aside to restore him. Three times Peter had denied Jesus, so the Lord gave him three opportunities to restate his devotion. But Christ also taught the disciple that real love for Him cannot be hindered by fear—it must proceed in obedience.

You may be struggling with whether God still accepts you after your failures. He absolutely does. Not only does He bring you restoration, comfort, and healing, but He will also challenge you to advance in faith by giving you a ministry to accomplish. Do you love Him? Then, like Peter after the resurrection, don't be afraid. Be courageous in your love for Jesus by repenting and serving His people.

....

Jesus, I do love You and will obey You. Show me how to serve Your people. Amen.

Why Prayer

*I will hear what God the LORD will
say; for He will speak peace.*

PSALM 85:8

The strength and vitality of relationships are built through communication. This is especially true when considering how you relate to God. If you don't talk to Him and listen to what He is saying to you, you miss out on so much, including the joy of close fellowship with Him. That's why prayer is so essential. It is a conversation with the Lord in which you open yourself to Him and get to know Him in return—which usually leads to praise and thanksgiving. In the process, God speaks to you through His Word, by the Holy Spirit, and through your circumstances—letting you know how great His love and plan for you truly are.

Prayer was never meant to be a burdensome responsibility. On the contrary, it is the immense honor and privilege of interacting with the Creator and Sustainer of everything in existence. He is all-powerful and all-knowing, and He wants to protect you, heal you, guide you, teach you, and help you succeed. There is nothing you could face that He can't handle. And He always invites you into His loving presence to remind you of His comfort, help, wisdom, and encouragement. So why wouldn't you want to enjoy time with Him? Go to Him. It's time to talk.

Jesus, here I am. Speak to me, Lord. Amen.

Reverent Honesty

The Spirit also helps our weakness; for we do not
know how to pray as we should, but the Spirit Himself
intercedes for us with groanings too deep for words.

ROMANS 8:26

Have you ever wondered, *Is there a wrong way to pray?* Do you ever question whether your words to the Father are acceptable or if there's anything you shouldn't say? Then realize that God always understands what you're thinking and feeling, and He knows exactly what you mean even when you cannot find the words to express what's inside you.

What is essential, however, is your *attitude* in prayer. The Lord's goal is not simply to grant your wishes and desires. Rather, He wants you to know that He is God Almighty, Creator and Sustainer of heaven and earth, who is good and loving toward you. When you approach Him, your supplication is to the highest throne—the supreme authority. So respect Him, offering reverence, awe, and deference to the King of kings and Lord of lords. The Holy Spirit will help you.

And yes, you can be honest about your feelings—He already knows them. Always tell God the truth. But also recognize the power and holiness of the Lord and respond to whatever He shows you with a repentant, willing, and worshipful spirit.

Jesus, You are God! I know that You are good and right in however You lead me. Amen.

Seek Him Always

Pray without ceasing.

1 THESSALONIANS 5:17

Most believers recognize the importance of praying and that they should do it more. So they seek God when they're in trouble or have a pressing need; however, when the burden wanes, so does their fellowship with Him. Yet the apostle Paul said that we should *always* be in prayer. That doesn't mean that you must be voicing a prayer every waking moment. Rather, his point is about priority—God's presence and perspective about the situations of your life should be first place in your heart and mind.

In other words, as you go through the day, bring to Him the needs and problems you encounter. If you're going to see someone with whom there is conflict, seek the Father's wisdom concerning that individual. If you face a challenge, pursue Jesus' direction about what to do. If a task goes well, thank Him for His help. If you are on your way to a meeting, ask Him to prepare your mind, give you clarity and insight, and give you ears to listen to your coworkers. Share all your experiences with Christ and rely on His moment-by-moment guidance. Soon prayer will be more than just a hit-or-miss activity; it will be a continual mindset and all-pervasive attitude.

Jesus, I want You in every moment of my life. Teach me to pray without ceasing. Amen.

Asking and Receiving

"Ask, and it will be given to you; seek, and you
will find; knock, and it will be opened to you."

LUKE 11:9

Maybe you've asked God for something—perhaps the most profound desire of your heart—and He didn't seem to answer. So when you read a passage like the one above, you wrestle with some hurt. You trusted Him, so why hasn't He responded to your request? You wonder, *Why doesn't God help me?*

But let's look more closely at how Jesus described this process of asking and receiving from your heavenly Father. In it, prayer isn't passive; it is active involvement in a relationship with the living God who wants to bless you. So when Jesus says to ask, He wants you involved every step of the way. Notice the progression. You begin with asking—telling the Father what you need and placing it in His care. Then you move to the seeking and knocking phase, looking for His answer and obeying Him in the opportunities He brings.

You won't wander in confusion and frustration when you ask the Father to show the way and then stay in fellowship with Him. Sometimes God won't respond in the way you hope or expect, but you'll always find that He leads you to the absolute best for you.

....

Jesus, in every way, You have my best interest at heart. Lead
me, Lord. Amen.

Praise and Power

When they began to sing, the LORD threw
the invading armies into a panic.

2 CHRONICLES 20:22 GNT

There is something about praising God that brings His presence into our circumstances in an astounding way. When Judah faced three overwhelming opposing armies, King Jehoshaphat sent his singers out to battle with the war cry, "Give thanks to the LORD, for His lovingkindness is everlasting" (2 Chronicles 20:21). Their enemies ended up destroying each other, while Judah's army never lifted a sword!

Praising God in our challenges focuses our attention on His very real and powerful help. Such exaltation fixes our emotions and thoughts on the greatness of our Deliverer, which in turn brings our troubles into manageable perspective. What relationship can He not heal? What enemy can He not conquer?

The more you praise, the more you magnify the One who is truly in charge of all things. So go to the Lord in worship and adoration when your soul is troubled and the night is dark. Confess aloud verses that describe God's loving-kindness and greatness and think about how good He has been to you. Then watch for the steady influx of His strength and hope. Because when you have rightly exalted the Lord, He will lift you up.

Jesus, I worship and magnify You. To You be all praise and adoration. Amen.

God Is Here

God is our refuge and strength, a
very present help in trouble.

PSALM 46:1

God is with you. Always. Maybe He seems distant, or perhaps there is some aspect of life that makes you feel very much alone. But the reality is that He is as near to you as your own heartbeat.

David understood the Lord's continuing presence and was greatly reassured by it. In awe, he wrote, "You go before me and follow me. You place your hand of blessing on my head. Such knowledge is too wonderful for me, too great for me to understand! . . . If I dwell by the farthest oceans, even there your hand will guide me, and your strength will support me" (Psalm 139:5–6, 9–10 NLT). Wherever David could go, God was already there. Therefore, there was never a reason for David to fear.

The same is true for you, which should be a tremendous comfort. The Savior is always available to you to strengthen, deliver, pardon, encourage, guide, rescue, and bless you. He will never abandon or forsake you no matter what you do or how you may try to run from Him. He claims you and calls you His own. So stop pushing Him away. Embrace His presence with you and trust Him.

Jesus, I am so grateful that I can always count on Your
presence and help. Amen.

MAY

God Knows

You keep track of all my sorrows. You have
collected all my tears in your bottle. You
have recorded each one in your book.

PSALM 56:8 NLT

God sees and remembers every one of your tears. That is how profoundly He cares for you. He understands that the tears you shed are the deepest expression of your being and communicate what words often cannot. Others may have no idea how many nights you've wept yourself to sleep, but your heavenly Father has been there every time, catching each tear from your eyes and hearing the most private and difficult cries of your heart.

God knows you—all of you. And He understands you. He realizes the burdens you bear and when you cannot go one more step. He also sees what this present challenge is doing to you. And He is gentle and affectionate toward you. He speaks to your innermost being in the most personal and healing manner.

So listen for Him—He tells you He loves you and wants to be your refuge. Quietly and attentively hear what He has to say because He deals with you tenderly to soothe your inner pain and set you free from the bondage that suffocates you. He cares for you, and He knows what He's doing. Allow Him to wipe away your sorrow.

Jesus, You are intimately aware of my suffering. Thank You
for loving me. Amen.

Testing and Refinement

He knows the way I take; when He has
tried me, I shall come forth as gold.

JOB 23:10

God allowed Job to suffer incredible loss for reasons that were His alone. It was not because Job did anything wrong. On the contrary, he was described as "blameless, upright, fearing God and turning away from evil" (Job 1:1). Yet God gave Satan permission to strike everything Job had, but not the man himself.

Job's situation perfectly demonstrates the mystery of trials in the life of the believer. Even the godly and faithful may undergo testing in this life that seems overwhelming and even unjust. However, throughout Job's pain and losses, the Lord never abandoned him for even a moment. Our sovereign God knew how greatly Job was being afflicted each step of the way and gave him the strength, clarity of mind, and resilience to stand it. Through it all, Job was being refined and gaining a more profound understanding of God (Job 42:5). And in the end, the Father cared for and blessed His servant (Job 42:10).

The same is true for us. Anytime we find ourselves being tested, we know our sovereign God is overseeing our transformation and refinement. He sees the beginning and the end and has a good future designed for us. So do not despair. Trust Him.

Jesus, You know the way I take. Mold me, my Savior.
Amen.

His Workmanship

We are His workmanship, created in Christ
Jesus for good works, which God prepared
beforehand so that we would walk in them.

EPHESIANS 2:10

Y ou may not feel very good about yourself at times—you may be so aware of your faults that you're convinced you're not as good as other people and are beyond redeeming. However, Scripture is emphatic that you are God's workmanship from start to finish. He created you and has good works that you are to accomplish for Him—assignments that require your unique mix of talents, personality, experiences, and abilities.

Jesus is the Author and Finisher of your story, and not the half has been told. You have a very limited perspective of the plot, and as long as you insist on forging your own path, He will not write His living will on your heart. However, once you acknowledge Him as your sovereign King and Lord, He will show you His viewpoint of your life—what He is accomplishing—and He will guide you into his wholeness, fruitfulness, and blessings.

So stop evaluating your worth and look to the One who continues to work on you. If He could take Joseph from prison and make him second in command of Egypt, there is no telling what He could do through you.

Jesus, thank You for seeing something worthwhile in me. Be glorified in my life. Amen.

Perplexed but Trusting

*We are afflicted in every way, but not
crushed; perplexed, but not despairing.*

2 CORINTHIANS 4:8

I f you are confused as to what the Lord is doing in your life, do not fear. Perplexity is to be expected in the Christian life. This is because we serve an infinite God who is always working to bring about His agenda, but we are limited and not privy to His schedule or what He will use to accomplish it. His ways and thoughts are completely different from ours, and so we are pretty much guaranteed to face circumstances that challenge our preconceived notions and raise questions.

But also understand that your trust in Christ is shaped and molded where human answers fail. The righteous, after all, live by faith. Trusting the Lord when few things make sense is how mature believers are established and how God works in you.

So do not fear when you don't have answers, when you don't know the way forward, or when your expectations are dramatically different from your reality. Your Savior is the only One who knows the end from the beginning, and He loves to lead you. What's important is not that you know *what* to do but *who* it is you follow. So relax in Jesus' care. He will show you what to do one step at a time.

Jesus, I don't know, but You do. I will follow You. Amen.

Christ Through You

They will see your honorable behavior,
and they will give honor to God.

1 PETER 2:12 NLT

I 'll never forget the amazing statement I heard from a young man as we talked about his upcoming mission trip. He had some of the normal anxieties that usually accompany such an endeavor, but he also had a tremendous amount of enthusiasm. And as he prayed, his words caught my attention: "Lord, I pray that those who meet me during my stay also encounter You." That struck me in a profound manner. He wanted the contact between him and others to be a genuine encounter with the person of Christ Himself.

Frankly, that is a goal for which all believers should strive. Indeed, I wonder what would happen if each of us adopted that same mindset. How would our days be different if each morning we asked Jesus to so permeate our words and deeds that others would sense the reality of His presence with us? How would it transform our families, coworkers, friends, acquaintances, and even our enemies? It would certainly change the world.

So consider: do others see Jesus in you? People desperately need His salvation. Don't keep Him a secret. Allow Him to work through you so others can witness His awesome presence and know Him as well.

Jesus, may anyone who encounters me find You and believe in Your name. Amen.

A Spiritual Operation

It is good for me that I was afflicted.

PSALM 119:71

In a sense, the trials we face are like surgery. Perhaps there is a medical issue that we must address, and the doctors say we will be better off if we have an operation. Though we believe them, that doesn't make the procedure any less invasive and excruciating. By submitting to the surgeon, we accept that our health comes at the cost of pain.

Adversity is the same way, though the problem is spiritual and often not as easy to diagnose. But it is God's tool for rooting out what is destroying us from within.

Perhaps this is difficult for you to accept. In light of the suffering you or a loved one has faced, it may seem like an easy excuse. If that's where you are in your thinking, I want you to contemplate this question: If adversity is not a tool in the hand of God, what is it? Too many deny the Lord's existence based on the presence of pain. However, that means that to validate His existence, God must conduct Himself according to our human wishes. Clearly, there are multiple problems with that. Thankfully, if we view trials as God's tools to help us mature, we'll learn from them and experience healing more profound than any mere surgery could ever hope to achieve.

....

Jesus, I believe my troubles are for my good. Heal me, my Great Physician. Amen.

Keep Representing Him

Blessed is a man who perseveres under
trial; for once he has been approved,
he will receive the crown of life.

JAMES 1:12

God understands the profound trauma adversity can cause us—especially when we face persecution due to our devotion to His name. He has not overlooked the sacrifices we are forced to make or how we are treated. Instead, He provides a special reward for those who "persevere under trial." This "crown of life" is reserved for those who willingly and lovingly represent Jesus regardless of the cost.

At times people—even other believers—will put you down, reject you, and even harass you because you remain true to Christ and His Word. This will be increasingly true as the culture turns further away from Him. Are you persevering? Or are you angry at God for what He is allowing others to do to you?

Remember that people mistreated Jesus the same way. But Christ encourages you by saying, "Blessed are you when people insult you and persecute you, and falsely say all kinds of evil against you because of Me. Rejoice and be glad, for your reward in heaven is great" (Matthew 5:11–12). So don't give up. Maintain a loving, Christlike attitude, and keep representing Him well.

Jesus, help me endure and maintain an attitude that honors You. Amen.

Choosing to Trust

God heard their groaning . . . and
God took notice of them.

EXODUS 2:24–25

As the pains of childbirth subsided, Jochebed held her new baby boy for the first time. She should have felt joy, but instead she felt a sickening knot forming in her stomach. Pharoah's decree demanded that her baby be killed immediately, simply because he was a Hebrew boy. However, under the threat of death, Jochebed made a choice—she decided to honor the Lord who had given her the child. Jochebed couldn't know that one day God would use her boy, Moses, to deliver the entire nation of Israel from Egyptian oppression. But through her act of faith, the Lord turned defeat into hope for countless generations.

Remember this whenever circumstances change—and especially when it's for the worse. The shift may cause you to question why the Lord is allowing such evil in the world and whether you should follow Him at all. The more unexplainable the situation, the easier it is to give in to doubt. However, when you see God's provision as part of a larger picture, it's easier to trust Him. Remember that there is much more going on than what you see. Honor Him, and He will take what is frightening and turn it into a reason for rejoicing.

Jesus, I don't understand what's going on, but I will honor
and trust You. Amen.

Giant Challenges

"The battle is the Lord's and He will give you into our hands."

1 SAMUEL 17:47

Every morning, the gigantic Philistine warrior named Goliath would shout at the Israelite army and dare them to fight him. The entire Israelite army would respond by turning and running back to their camp in fear. This pattern of events had been repeated for some time when the boy named David appeared on the scene.

We all know how David gathered five stones and went down into the valley to challenge Goliath. It must have been terrifying to watch as this teenager with a slingshot confronted the giant armed to the teeth with his weapons of war. Why would the Lord choose David to confront Goliath? He was untrained, inexperienced, and young. Humanly speaking, he had nothing going for him.

You may wonder why the Lord has chosen you for certain battles as well. But the greater the odds against you, the better for God. Our heavenly Father gets far more glory when He works through people the world considers weak because no one can deny He is the One who provides the victory. Remember this truth whenever you're confronted with enormously scary giants. The battle belongs to Him. Trust Him, and, like David, He will lead you to triumph as well.

Jesus, these challenges belong to You. Thank You for delivering me. Amen.

Go Where He Sends

"I am has sent me to you."

EXODUS 3:14

As Moses tended the family's sheep in the wilderness, he saw flames shooting upward, encompassing a bush without even singeing a single twig. Then, just as surprisingly, God spoke from the fire, saying, "I will send you to Pharaoh, so that you may bring My people, the sons of Israel, out of Egypt" (Exodus 3:10). As one may expect, Moses was filled with self-doubt and fear at the sudden and immense responsibility.

Perhaps you can empathize with his trepidation—especially if the Lord has ever called you to a task outside of your skill set or educational preparation. Maybe, like Moses, His invitation shocked you, as did the scope of the assignment. However, remember that when Yahweh called Moses, He was not relying on the Hebrew's talents or strengths, and He doesn't depend on yours either. The eternal God who has no beginning or end is sovereign, all-powerful, and fathomlessly wise. He anticipates every obstacle and has a plan that cannot fail.

When Moses finally accepted the Lord's authority, he had a clearly defined mission and reason for living. And no matter what happened, God helped him through it in miraculous ways. The same can be true for you. Yield to Him in faith, go where He sends you, and watch Him work.

Jesus, I will go wherever You send me and rely on You to deliver. Amen.

Small Steps of Faith

Had the prophet told you to do some great thing, would you not have done it?

2 KINGS 5:13

Sometimes our greatest acts of faith will come through small steps of obedience. This was certainly true for the highly respected captain of the Syrian army named Naaman. He traveled to Israel and sought the prophet Elisha to be cured of his leprosy. However, Naaman felt insulted when Elisha sent a lowly servant to instruct him to wash in the Jordan seven times.

Naaman was so outraged that he refused to perform the one act that would save him from his very painful disease. Thankfully, his servants confronted him in his pride and pointed out that the Lord had promised healing through that small step of faith. Naaman realized that if he refused to humble himself before God, it could cost him his life. So he obeyed, and his flesh was made whole.

You may not pay attention to the little things God calls you to do because they seem insignificant. However, you don't know the amazing way He may want to work through your obedience. Say yes to the Lord regardless of how small, mundane, dull, or inferior the task seems—He will reward your humble steps of faith.

Jesus, whatever You command is great and worthy of my obedience. I will do as You ask. Amen.

Worship by Listening

"This is My Son, My Chosen One; listen to Him!"
LUKE 9:35

Jesus took Peter, James, and John to a high mountain to reveal Himself to them. However, they never imagined they would see their Teacher in the way He transfigured before them. Suddenly, He shone forth in brilliant, dazzling radiance like the sun, and His clothing gleamed like the very purest white light. Then the Father spoke: "This is My beloved Son, with whom I am well-pleased; listen to Him!" (Matthew 17:5).

What was the disciples' reaction? Immediately they began to worship Christ. As God's glory engulfed them, they were struck by His absolute holiness, wisdom, power, and authority. They prostrated themselves before Him. At first, Peter was focused on what they could do in their own strength to show their love. But God told them that the greatest act of reverence was to listen to what He had to say.

This is instructive for us. Too often we may picture Jesus as the lowly rabbi, clad in rough carpenter's garments and sandals. But we must see Him for who He really is—the almighty, magnificently victorious King of kings and Lord of all. Then we will recognize Him as the glorious, all-powerful Sovereign of our lives and submit to Him without reservation.

....

Jesus, You are worthy of all the honor, glory, power, and praise! May I honor You for who You are. Amen.

145

Seek Intimacy

Having risen a long while before daylight,
He went out and departed to a solitary
place; and there He prayed.

MARK 1:35 NKJV

Intimacy with God is one of the most essential elements of the Christian life. A profound, abiding relationship with Him is the key to a lifelong journey filled with joy, contentment, significance, and fruitfulness. Of course, learning to love the Lord takes time, diligence, and willingness. This is why Jesus demonstrated the importance of being alone with the Father by consistently rising early and going to a solitary place where He could pray without interruption.

Do you need a place where you can find refuge, hope, strength, and a greater love than anything this world has to offer? If so, your soul is longing for God's presence. Thankfully, He is always available to you. He gives you profound wisdom, unfailing strength, and unshakable hope for even the toughest situations.

But as complicated as your life is, how do you start—especially if you've never scheduled regular time to be alone with God? Begin this very minute. Close your eyes and sit for a moment without saying anything. Simply focus your heart on the Lord and the fact that He loves you unconditionally. Then pray, asking Him for the desire to know Him better. That's a prayer He loves to answer.

Jesus, teach me to draw closer to You in every way. Amen.

Not Alone

"I will not leave you as orphans;
I will come to you."
JOHN 14:18

Loneliness can be one of the most crushing human emotions—one that can create an overwhelming sense of abandonment, helplessness, and despair. And you don't have to be alone to experience it. Indeed, you can be surrounded by people, but if they don't understand you or appreciate who you are, it can feel incredibly isolating. When you're lonely, you must be especially careful because you are more vulnerable to temptation. It's a dangerous place to be.

This is when it's important to remember that Jesus knows what it's like to be lonesome. As the perfect Son of God, He was unlike all the other children in Nazareth. And when a person is different from the crowd, they usually spend a good deal of time by themselves. We also know that right before the crucifixion—the time of His greatest sorrow—His disciples scattered, leaving Him utterly alone.

As your sympathetic High Priest, Jesus was made like you in every way and has experienced all the pain you do. He is intimately acquainted with the devastating effect of loneliness, so He guarantees He will never leave or forsake you. He will always come to your aid, assure you of His presence, and remind you that He sees and loves you.

....

Jesus, thank You for always being with me. Amen.

He Hears You

"I am with you and will keep you wherever you go."

GENESIS 28:15

J esus hears you. Others may not, but He does. Your faintest whispers of pain, confusion, and loneliness reach your loving heavenly Father, who goes to extraordinary lengths to comfort you. You can see this throughout Scripture. When men and women of faith faced great challenges, God reminded them of His powerful presence, saying to them, "I am with you" (Genesis 26:24; Isaiah 41:10; Jeremiah 1:8; Haggai 1:13; Matthew 28:20; and Acts 18:10 to name a few). They were afraid, anxious, doubtful, and bewildered, but the awareness of the Lord's presence became their strength to overcome truly formidable odds victoriously.

God is with you too. He is the Lord Almighty who is able to help you. He is kind, merciful, faithful, and tender toward you, caring for you with everlasting love. He knows all your needs and works all things together for your good. Through the indwelling presence of His Spirit, He listens intently to the groans of your heart. So turn to Him and find the solace and help you need. It may come through Scripture, through the awareness of His presence while you sit quietly in prayer, or in any number of ways. But He will speak to you. And He will never, ever leave you.

Jesus, thank You for always being with me and hearing the cries of my heart. Amen.

Try Serving

Anyone who serves Christ in this
way is pleasing to God.

ROMANS 14:18 NIV

There will be times in your spiritual journey when you'll feel your relationship with the Savior is stale and lifeless. Perhaps your prayer life seems unfruitful, or your sense of God's presence is dulled. Attempts to invigorate your spiritual health seem to fail miserably. You pray harder, and you read Scripture longer but to no avail. What can you do?

May I suggest something quite practical that I have discovered always helps? Find someone to serve.

There are, of course, many reasons why we occasionally find ourselves in a spiritual funk, but demonstrating a servant spirit can frequently be just the remedy we need. This is because we're often so absorbed with our own issues and problems that the only way out is to concentrate on the needs of others. And acts of service are a wonderful way to get our minds off ourselves and onto what the Father is doing in the lives of those around us.

It is amazing how your perspective will change when you reach out and help someone. Pray for God to open a door of service and watch how He reinvigorates your relationship with Him.

Jesus, I want to experience the fullness of a relationship with You. Show me who to serve in Your name. Amen.

Serve Like Jesus

*"The Son of Man did not come to
be served, but to serve."*

MATTHEW 20:28

You are never more like Jesus than when you exhibit a heart of service. Jesus, Lord of all, came to serve us. "He made himself nothing by taking the very nature of a servant" (Philippians 2:7 NIV). So the more we humbly minister to others in His name, showing His love, sacrificial generosity, and compassion, the more Christlike we become.

This attitude of service is so important to Jesus that He said, "Whatever you did for one of the least of these brothers and sisters of mine, you did for me" (Matthew 25:40 NIV). Of course, serving Christ in this manner requires us to humble ourselves, lay aside our rights and desires, and do the Father's will as He did. We don't do it for the notoriety or the accolades but to be a living example to others of how much God cares for them. We encourage the prisoner, strengthen the fainthearted, build up the weak, clothe the naked, and feed the hungry so that they will glorify the Father who is in heaven and understand how important they are to Him.

So enter into the joy of the Savior by embarking on a lifestyle of Spirit-led servanthood—because that's when you're truly most like Him.

*Jesus, help me to serve others as You would, to Your glory.
Amen.*

Get Back Up

*Though the righteous fall seven
times, they rise again.*

PROVERBS 24:16 NIV

A braham lied about his wife's identity to save himself. Moses murdered a man. David was an adulterer and killer. The disciples fled after Christ's crucifixion. The failures of humanity mark the pages of Scripture, yet they aren't the story-enders that we might imagine they would be. God specializes in picking us up after we fall and restoring our confidence and dignity.

Of course, when you fail, you may feel worthless and like God will never accept you again. But remember that no matter what you've done, the Father freely offers you forgiveness (1 John 1:9). You don't have to remain trapped in self-condemnation—that doesn't help anyone. Instead, accept that Christ determines your self-worth and identity. And because of His infinite wisdom and kindness, the events in your life that you would consider disappointing, even crushing, can be redeemed. Through the Lord's rich and plentiful grace, they can even work together for good.

Failure is never final with God, because with Him all things are possible. When you fall, He will pick you up. If you falter, He will come to your rescue. So don't let your failures keep you down. Turn to the Lord and allow Him to show you the path forward.

*Jesus, thank You that my failures don't define me and that
You help me up when I fall. Amen.*

151

Spiritual Sources

*Our struggle is not against flesh and
blood, but against . . . spiritual forces of
wickedness in the heavenly places.*

EPHESIANS 6:12

When we begin to see our circumstance the way God sees them, we realize that everything in our lives flows from the spiritual dimension. In fact, all that we do in the physical, relational, mental, and emotional realms has a spiritual component to it.

Unfortunately, when we think about the adversity in our lives, our natural tendency is to look only on the surface—the relational or physical pain we experience—rather than the underlying spiritual realities. But in times of brokenness, we should always consider: What is happening in my spiritual life? What might God want to change in my relationship with Him? How is the Redeemer working through this time of trial to restore, renew, and remake me? How might the Father be leading me to greater wholeness through this season of difficulty?

These questions bring us back to God's ultimate purpose of developing our faith in Him so He can work through us as Christlike people, strong in Spirit, completely obedient to Him, and utterly dependent on His supernatural wisdom and power.

*Jesus, give me spiritual eyes so I can always recognize how
You are working. Amen.*

Different Goals

"He who has found his life will lose it, and he who has lost his life for My sake will find it."

MATTHEW 10:39

So much about the brokenness we experience in the Christian life goes against what we are taught in our culture. We're taught to be self-confident, to make our plans and refuse to move or budge from our purposes, and to get what we can. However, the Father's goals for us are just the opposite. This is because His purpose is not to make us famous, prominent, prestigious, or wealthy. His objective is to bring us to the point where we recognize that nothing in this world lasts and that all we have of true eternal value is God.

As believers, we are to depend on Christ, let Him set the agenda for our lives, do whatever He asks, and be sacrificial just as He has. Eventually, by His grace, we're able to say, "All that I am and all that I have belongs to Jesus. He is in me, and I am in Him, and that's what really matters." So today consider, what goals does God need to change in you? Do not be afraid of total surrender, because what He has for you is life at its very best.

Jesus, all I am and all I have belongs to You. You are everything to me. Amen.

Good Scars

*Join with me in suffering for the gospel
according to the power of God, who has saved
us and called us with a holy calling.*

2 TIMOTHY 1:8–9

The apostle Paul had plenty of scars—the physical kind, from brutal lashings, and the kind you don't see, from rejection by others and loneliness from years of unjust imprisonment. But Paul became the great apostle through his sufferings, with many of his epistles inked in the dim light of a jail cell. The key is that Paul refused to look at his problems with bitterness or defeat. Instead, he recognized them as the way the life and power of Christ were demonstrated in him. He exclaimed that he would "press on toward the goal for the prize of the upward call of God in Christ Jesus" (Philippians 3:14).

In the same way, the Father works through your scars to conform you to the character of Christ, to produce an indomitable spirit of faith and courage in you, and to make you an effective minister to others. So, like Paul, press on, trust the Lord, and pursue His upward call. He will work through you to accomplish feats unattainable apart from your trials. And when you meet Christ face-to-face, you will see the scars that made Him your Savior and see His likeness in you.

Jesus, I trust You in my trials and press on to Your upward call. Amen.

Faithful in All

*"He who is faithful in a very little
thing is faithful also in much."*

LUKE 16:10

My teaching ministry began in a small town in the mountains of North Carolina. The Bible institute where I taught and the church that I pastored were quite small and unpretentious. Like any eager young pastor, I sometimes thought about moving on to larger churches. But I clearly remember God's plain message to me that laid the foundation for my future ministry. If I wanted to succeed in my walk with Christ and be productive in my work, He expected me to be faithful in *everything*—especially the small steps of obedience He instructed me to take. So I promised God that I would give Him my very best every day and would remain in that rural community for the rest of my life if that was His will.

The Lord wants us to work for His honor, not our own. If we're distracted by our importance, how people see us, or grand goals, it's a hindrance to God working through us. But if we'll submit to Him and apply His truth to our daily struggles, He will strengthen us for His greater purposes. Therefore, never underestimate the power of small steps of obedience. They pave the way to God's wonderful plan.

....

*Jesus, I want to honor You. Teach me Your will step-by-step.
Amen.*

Strength for All

To get this done I toil and struggle,
using the mighty strength which Christ
supplies and which is at work in me.

COLOSSIANS 1:29 GNT

Perhaps in serving the Lord, you've wondered, *When it comes to strength for my tasks, what is God's part, and what is mine?* The apostle Paul certainly gave everything in him—when he wasn't teaching the church, evangelizing the lost, and defending against false teachers, he was plying his trade as a tentmaker. Yet he found the spiritual equilibrium that is required for sound Christian living. So how did he continue without faltering? Paul did all he could, but he never viewed his ventures as an individual undertaking. He recognized that undergirding everything he did was the great power of God supernaturally enabling him.

Your part, like Paul's, is to put forth all the effort you can muster obeying God. Pray, investigate, plan, prepare, and do whatever else He shows you to do. The Lord will not move forward until you do as He says. However, you can depend on Him to actively accomplish His purposes—especially in areas where you have no control. You can also count on His strength, wisdom, love, direction, and grace on the journey. So do all you can, and trust God for the rest. The outcome rests safely in His hands.

Jesus, I obey Your commands and trust Your strength. Amen.

Let Go

*Cast all your anxiety on him
because he cares for you.*

1 PETER 5:7 NIV

At times, when there are heart-wrenching situations that steal our hope, there is only one thing we can do—let go. As much as we would like to control the situation and have our will be done, we must acknowledge that in His wisdom and love, the Lord will decide what is best. And it may hurt terribly. But we recognize our responsibility is to honor Him as God, trust in His goodness, and put no other thing before Him.

So when you encounter trials where the consequences are monumental, do not bow to despair or bitterness. Instead, deliberately submit your life to God. This does not mean you will stop wrestling in prayer. Rather, it means that even as you pray, you put your wholehearted trust in God, seek His will, and intentionally relinquish the outcome of your circumstances to Him. This is not resignation or fatalism, and arriving at this point is seldom easy. You may wrestle with the feeling that you can do at least one more thing to solve your dilemma. But releasing your situation to the Lord is a mature step of faith, indicating your trust in His wisdom, goodness, and power. So let go. And allow Him to reveal Himself to you.

Jesus, I let it all go. Help me to trust You completely. Amen.

Earthen Vessels

We have this treasure in earthen vessels, so
that the surpassing greatness of the power
will be of God and not from ourselves.

2 CORINTHIANS 4:7

D o you feel ordinary? Perhaps you have your unique quirks and your exceptional moments, but when all is said and done, you don't see yourself as very special. However, always remember that there's nothing mundane or commonplace about what God is doing in and through you. Your life is the platform for the Lord's extraordinary presence. Yet also understand God shines through you because He wants people to look to *Him.*

Paul equated our lives with the clay pots that were so common in biblical days. Their value was based on whatever was *in* them—water, wheat, oil, gold. In like manner, our unshakable eternal worth comes from the One who indwells us. Our matchless Redeemer is the One other people need. And His ultimate goal is to draw others to Himself in faith and salvation through us.

Friend, you were created to be a vessel that shines forth His glory. So allow Him to work through your life in such a way that people are attracted to His awesome presence. Fill yourself up with Him because the more He lives through you, the more people around you will want to know Him.

Jesus, please shine through me so that others can know Your
awesome salvation. Amen.

The Futility of Worry

*"Which of you by worrying can add
a single hour to his life's span?"*

LUKE 12:25

D o you realize that most of the things you are worried about today will never come to pass? If you think about it, you've probably fretted about many calamities over the years that never happened. And the stark reality is that worry is a debilitating state of mind that can erode your joy, peace, and sense of God's presence. Perhaps it is your job that has you anxious, or your loved ones, or the future. The perpetual worrier carves emotional channels through which deeper and stronger fears may eventually take root.

Yet worry is essentially an assault on the character of God, since most of our concerns stem from the notion that somehow God will not come through for us. When we confront worry with the truth of Jesus' goodness, mercy, and faithfulness, we can disarm the explosive nature of our fears. And when we deliberately choose to trust Him to take care of our circumstances and concentrate on the business the Lord sets before us each day, we can experience newfound contentment and stability. So do not fret. Instead, "commit everything you do to the LORD. Trust him, and he will help you" (Psalm 37:5 NLT).

*Jesus, help me to stop worrying. I trust in Your wisdom,
power, and love. Amen.*

Rebuffing Worry

Rest in the LORD and wait patiently for Him.

PSALM 37:7

It is virtually impossible to enjoy God's presence and also worry at the same time. So, if you are fretting about something today and don't know how to stop thinking about it, try directing your thoughts to God. Open Scripture and read about how faithfully He has helped others in the past.

You see, anxiety compels us to focus on what we cannot control, keeping us agitated, uneasy, frustrated, and grasping for solutions that will not work. Ultimately, it leads us to destructive ways of coping with our circumstances. However, when we center our attention on the Lord through worship and prayer, the effects of worry are diminished because there is absolutely nothing outside of God's sovereign care. We realize we can trust Him to help us in the ways He's faithfully helped others.

So deliberately turn aside from the inner noise of anxiety, and gaze steadily into the wonders of God's person. Quiet your soul by sitting before the Lord and listening to whatever He has to say to you through His Word. Wait for His guidance. He has a plan, and He will show you what to do when you wait patiently before Him.

Jesus, help me to place my focus on Your good and glorious greatness instead of my problems. Amen.

Who Reigns?

As long as he sought the LORD, God gave him success.

2 CHRONICLES 26:5 NIV

King Uzziah's reign over Judah began well. He sought the Lord, conquered enemies, restored important buildings, improved the agrarian economy, and built a superior fighting force. But something devastating happened along the way—Uzziah developed a conceited spirit. Though his early achievements were initially centered around a healthy, reverent relationship with God, later "his heart was so proud that he acted corruptly, and he was unfaithful to the LORD" (2 Chronicles 26:16). Instead of looking to God for direction and success, he barged into the temple—where only the priests were allowed—and burnt incense, desecrating the holy act that represented prayer. And the Lord punished him.

Excessive pride turns our attention away from God and to ourselves. It puts our focus on our own efforts, where "I" reigns instead of the Lord. If you've found yourself increasingly centering on *your* goals, *your* reputation, *your* authority, *your* success, *your* talents, *your* progress, *your* dreams, take a moment and evaluate where God is in your life. Is He on the throne, or are you? King Uzziah is a cautionary example for you—it never ends well when you attempt to take the Lord's place or think you can make your own rules. Humble yourself and get back on the right track.

Jesus, please examine my heart and purge whatever pride You find. Amen.

Defeating Pride

When pride comes, then comes dishonor,
but with the humble is wisdom.

PROVERBS 11:2

Inordinate self-centeredness is a deadly enemy when it comes to God's power. Although our journey to self-reliance may be ingrained when we're children, our *spiritual* path is inverted—from independence to dependence on Christ. The Lord wants us to acknowledge Him as our Sovereign and the Source for all things.

This is why pride is such a dangerous foe to us spiritually—because it takes the credit away from God and deposits it into our account. Instead of glorifying Christ, we see our accomplishments as completely our own. But do not be fooled—it is God who grants us success. And the Lord delights in helping us succeed. However, our achievements should never come at the expense of our intimacy with Him.

So if you sense your heart has been hardened by pride, stop for a moment and appreciate God's greatness. You may be clever, but by the Lord's wisdom the universe was established. You can do a great deal, but nothing is impossible with God. You may be capable of some noble endeavors, but Jesus came to serve and give His life for us all. In this way, you will develop a reverent understanding of who He is. And as you exalt the Lord, He will honor you.

Jesus, only You deserve all the honor, glory, and praise.
Amen.

He Stands with You

The Lord stood with me and strengthened me.

2 TIMOTHY 4:17

Paul was in prison again, and he knew that the end was near—soon Nero would put him to death. Even worse, he was alone. Most of his friends had either deserted him or were scattered abroad. The impending execution, loss, and abandonment could have been completely devastating, but they did not leave Paul hopeless because he knew God would never forsake Him.

Standing alone takes strength. And if, like Paul, you find yourself in a battle where no one else will defend you or come to your aid, here is wonderful news for you today: the Lord is with you to fortify, guide, support, and deliver you. God has spoken to you through His Word, and His powerful promises can break through the darkness of your worst night and defeat your most profound fears with His comfort and unshakable hope.

This is one of the reasons it is so important to hide Scripture in your heart. At just the right moment, the Lord can bring His encouraging Word to mind so that you can endure. If you feel alone and need a reminder that God stands with you, ask Him to lead you to a promise in Scripture. He will be the strength of your heart and your portion forever.

....

Jesus, thank You for always standing with me. Strengthen me with Your Word. Amen.

Spiritual Hindrances

*Let us strip off every weight that slows
us down, especially the sin that so easily
trips us up. And let us run with endurance
the race God has set before us.*

HEBREWS 12:1 NLT

Are you spiritually lethargic? Is your soul sapped of energy?
Perhaps you would love to know God better and grow in
godliness, but your progress is slow at best. You don't understand it
because you're not slacking—you read the Bible and pray every day.
The spiritual momentum just isn't there. What's going on?

Today's verse provides a clue. Many believers are weighed down
with excess baggage—burdens like anger, pride, bitterness, lust,
greed, jealousy, and unforgiveness, to name a few. Any sin we enter-
tain will drain us of our spiritual energy and kill our progress in
the Christian life.

God stands ready to supply His power and wisdom once you
realize you must rid your heart of these entanglements to receive
His strength. If the Holy Spirit is convicting you of some area of sin
in your life, do not ignore Him. You won't be able to run the race
the Lord has for you until you obey Him. Throw off the encum-
brances through confession and repentance. Then enjoy the race as
He energizes your spiritual life and teaches you to soar.

*Jesus, reveal every sin in me so I may repent and walk in
Your will. Amen.*

JUNE

Loving Motives

Whom the LORD loves He reproves, even as a
father corrects the son in whom he delights.

PROVERBS 3:12

L ove is the motivation behind everything God does in us and
everything He allows into our lives. The Father is never act-
ing in anger or wrath when He allows trials to assail us. Rather,
He cares about us too much to see us continue in sin, remain in a
lukewarm spiritual state, or go unfulfilled in His purposes for our
lives. He moves to help us change, grow, and become both spiritually mature and whole in spirit, mind, and body. This also means
He disciplines us for our good when necessary.

God's purpose is not to break our spirits but, rather, to breach
the stubbornness of our wills in order to carry out His will through
us. A good parent knows that any streak of obstinacy in children
must be lovingly prevailed over so that they can grow up to be productive, law-abiding, generous, and loving spouses, friends, parents,
citizens, and members of the body of Christ. In the same manner,
God seeks to eliminate the pride, self-focus, and disobedience that
keep us from being the loving, generous, fruitful, Christlike people
He created us to be.

Jesus, I know You love me. Help me to endure this trial in a
manner that honors You. Amen.

Spiritually Transparent

*I acknowledged my sin to You, and my iniquity I
did not hide . . . and You forgave the guilt of my sin.*

PSALM 32:5

S ince the time of Adam and Eve, it has been normal for us to
try to hide our weaknesses and failures from God. But spiritual authenticity and growth begin with a transparent admission of
our struggles. We can see this in the letters of the New Testament,
which were written not only to encourage and instruct believers
in their faith but also to reveal and confront the problems that
had crept into the churches. For example, the Galatians needed
to continue their walk in the Spirit and not revert to the law. The
Corinthians were dealing with moral issues. Some Thessalonians
were confused about Christ's return, while others were troublesome
busybodies. These issues had to be confronted for the health of the
believers in those churches.

This is a vital principle for all who want to make progress in
their relationship with Christ—we can deal effectively and victoriously with our problems, but we must first bring them before the
Lord, not suppress them.

God encourages you to be honest with Him. Therefore, do not
hide yourself from Him. Instead, be forthright and allow Him to
lead you to spiritual maturity.

....

*Jesus, I confess my sins to You, trusting You to lead me to
victory over them. Amen.*

Emotionally Transparent

*O my God, my soul is in despair within
me; therefore I remember You.*

PSALM 42:6

G od already knows everything about you. *Everything.* Still,
He asks you to be honest with Him about your emotions,
ambitions, aggravations, and failures so He can lead you to freedom
in them. Of course, we all harbor secret fears and longings that we
think we can't discuss with the Father. But as long as we stay silent
about them, the troubles and wounds wear us down.

All throughout the Psalms, the writers recorded their most profound feelings, frustrations, and disappointments. They wondered
where God was in their adversity. They acknowledged that they felt
abandoned. They questioned His justice. Yet God wasn't threatened by any of it. He already knew how they felt and answered their
questions with compassion and wisdom.

Until you acknowledge the most profound pains, feelings, and
fears of your heart to the Father, you will not develop a completely
trusting relationship with Him. So allow the Holy Spirit to identify
areas of your life where you haven't been completely honest with
Him. And trust the Lord to meet you at your point of need with
His grace and wisdom, which will undoubtedly put you on the road
to recovery and wholeness.

*Jesus, help me bring my deep needs before You so I can
experience the truth that sets me free. Amen.*

Thirsty for Him

Springs of water will satisfy the thirsty land.

ISAIAH 35:7 NLT

Have you ever felt as if your life were a dry, barren desert—as if you were parched, depleted, and unable to produce anything fruitful? The prophet Isaiah has encouragement for you. He reports a time when Israel was spiritually and physically desolate. The people had wandered from God; became preoccupied with their own desires, goals, and troubles; and subsequently faced terrible defeats. However, when they came to their senses, they cried out. The Lord redeemed them and made them fruitful once again.

The wonderful thing about the Lord is that He is never distant—He is always beside us. He is faithful, which means that even when we are faithless, He remains steadfastly true. He sees the areas we've destroyed through our unwise actions and sets about restoring us, giving us His living water, and bringing life to our barrenness.

Likewise, the Father always works in the present but looks to the future. Life at its best is not lived in the past, worrying about what happened or what once was. Instead, it is lived now, aware of one thing: our Savior loves us, and He is always working for our good and His glory. Cry out to Him and trust Him to restore you.

Jesus, You are the living water—renew me and make me fruitful once again. Amen.

Approval Anxiety

Am I now seeking the favor of men, or of God?

GALATIANS 1:10

A deep inner cause of anxiety that many people wrestle with comes from a desire to prove themselves—especially to others. The things they do for acceptance seem unending—the ways they dress, change their appearance, buy houses they can't afford, act out, engage in illicit activities, strive for power, and seek out social status. And they do it all because they are concerned about what others think. They are constantly worrying about how they stack up, so they work harder with longer hours and overschedule their lives in an effort to impress others with their productivity and performance—or at least to satisfy their own internal need for success.

Is this you? Understand that Jesus tells you that all that truly matters is your heavenly Father's opinion about who you are. If He approves of you, that's all the endorsement you need. He gives you your identity and an inner beauty that far surpasses anything related to what you might wear, own, drive, or live in. As for performance, what more does your heavenly Father expect than that you do your best? You are responsible to work wholeheartedly in obedience to Him, honoring Him with whatever you do.

Jesus, thank You for always accepting me. Help me to embrace my identity in You. Amen.

His Life Through You

*It is no longer I who live, but Christ lives
in me; and the life which I now live in the
flesh I live by faith in the Son of God.*

GALATIANS 2:20

When I was in seminary, I had a wonderful professor who impacted my life. Whenever he taught, I listened attentively because his actions and demeanor vividly demonstrated the presence of the living God. Likewise, the occasions I had to visit with him in his study were memorable because he was so godly in everything he said and did. I always came away from my interactions with him with a sense of drawing nearer to Jesus.

This professor was a wonderful example of how allowing our old, earthly ways to be crucified with the Savior can make us into truly impactful witnesses. Jesus takes up residence in us and works through us in a manner that profoundly touches and transforms other people's lives.

You can be a mighty testimony of Christ's power, just like my professor. If you'll permit the Lord to live through you, the people you meet can have genuinely life-changing encounters with Jesus. However, you must relinquish control to Him. I hope you will. Because having Christ live through you is the most awesome experience you'll ever have.

*Jesus, I surrender my old nature; live through me, my
Savior. Amen.*

Where Are We Going?

"Go forth from your country, and from your relatives . . . to the land which I will show you."

GENESIS 12:1

Suppose you plan a wonderful surprise trip for your loved ones. The supplies are loaded, and the tank is full of gas. Everyone piles into the car and fastens their seatbelts in anticipation. Finally, someone asks the question, "Hey, where are we going?" And the only thing you can say is, "Well, I don't know exactly."

This may sound like a silly scenario, but it is precisely what God asked of Abram and his family. He asked them to leave everything they knew and travel to a land that was completely foreign to them. Of course, even back then, people didn't usually make big trips like that without knowing where they were going.

But like Abram, when God calls us, we must go. And He probably won't give us a road map—any journey He asks us to take is a training ground for faith. But we can be confident that the future will be blessed more than we can conceive because the Lord is leading. That was certainly the case for Abram. So even when you don't have a travel plan, let God guide you in His way and time because the destination is certainly worthwhile.

....

Jesus, I don't know the way forward, but I will obey You step-by-step. Amen.

Perfected Power

*I will rather boast about my weaknesses, so
that the power of Christ may dwell in me.*

2 CORINTHIANS 12:9

The nature of adversity is that it robs us of the resources we
need to function properly—strength, energy, concentration,
and the like. It becomes difficult to focus on anything else, and we
feel physically and emotionally drained because of it.

The apostle Paul certainly understood this, which is why he
asked God three times to remove the thorn in his flesh. It was painful and made him weak. Certainly, the Lord would want to remove
it, right? Yet the Father allowed Paul's thorn to endure because He
wanted to diminish Paul's dependence on his own strength and
wisdom. And He taught Paul that "power is perfected in weakness"
(2 Corinthians 12:9). The term *perfected* signifies being completed
or fulfilled. In other words, the frailer a person is, the greater their
capacity to accept and exhibit God's might.

For this reason, one of the best ways for the Lord to glorify
Himself is to manifest His power through an inadequate vessel. So
God allows adversity in our lives—not to hurt us but for the purpose of enabling us by His strength to do what otherwise would be
impossible. Therefore, embrace your limitations and allow Christ's
supernatural ability to work through you.

*Jesus, I rejoice in my limitations because I know that You
strengthen me in my weakness, and that glorifies You. Amen.*

175

Strength Through Weakness

I am well content with weaknesses . . . for Christ's
sake; for when I am weak, then I am strong.

2 CORINTHIANS 12:10

The idea of being content with weakness contradicts the message society sends us. In an age characterized by the pursuit of power, it's unusual for people to be happy with living in a state of limitation. But upon examining Paul's life, one hardly gets the impression that he was a helpless man. On the contrary, he spent his life boldly preaching the gospel to hostile crowds. He planted churches throughout the major cities of Asia Minor and in the port cities along the Aegean Sea. Paul trained the first pastors and elders of these early congregations. And he wrote half of the New Testament. That certainly doesn't sound like a weak man.

So how do we reconcile Paul's claim to weakness with his amazing accomplishments? Simple. The answer is in the phrase "for Christ's sake; for when I am weak, then I am strong." Paul surrendered to Jesus' power to do all he couldn't—to achieve the Lord's goals, which were unreachable in his own strength. The same is true for you. God will always do more through you than you can possibly imagine. So admit your weakness, submit to Him, and let Him be strong in you.

Jesus, I submit to You. Be strong in me. Amen.

Regular Practice

Job . . . was blameless, upright, fearing God.

JOB 1:1

Job knew what it meant to be caught off guard by disaster. He lost family, property, and wealth all in a matter of moments. Yet somehow he managed to honor God with affirmations of trust. How? We know that Job was a godly and upright man and that he made sacrifices to the Lord. But here is the key to why Job was able to endure: "This was Job's regular practice" (Job 1:5 NLT).

Certainly, Job had questions about his losses, but ultimately, he trusted in God's goodness and sovereignty to the end because he had a solid relationship with the Lord in the day-to-day. In this we see a valuable principle: *never underestimate the value of a God-honoring routine.* Our daily times alone with the Father build strength within us that sustains us when we're thrown headlong into adversity.

So don't wait until times of trouble hit to get ready spiritually—that only leads to a more difficult battle. Train for those seasons now by safeguarding your quiet times with the Lord. Because every day that you enjoy His presence, delve into His Word, and pray about what concerns you, He strengthens your soul. You may not see the benefits immediately, but when the trials come, you'll be surprised at how He's prepared you.

Jesus, I love meeting with You daily. Thank You for strengthening my soul. Amen.

He Is Greater

"With him is only an arm of flesh,
but with us is the LORD our God to
help us and to fight our battles."

2 CHRONICLES 32:8

When Judah faced a siege from the brutal, clearly superior, and completely overwhelming Assyrian army, King Hezekiah encouraged his people, reminding them that mere men are never a match for God. He said, "Do not fear or be dismayed because of the king of Assyria nor because of all the horde that is with him; for the one with us is greater than the one with him" (2 Chronicles 32:7). And true to form, God sent a supernatural response for their problem: "The LORD sent an angel who destroyed every mighty warrior, commander and officer in the camp of the king of Assyria. So he returned in shame to his own land" (2 Chronicles 32:21).

This is the marvelous truth that every Christian can embrace: *God Himself fights our battles for us, and He is far greater than any enemy we might face.* The difficulties we face may seem insurmountable, but He can do the impossible. Whatever our problems may be, regardless how big or frightening they are, they are not equal to the matchless power of our sovereign, omnipotent, omniscient God. His purposes will be accomplished—always. So count on His help today.

....

Jesus, You are greater than anything I face today. I praise
Your mighty name! Amen.

178

The Great Pursuit

Surely goodness and lovingkindness will
follow me all the days of my life.

PSALM 23:6

D o you understand how lavishly God loves you? David did. In fact, he recognized that the Lord actively pursues us with His goodness and loving-kindness. What a delightful way to think about the Father. Every day of your life, in sickness and health, His kindness and mercy unceasingly accompany you.

Perhaps you're wrestling with this concept today. Certainly, God dispenses His blessings, but perhaps you feel He does so in a more measured manner. It's difficult to accept that He's chasing you down to demonstrate His great love for you.

Even so, I encourage you to embrace the truth that your heavenly Father has arranged untold ways to express His kind-heartedness and mercy to you. Begin by doing this simple exercise: Start your day saying Psalm 23:6 aloud—that God is energetically pursuing you with His goodness and loving-kindness. Repeat this to yourself several times a day and continue for the next few months. You'll build a new mindset that anticipates and recognizes God's activity. Then you'll begin to see what David did—that the Lord is intensely pursuing you to comfort you and show you His love.

Jesus, thank You for pursuing me with Your goodness and loving-kindness. Amen.

A Better Way

*They who seek the Lord shall not be
in want of any good thing.*

PSALM 34:10

Today, embrace this crucial and life-transforming principle: behind every command and exhortation of Scripture is the inherent goodness and protection of the living God. When the Lord prohibits us from engaging in certain behaviors, it isn't because He is opposed to our happiness. On the contrary, it is because He so delights in our joy and well-being that He warns us of what would be destructive to us.

God understands that at times we will try to fill our needs in the manner that seems most expedient to us. Perhaps we attempt to dull our pain or fill the emptiness with illicit substances, inappropriate relationships, or damaging forms of entertainment. But He also knows the devastating consequences of doing so. Therefore, in His profound loving-kindness to us, He warns us not to participate in them. And He faithfully shows us what will truly fulfill those profound longings.

So today, accept that all the Father's promises, precepts, and commands are for your good—even if you're not quite sure how. Ask Him what it is you really yearn for and then trust Him to satisfy your soul.

Jesus, please forgive me of my sin and show me Your better way. Amen.

Agree with Him

*If we confess our sins, He is faithful and
righteous to forgive us our sins and to
cleanse us from all unrighteousness.*

1 JOHN 1:9

Today's verse sounds easy enough—the Father calls us to admit that we've done something wrong, and He will forgive us. However, John penned this verse with a specific Greek word that indicates that when we *confess* our sins, we *agree with God* that we have violated His law. In other words, we acknowledge that not only does He have the authority to command us, but He is good and right about His instructions. He really does know the best way for us to live.

But do not mistake *why* the Father makes the promise above—it isn't merely so you'll recognize Him as God, though that is part of it. Rather, He is so ready and willing to forgive you when you fail because of His unconditional love for you. He wants you back, and He wants the most joyful and fruitful life for you. Confession restores your intimacy with the Lord and removes the obstacles to His brightest and best future for you.

So be grateful when the Holy Spirit targets specific areas of your life that disagree with God's ways. Accept His loving call, agree with Him, and be cleansed.

*Jesus, I agree with You—You are God and worthy of my
obedience. Amen.*

Turn It Around

The kindness of God leads you to repentance.

ROMANS 2:4

Yesterday we discussed confession. Today's focus is repentance. *Repent* and *confess*—not the most pleasant words, are they? They are associated with faults and failings we would rather forget or ignore. So how is it that Paul suggests it is God's kindness that reveals them to us?

As we saw yesterday, the word *confess* signifies *agreeing with God*. However, the Greek word for *repent* conveys the idea of turning around and going in the opposite direction. The Father realizes we'll be attracted to the solutions this world has for our problems, but He also knows that they will only make matters worse. Once we acknowledge that we've done wrong, in His goodness He turns us around, puts us on His path, and leads us to His best for us.

God's guidance is important because our human inclination when we are in a hole is to keep digging. We think if we try harder or do more of the wrong thing somehow it will become right. We realize the consequences of such behavior—we've lived them. Thankfully, Jesus saves us from all that. In His kindness, He shows us how to be different. So today, praise Him for showing you a better way. Confess, repent, and give Him the glory.

Jesus, I want Your path in all things. Show me the way, my Redeemer. Amen.

When You're Ready

"It is He who reveals the profound and hidden things."

DANIEL 2:22

We live in an age where volumes of information can be accessed in a few moments on the internet. If there's a question on our minds, we can simply google it and find what we need. So it can be frustrating and confusing when God doesn't tell us all we ask of Him right away. After all, He promises, "Call to Me and I will answer you, and I will tell you great and mighty things, which you do not know" (Jeremiah 33:3).

Although it's indeed true that the Father will reveal a great deal when we seek Him in prayer, He alone knows what we can handle. Out of wisdom and kindness, He keeps the curtain drawn tightly on some of the things we'd like to know. Why? Because we can get into a lot of trouble with the wrong information—or with the right information at the wrong time. We're not equipped to handle God's full revelation of His plan for us. So as our good and loving Father, He only gives us what we are ready to receive and prepares us for the rest.

Therefore, trust He will tell you what you need to know, when you need to know it, and that He will never, ever lead you astray.

Jesus, I trust You to reveal Your plan in the best way and time. Amen.

What Does God Require?

What does the LORD require of you but
to do justice, to love kindness, and to
walk humbly with your God?

MICAH 6:8

Life can be complicated, but your relationship with God doesn't have to be. Instead of relating to the Lord based on a demanding set of rules, the prophet Micah gave us some simple guidelines to help us keep our faith uncluttered. What does God require of you?

First, do justice. Do what you know is right. Don't compromise the truth or rationalize away what the Word of God instructs. Obey whatever God has shown you to do and quit worrying about the rest. *Second, love kindness.* Put others first and view them with compassion—even if they've hurt you or you disagree with them. Instead of insisting on your rights, trust the Lord to defend you. God will take care of both your reputation and rewards. *Third, walk humbly with your God.* Esteem the Lord for who He is—the living, eternal, all-knowing Sovereign of all that exists. He knows what He is talking about. So do whatever He says, acknowledge Him in all your ways, and keep Christ at the center of your life.

Put these principles into action and be at peace with the knowledge that you're being pleasing to God.

Jesus, thank You for showing me how to please You and empowering me to do so. Amen.

Threefold Presence

The grace of the Lord Jesus Christ, and the love of God,
and the fellowship of the Holy Spirit, be with you all.
2 CORINTHIANS 13:14

Have you ever considered that every time you experience the presence of God, you're encountering the Trinity? The Lord reveals Himself as triune—He is one God, but He exists in the persons of the Father, the Son, and the Holy Spirit. And each is a special expression of His relationship with you as a believer.

You have communion with God the Father, who sits on the throne of heaven. He is the Creator and Sustainer of all things, and He calls you and cares for you as His beloved child. You have fellowship with God the Son, Jesus, your Savior and Lord, who fought sin and death and overcame both on your behalf. He is the Word—the active agent through which the Father accomplishes His will, which makes Him your perfect High Priest and Redeemer. And you walk in intimate union with God the Holy Spirit, who indwells you. He is your divine Counselor and Advocate—the One called alongside to help you in every way imaginable, including directing you, illuminating Scripture to you, and transforming you from the inside out.

The threefold Godhead is with you. Embrace the privilege you enjoy and praise His name.

Lord, I praise You in awe and amazement. To You be all
honor and glory. Amen.

Cast It Away

Let all bitterness and wrath and anger and
clamor and slander be put away from you.

EPHESIANS 4:31

A re you struggling with memories of people who've treated you badly? Whether or not you deserved what they did to you, it may still hurt terribly and have continuing repercussions. And it may be difficult to stop thinking about it. Yet God instructs you to cast off your anger and forgive. But how can you do so—especially if you've been disrespected, treated cruelly, or even outright betrayed? It's not easy, but it is necessary.

The best way to keep your heart from succumbing to bitterness is to see the Lord's hand in every circumstance that touches your life. Believe that He can work through whatever has been done to you for your good and His glory—and praise Him. Because when you say to God, "My times are in Your hand" (Psalm 31:15), you acknowledge His ultimate sovereignty over your life and His good plan. You take the power away from your destructive thoughts and give Him room to heal your wounds, deliver you from bitterness, and set you free from whatever bondage is in your life. So regardless of what others have done, forgive them, trust God to vindicate you in His time, and be grateful that He always has the last word.

Jesus, I will obey You and forgive—help me to do so
completely. Amen.

Be Joyful to Grow

Consider it all joy, my brethren, when
you encounter various trials.

JAMES 1:2

Upon first glance, James seems to be demonstrating an incredible amount of insensitivity. When I'm facing a crisis in my life, the last thing I want is someone telling me to rejoice. However, James was not suggesting that we be joyous *because of* our trials. We are only deceiving ourselves when we dutifully say, "Praise the Lord," every time something goes wrong.

Rather, James was clear as to why we are to be glad *in the midst of* adversity. You see, James assumed that his readers were committed to spiritual growth and that when we understand that trials help us to advance quickly, we will be pleased because of the end result—maturity. After all, the testing of our faith produces endurance, which is necessary if we want to please God and be like Jesus.

So when you face a challenge, don't think, *Why is God punishing me?* Don't short-circuit the maturation process by resisting it and putting off the very thing the Lord sent the trial into your life to accomplish. Instead, realize the Father sees something precious in you to develop. Make the most of the difficulty by turning into it and learning all you can. And thank God for the spiritual growth that is ahead.

....

Jesus, I accept this lesson of spiritual maturity. Teach me,
Lord; I am listening. Amen.

Wisdom for Growth

If any of you lacks wisdom, let him ask of
God, who gives to all generously and without
reproach, and it will be given to him.

JAMES 1:5

D o you find it difficult to accept the connection between
adversity and spiritual growth? If so, ask the Lord to help
you understand it. That's what James meant by asking for wisdom,
which is the ability to see things from God's perspective. He will
reveal to you His big picture of your life and how He is maturing
you spiritually.

For a long time, I had trouble accepting this connection
between suffering and maturity in the Christian life. But this was
a faith problem on my part, where I gave into the pain and the
feeling that things would never change rather than accepting God's
good purposes every step of the way.

Like me, it may be difficult for you to accept that the Father
is so intent on bringing you to maturity that He is willing to let
you suffer. Indeed, you may not even think yourself worthy of this
attention from Him and divorce the concepts of adversity and spiritual growth in your mind. But in His economy, trials are a small
price to pay for the immense and eternal benefits that He wants to
bring you. So ask Him for the wisdom to grow in them.

....

Jesus, thank You for Your wisdom to endure and grow.
Amen.

Higher Perspective

*For Your name's sake You will
lead me and guide me.*

PSALM 31:3

In some elaborate English gardens, the landscapers arrange hedgerows in the shape of a maze. A person wandering between the lines of bushes may feel as if they must find their way out by trial and error because the bushes are too high to see over. However, someone watching from an upper window or balcony of the house can see the pathways clearly and give direction to the one wandering below.

Perspective matters. You might feel surrounded by a maze of bewildering details today. Though you can see where you are now and where you've been, you have no idea what's around the bend. But the Lord can see the entire span of your life and every step along the way. You don't have to be lost in this situation. You can trust Jesus to lead you.

Of course, leaning on Christ for the way forward comes more naturally when you cannot see the road ahead, but it's just as crucial to rely on His direction even when you think you have the whole picture. So don't wait until you're directionless to turn to Him. Seek the Lord's guidance every day, trusting that He sees farther ahead than you could possibly imagine.

....

*Jesus, thank You for giving me Your perspective for the path
ahead. Amen.*

Stay or Go?

The LORD said to Moses, "Why are you crying
out to Me? Tell the sons of Israel to go forward."

EXODUS 14:15

E cclesiastes 3:1 wisely teaches, "There is an appointed time for
everything." Though not included in the list, this principle
rings just as true: "There is a time to wait and a time to act." This
was certainly true for the people of Israel. When God parted the
Red Sea so they could escape Pharaoh's army, the time for praying
about the problem was over. It was time for them to accept the
Lord's route for deliverance.

So how do you know when to tarry and when to go forward?
Waiting on God is always necessary and right—never rush into
a situation without consulting Him. However, if you're in a position where a decision must be made and you've done everything
you know to discern the Lord's will—you've prayed, searched the
Word, sought godly counsel, and submitted every area of your
life to Jesus—then move forward with confidence in what He's
shown you.

God knows the future and wants to lead you, so have faith
that He will direct you wisely. And when He calls you to go forth,
entrust yourself to Him fully and do it because He is faithful and
will never steer you wrong.

Jesus, I will trust You—whether to wait or go forward.
Show me what to do. Amen.

Good Planning

The mind of man plans his way,
but the LORD directs his steps.

PROVERBS 16:9

S ome believers live in bondage to the idea that they should not plan ahead or look forward to the future because they don't know what God has in store for them. The good news is that God didn't design faith to operate that way. He instilled within you the desire to work and be forward-thinking; He wants you to anticipate His good plans for tomorrow.

This doesn't mean you inflexibly set your agenda and expect God to bless it. Instead, goals are really a natural outgrowth of godly priorities, the things on which you place the most value. The first step in setting up a list of Christ-centered objectives is to ensure that your focus lines up with His—you "seek first His kingdom and His righteousness" (Matthew 6:33). God promises to fill your life with abundance as you learn to love Him first. Then, when your value system is shaped by His, you're on the positive road to a godly understanding of what it means to set personal goals that fit His purposes. You're well prepared to make a plan based on His principles and to reach it through the strength, wisdom, and direction He provides.

....

Jesus, I want to carry out Your plans. Lead me, Lord. I seek
You first and foremost. Amen.

Evaluating Your Plans

Those who plan what is good find
love and faithfulness.

PROVERBS 14:22 NIV

A re there plans in your heart that you want to ensure come from God? Write down the areas in which you feel the Lord is leading you to take action, and then determine if your goals fit your walk of faith by submitting them to the following criteria: Does this objective glorify God? Will I be a better person if I pursue this course of action? Does this goal mature me in Christ? Does it benefit others in a manner that God instructs? Will anyone be harmed by my actions, or will others enjoy the rewards too?

If you can respond with a yes to these questions, you are most likely headed in the right direction. Otherwise, examine your heart and allow Scripture to adjust your path. Either way, never stop seeking the Lord as you proceed.

Nothing is as refreshing as the satisfaction of knowing you're working for a God-given purpose. Of course, walking by faith and striving toward Christ-centered goals is a process that may involve some occasional disappointments. But that does not mean that you are a failure or that somehow God has let you down. Instead, when setbacks come, treat them as a learning experience, keep clinging to Jesus, and continue moving on in wholehearted faith.

Jesus, help me to walk in obedience with plans that align
with Your will. Amen.

Transforming Praise

Be exalted, O LORD, in Your strength;
we will sing and praise Your power.

PSALM 21:13

Praise is the overflow of appreciation to God for who He is and what He's done. It isn't to be limited to seasons of blessings but is more than appropriate in difficult seasons, hardships, trials, and times of persecution as well. Indeed, we may not fully understand the power of praise until we've seen it transform our adversity. Worship invites the Lord to intervene in our circumstances—not necessarily by bringing an end to our struggles but by changing our perspectives and the spiritual landscape.

You see, when you praise the Father in times of heartache or stress, you're showing Him that you truly trust Him despite how everything looks. This is one of the most spiritually powerful things that you can do—it shakes the unseen realm in ways we can barely conceive.

Of course, the Enemy may try to deceive you into believing that God mustn't be concerned about you because He allowed the trouble in the first place. However, when you worship the Lord, you're saying that you'll trust Him no matter what befalls you because you believe His Word, which declares that He is faithful and never fails. So refuse to waiver in your faith. Praise Him right now. And rejoice that victory is ahead.

Jesus, I praise You, knowing my life is securely in Your hands.
Amen.

Supernatural Service

*The same Spirit works all these things, distributing
to each one individually just as He wills.*
1 CORINTHIANS 12:11

D o you realize that there's a ministry that God has planned in advance for you to accomplish? That may sound like it's true for people called to be pastors, ministers, and missionaries, but perhaps you are doubtful about yourself. Yet the Father has opportunities to serve designed especially for you—where your unique mix of talents, personality, and spiritual giftedness would be perfect for the task. He has placed you in this specific time and among specific people to be His representative. That's why He grows you spiritually—so that you'll be able to minister to others with supernatural wisdom, compassion, and generosity.

Do not miss the important word used in that last sentence: *supernatural.* That's because God Himself inspires and empowers you for the job by His Spirit. Stay connected to Him and He will show you what to do. And when you serve others under the Lord's guidance and by the power of His Holy Spirit, their lives will be transformed eternally.

So how has the Lord directed you to represent Him to others? Do not fear what He's calling you to do. Depend on the Holy Spirit to work through you and trust Him to bring Himself the glory.

*Jesus, I will serve as You desire. Work through me, Lord.
Amen.*

God-Accomplished Missions

*"The LORD is the one who goes ahead
of you; He will be with you."*

DEUTERONOMY 31:8

I magine how Moses must have felt when he heard God's assignment. Go into Pharaoh's court and demand that he let all the Israelites go. Then organize those more than two million people so they can leave the only home they've ever known and go to a land they've never visited. The Lord's mission for Moses was certainly vast and complicated—as may be the ministry He's called you to. However, the overly immense nature of the task is part of His plan because He wants you to rely on Him *completely* for its accomplishment. If we can do our ministry in our strength and wisdom, we may quickly conclude we don't need God.

But Moses brought nothing to the task—he had to thoroughly trust the Lord. And God came through repeatedly. Moses didn't convince Pharaoh, open the Red Sea, or provide water or manna. The Lord did. Moses simply obeyed Him. Ministry inevitably follows that pattern. We may plant the seed of the gospel, but God grows it. We may provide bandages and medicines, but He does the healing. So anytime the Lord calls, obey what He tells you and trust He will do His part—accomplishing the mission in a manner beyond your imagination.

*Jesus, I will obey Your call. Empower me to do Your will.
Amen.*

Hemmed In

*"Do not fear! Stand by and see
the salvation of the LORD."*

EXODUS 14:13

W hen you are hemmed in and there are no good options for which way to turn, remember that it is for a purpose. God Himself is about to deliver you. This was the case for the people of Israel as they camped along the banks of the Red Sea. The Egyptians descended on them "with all the forces in Pharaoh's army—all his horses and chariots, his charioteers, and his troops" (Exodus 14:9 NLT). There was nowhere they could go to escape. But Moses commanded them to stand still because the Lord was about to save them.

This is God's command to you when you're surrounded by extraordinary difficulties as well. You cannot retreat; you cannot go forward; you're shut in on the left and on the right. What can you do? Stand still. Recall the mighty things the Lord has done in the past to deliver His people. He made a miraculous corridor of escape through the divided waters of the Red Sea. The sovereign God who can do that has no problem making a way for you. So keep your eyes on Him and wait. Soon enough, He will open the way for you, and when He does, walk through with confidence.

Jesus, thank You for being my wise and faithful Deliverer. I will keep my eyes on You. Amen.

Be Set Apart

*The LORD will establish you as
a holy people to Himself.*

DEUTERONOMY 28:9

When God brought the Israelites out of Egypt, He saw that it was necessary to de-Egyptianize them in order to make them His chosen people. Toward that end, He led them through the wilderness, cut off their dependency to earthly forms of provision and security, protected them from enemies, gave them the Law, and fed them with manna. The Lord changed every area of their lives so they'd rely wholeheartedly on Him and be different from the nations around them.

Why did God go to such lengths with the Israelites? Because He wanted it to be obvious to the whole world that they were *His* special people—a nation that would be the platform for the Lord's greatest works. And, of course, it was through Israel that God sent His Son, Jesus, to be our Savior.

On this side of the cross, the Father draws people to Christ through you, which is why He instructs you to be set apart as well. True, it's not easy being different or following God. But don't be afraid or resist how He's transforming you. Because ultimately, being like Jesus is the way you best "proclaim the excellencies of Him who has called you out of darkness into His marvelous light" (1 Peter 2:9).

*Jesus, make me different like You, and draw others to
Yourself through me. Amen.*

JULY

God, Your Strength

My flesh and my heart may fail, but God is the
strength of my heart and my portion forever.
PSALM 73:26

More times than I can remember I've faced challenges that I knew were completely beyond me. I've suffered rejection and betrayal from men I thought were my best friends. There have been occasions when I've been hurt so deeply and cried so intensely that I told God I was ready to die. But as I've rehearsed for the Lord what I could and couldn't do because of my pain, He's gently reminded me, "I wasn't interested in your strength and abilities when I called you. And I'm still not interested in them now. What I want to know is, are you available to Me now? If so, then let's go. My grace is sufficient."

Realize that your biggest weaknesses and trials are God's greatest opportunities to shine His glory through you. The Lord has allowed adversity into your life to break your reliance on your own abilities. So instead of begging Him to change your circumstances, why not ask Him to fill you with His strength? Learn to live in dependence on Him for what you lack. Because as you do, His power will be demonstrated through you to others. And they will learn to trust Him as well.

Jesus, I am available to You. Let Your power shine through me. Amen.

It's Personal Now

"None of them will have to teach a neighbor to know the LORD,
because all will know me, from the least to the greatest."

JEREMIAH 31:34 GNT

In the Old Testament, the Lord spoke to His people through the prophets. Men such as Moses, Isaiah, Jeremiah, and others exhorted Israel to worship Him, seek Him, obey Him in holiness, and serve Him wholeheartedly. God's reason for speaking today is the same as it was then; however, His method has changed. In seeking to build an intimate relationship with us, the Father now communicates directly and personally to us through Scripture and the illuminating presence of the Holy Spirit.

While God still speaks through spiritual leaders, He delights in communicating with you one-on-one. So consider: Do you actively seek to know Him as your Redeemer, Lord, and intimate Friend? Do you personally take time to have a relationship with Him? Or are you relying on other people to tell you who Jesus is and what He desires from you?

From the beginning of your life, the Lord has sought to fellowship with you. Now it's your choice. Don't miss out on the awesome privilege of knowing God and building a close relationship with Him. Don't delegate that honor to others. Seek Him for yourself because you will surely find Him.

Jesus, I want to know You for myself. Thank You for
speaking right to my heart. Amen.

Test with Scripture

The people of Berea . . . searched the
Scriptures day after day to see if Paul
and Silas were teaching the truth.

ACTS 17:11 NLT

P erhaps you've heard the phrase, "Don't believe everything you read." It's good, commonsense advice. It's always wise to treat the information you receive with caution and verify facts before you repeat them. This is especially true regarding spiritual matters, which is why 1 John 4:1 warns, "Do not believe every spirit, but test the spirits to see whether they are from God." Ask the Lord to help you discern whether what you've heard is from Him, and He will show you if it aligns with the whole counsel of Scripture.

That's what the people of Berea did when they heard Paul's message about Christ. As Jews, they knew the prophecies concerning the Messiah, so when Paul insisted that Jesus was the Deliverer that God had promised, they went back to the source—Scripture. Because of this, the Berean Jews were considered "noble-minded," and "many of them believed" in Christ as their Savior (Acts 17:11–12).

So whenever you hear a sermon or Bible lesson, make it a personal habit to test the principles against the infallible Word of God. Not only will you avoid error, but you'll learn a lot along the way.

Jesus, may Your Word be the standard by which I judge all other voices. Amen.

JULY 4

Free Indeed

"If the Son makes you free, you will be free indeed."

JOHN 8:36

Jesus Christ is the Great Emancipator. He came to set us free—not necessarily from political or military tyranny, though that is sometimes the case—but from the far worse grip of sin and its everlasting destruction. When you embrace Christ as your Savior and Lord, you are liberated immediately from the *penalty* of sin—eternal death. But that's only the beginning. Christ also came to unshackle you from sin's power, which still enslaves your emotions, will, and personality.

This is because true freedom is spiritual. The oppression we experience due to sin cannot be medicated, fought off, or legislated into submission, because earthly measures cannot touch it. Instead, this liberty can be received only as a gift from God. And it makes all the difference in the world wherever you are—whether with political autonomy or behind barbed-wire walls, at home or within a prison camp, in success or while enduring injustice. Christ's freedom in you cannot be stifled, regulated, or executed. His is the ultimate emancipation.

Jesus wants you to experience the most wonderful life you can imagine—His life expressed through you. So refocus your quest for liberty on Him, and you will be free indeed.

Jesus, thank You for truly setting me free. Lead me into the fullness of Your liberty. Amen.

203

Loving the Lost

"They hated Me without a cause."

JOHN 15:25

It may be both difficult and confusing to watch as Christians around the world are persecuted simply for confessing the name of Jesus. Why would people despise believers—especially when they're just trying to show the love of God? However, remember this is a fallen and sinful world. Jesus said, "If I had not come and spoken to them, they would not have sin, but now they have no excuse for their sin" (John 15:22). That conviction they feel is painful and leaves them feeling vulnerable—so they attack out of a desire to maintain control. The Lord knew this would happen. He warned, "If the world hates you, you know that it has hated Me before it hated you" (John 15:18). It's not you—it is Jesus within you they despise.

But also remember that at no time did Jesus ever say, "Hate them back." On the contrary, we're to follow His incredible example of sacrificial love and service. Remember, "While we were yet sinners, Christ died for us" (Romans 5:8). While we were still horrible to Him, Jesus gave everything for us out of love. So no matter what they do, love them back by remembering where they're headed without Him, and with the hope that they'll accept the truth that sets them free.

Jesus, help me to love the lost and lead them to You. Amen.

Meaningful Work

*God is not unjust so as to forget your
work and the love which you have shown
toward His name, in having ministered
and in still ministering to the saints.*

HEBREWS 6:10

D o you feel at times that all you do in obedience to Jesus seems
to go unnoticed? Perhaps you don't see the fruit, or the tasks
He calls you to feel hidden, mundane, or even unimpactful to His
kingdom. Remember that in His goodness, our heavenly Father
has promised that not even the smallest deed of kindness is ever in
vain when done in the name of Jesus. Indeed, Christ said, "If, as my
representatives, you give even a cup of cold water to a little child,
you will surely be rewarded" (Matthew 10:42 TLB). No diligently
completed task goes unnoticed—every word and effort are noted
by our omnipresent, all-caring Father.

So never give in to the debilitating despair of thinking your life
doesn't count or that your contribution to the kingdom is insignificant. God is very strategic about how He directs you, and He will
bring fruit from your obedience at the right time. Remember, you
reap what you sow, more than you sow, and later than you sow.
So continue to serve with confidence, knowing that what you do
matters exponentially in eternity.

*Jesus, thank You that all I do in obedience to You is
meaningful and eternal. Amen.*

God Can Do More

*Even though, at about 100 years of age, he
figured his body was as good as dead . . . Abraham
never wavered in believing God's promise.*

ROMANS 4:19–20 NLT

Y ou may be able to imagine a great deal for your life, but have
you ever considered how much more God can do? Abram
did. Since he and Sarai were well past their childbearing years and
still childless, Abram asked the Lord to make his servant Eliezer his
heir. Yet God had much better for him. He promised Abram a son
whose offspring would be more numerous than the stars of heaven.
With no city lights to obscure Abram's vision, he looked upward
into the dark night and saw a multitude of shining lights.

Here was a man whose likelihood of having one child was nil.
But Abram believed God, and the Lord did immeasurably more
than Abram could possibly conceive.

This is instructive for us. We often ask for so little when the
Lord is ready to do the miraculous, and our unbelief limits what
Christ's superabundant power can do in us. Don't make that
terrible mistake. Today, expect the Father to do great things in
your life. And like Abram, show you believe Him by obeying His
every direction. Certainly, He will defy your hopes in ways that are
truly surprising.

*Jesus, I will trust You to provide beyond what I can imagine.
Amen.*

The Key Feature

A man's pride will bring him low, but
a humble spirit will obtain honor.

PROVERBS 29:23

Would you like to impress God? If so, you may think that to do so, you'll have to give more money, serve a lot of people, pray several hours a day, and attend many Bible studies. Those are the activities we often engage in to earn His love, even though He already cares for us unconditionally. However, there is a virtue revealed in Scripture that truly moves the Lord's heart. Indeed, it is the key to answered prayer. What is that powerful characteristic? *Humility.*

The Lord tells us, "These are the ones I look on with favor: those who are humble and contrite in spirit, and who tremble at my word" (Isaiah 66:2 NIV). God is not looking for men and women who possess superior intelligence, affluence, or acumen. He's searching for those rare Christians who exalt Jesus with everything they are because they honor Him as the King of kings and Lord of lords. So if you really want Him to bless you with His favor and use you for His kingdom, stop trying so hard in your own strength. Instead, humble yourself before Him, admit your inadequacy, acknowledge His authority, and submit to His wisdom. His power flows to those who lean heaviest on Him.

Jesus, I humble myself before You and devote all I am to You. Amen.

True Knowing

*"I have heard of You by the hearing of
the ear; but now my eye sees You."*

JOB 42:5

Y ou may have heard it said that a person does not really know
who his friends are until the bottom drops out. In much the
same way, we will never personally know how truly faithful, strong,
and wise Jesus is apart from adversity. Indeed, if our lives are free
from pain, turmoil, and sorrow, our experience of God will remain
purely academic. Our trust in Him would never increase, mature,
or be strengthened. Our relationship with Him could be compared
to that with a great-great-grandfather about whom we've heard stories yet never met personally. We would have great admiration but
no intimacy or fellowship. That is not the kind of relationship God
wants with His children.

Through the costly death of Christ, the Lord has opened the
way for us to have direct access to Him, and He wants nothing to
stand between us. So He engineers circumstances through which
He can reveal Himself to us in a personal and profound way and we
can bond with Him emotionally, relationally, and spiritually. When
difficult seasons arise, do not despair. Instead, rejoice that God is
about to reveal Himself to you in a powerful way, and get ready to
experience His faithfulness firsthand.

*Jesus, thank You for revealing Yourself to me through all my
circumstances. Amen.*

Dealing with Anger

*Cease from anger and forsake wrath; do
not fret; it leads only to evildoing.*

PSALM 37:8

Everyone struggles with anger at one point or another. We can
lose our composure in a heated moment or may be legiti-
mately disturbed over injustice. However, when we get mad, it's
important for us not to stay there, because anger is the enemy of
joy. When we're continually upset with others, ourselves, or our
present circumstances, we become vulnerable to bitterness, depression, isolation, and discouragement. Our inner turmoil makes it
virtually impossible to enjoy life or God's blessings.

However, there is a way of escape. Of course, the most important step is to honestly confess our fury to God. He leads us to think
through the reasons for our animosity and leads us to the root of why
we've reacted as we have. We may actually be responding out of our
woundedness or some wrong done to us in the past. Then, once God
has identified why we've become angry, He can begin the healing
process—and that usually includes forgiving those who've hurt us.

The problems that made you furious may not disappear, but
you can face them with a much better attitude and greater under
standing of yourself and others. So don't stay angry. Go to God and
let Him set you free.

. . . .

*Jesus, please deliver me from the anger within me and heal
me. Amen.*

Forgive Yourself

As far as the east is from the west, so far has
He removed our transgressions from us.

PSALM 103:12

I s your life haunted by past sin? Are there mistakes you've made that continually make you feel unworthy and unacceptable to God? If so, then you'll likely have trouble enjoying life to the fullest. Much of the depression that besieges our society comes from people laboring under an enormous load of unresolved guilt. However, once we confess our sin to God, He forgives us completely and restores our fellowship with Him. Still, sometimes we misguidedly feel we must continue punishing ourselves.

If you've repented of your sin before God, He has wiped it away and remembers it no more. To continue in unforgiveness toward yourself is useless and disrespectful to Christ's provision.

Therefore, to put an end to those old condemning thoughts, write out a confession to God, sign it, and date it. Next, go through all the passages in Scripture concerning forgiveness and write out each verse completely. Once you've done that, re-read what you've written and what the Father has to say about you. Then, across your confession in big, bold letters write, "Forgiven by God because of Jesus' love and death on the cross." You stand unconditionally loved and accepted by God. Believe it and enjoy all He has for you.

Jesus, thank You for forgiving me and helping me forgive
myself. Amen.

Why Pray?

Can two people walk together without
agreeing on the direction?

AMOS 3:3 NLT

Are there times you wonder if your prayers are making a difference? After all, God will do as He pleases. So why pray at all? Why approach His throne when He already knows what He's going to do?

Always remember that whatever the Father is up to, He will be accomplishing gently, patiently, and quietly in the unseen over time. He transforms your mind and desires and shapes your path through your times in the Word, in fellowship with Him and other believers, through the sermons you hear, and in the circumstances of life to position you for His purposes. And what happens through your times in prayer is that He's bringing you into harmony with His will. After all, you need to be in agreement with God to receive His best.

Sometimes it'll seem as if trials or opportunities appear quickly out of the blue—and those may be the ones you're most motivated to pray about. But remember that over time, He's been working to position you for them. He is actively working through the very things you're praying about to reveal Himself and His will to you. So keep seeking Him and be confident that what you're doing is indeed powerful and worthwhile.

Jesus, I set all my requests before You. Guide me so I may
walk in harmony with You. Amen.

Keep Praying

"Keep watching and praying that you
may not enter into temptation; the spirit
is willing, but the flesh is weak."

MATTHEW 26:41

D o you realize that when you fail to pray, you cut off the power, wisdom, strength, and blessings you could be enjoying? Perhaps you are noticing the effects of prayerlessness in your life today. Maybe you're experiencing the weight of your sin, or you just can't shake a sense of confusion. It's also possible you're feeling unusually discouraged, weak, or depressed. That's what happens when you don't spend time with God.

So why does failing to pray make you feel this way? Understand that the Lord isn't intentionally making you feel bad; rather, this is the natural outcome of being disconnected from Him. This is because prayer is like a powerline that plugs you into the Source. Through it, you're given His wisdom and guidance, His identity and purpose, His strength and peace, His love and acceptance. Prayer is the conduit through which you receive all of it. And that's why when you cut it off, you've got a problem.

So don't quit praying when things don't go your way or according to your time schedule. Stay connected because you need the presence and power of God in your life.

Jesus, help me to keep praying and seeking You in every
season. Amen.

Persecuting Jesus

*"These things they will do because they
have not known the Father or Me."*

JOHN 16:3

J esus warned the disciples that a season was approaching when the
religious leaders would mistreat them—putting them out of the
synagogue and persecuting them. He said, "An hour is coming for
everyone who kills you to think that he is offering service to God"
(John 16:2). Indeed, we see Saul—who'd later be called Paul—do
that very thing. He ardently persecuted believers, wholeheartedly
believing he was honoring the Lord. So Jesus put him back on track,
saying, "Saul, why are you persecuting Me?" (Acts 9:4).

Imagine being so caught up in serving God that you completely
lose sight of who He is. It can happen to the brightest and best in
the church. Jesus doesn't question the sincerity of such actions—He
recognizes that people do so because they want to show devotion
to Him. However, He also identifies the root problem—they don't
actually know Him.

Getting so caught up in religion, righteous agendas, or church
politics that you lose sight of God Himself is dangerous indeed. You
may actually be thwarting His work—persecuting Jesus Himself by
your actions. So make sure your relationship with Him is first and
foremost. He will certainly direct you to what truly honors Him.

*Jesus, I want to truly know You and serve You faithfully.
Teach me Your ways. Amen.*

Look to God

*"With people it is impossible, but not with
God; for all things are possible with God."*

MARK 10:27

When you encounter a difficult situation in life that looks impossible, what is the first thing you think? For most people, it is, "Oh Lord, what am *I* going to do?" But that's the wrong question. Instead, the right thing to ask is, "Lord, what are *You* going to do?" Because, as we are well aware, He is all-powerful, and nothing is too challenging for Him.

Of course, all of us know that in our minds. But often, when our back is against the wall and we don't know where to turn, we become gripped by the immensity of our predicaments and the disconcerting details that accompany them. It's natural for us to immediately envision the worst-case scenarios and how helpless we are with our limited resources. We become trapped by what we see and hear rather than recall who comes to our aid.

This is why we must train ourselves to look to the Lord rather than our circumstances. Because when we invite the supernatural, powerful presence of the living God to take hold of our situation, He deals with our difficulties in ways far beyond our imagination. He can get us to the right solution regardless of what we face.

*Jesus, I fix my eyes on You, grateful that my challenges are
no match for You. Amen.*

Christlike Treatment

*"In everything, therefore, treat people the
same way you want them to treat you."*

MATTHEW 7:12

I n today's verse, Jesus taught a principle that we might be able to
quote but may also have some difficulty living out. Of course,
it's easy to love people who are kind and generous to us, but when
people are belligerent, arrogant, or cruel, it's another story. Some
people believe that Christ's command to treat *all* people well is
unreasonable. But whatever Jesus instructs us to do, He empowers
us to carry out. So we must take it seriously when He says this
is our standard *in every situation*—not just when it's convenient.
Because everyone we encounter is someone He loves and died to
save, whether they treat us well or not.

To help you when people are difficult, always remember Jesus'
example at the cross. Even as the Roman soldiers nailed His hands
and feet to the rough wood, He said, "Father, forgive them; for they
do not know what they are doing" (Luke 23:34). He had come to
purchase forgiveness for sins, and He stayed true to His mission
even when it was most painful. Today, you are His representative
to carry forth the message of salvation. So treat people well, and in
so doing, lead them to Him.

*Jesus, help me to be as kind and loving to people as You are
to me. Amen.*

Comfort in His Direction

*I will instruct you and teach you in
the way which you should go; I will
counsel you with My eye upon you.*

PSALM 32:8

T oday, here are three things you need to know as you wait on
the Lord's direction.

First, God *will* show you His will. He desires that you walk
according to His plan and assumes responsibility for teaching you
how to do so. It is, however, your responsibility to obey what He
leads you to do.

Second, the Father is committed to your success. From the time
you were born, God has been working through the circumstances
of your life to train you for His purposes. So commit yourself to
following wherever the Lord leads you with confidence that He
will equip and empower you to accomplish whatever He's planned
for you to do.

Third, God will redirect you when you make a wrong turn.
So do not fear going forward when He calls. No matter how badly
you mess up, the Father will take the broken pieces of your life and,
with the glue of His unconditional love, put it back together. He
will take you where you are and help you get back on the right track
with His wisdom and strength.

*Jesus, thank You for teaching, leading, equipping, and even
redirecting me because of Your great love. Amen.*

You Too

He protects the lives of his godly people and rescues them.

PSALM 97:10 NLT

The people in the Bible were just like you—they were similar to you in their struggles and feelings, their successes and failures, and their desires and goals. Technology may have advanced, but the human heart has not changed throughout the ages. So you may read about how powerfully God worked through saints like Abraham, Moses, David, or Joshua, and imagine, *That could never be me.* But the truth is, their lives were marked by the same challenges, limitations, fears, and pressures yours is. They didn't live on a spiritual mountaintop; hearing and trusting the Lord were not easier during their time. If anything, you're in a better position to serve God because you're permanently indwelt by the Holy Spirit and have the full counsel of Scripture at your fingertips—two privileges Old Testament saints didn't have available to them.

The point is, Scripture recorded the astounding moments God worked through the saints, but their successes were based on the commonplace ways they walked with the Lord day in and day out—with faith in Him and endurance in the struggles, heartaches, setbacks, and challenges. The Father will operate in the same way through you. Faithfully follow wherever He leads; persevere, and you will see Him work too.

Jesus, I will surrender myself to You fully, day by day. Work through me, Lord. Amen.

Surrendered to Faith

"It shall be done to you according to your faith."

MATTHEW 9:29

Do your life and relationship with Jesus feel lackluster—as if something crucial is missing? This is the condition of far too many believers today; they're simply not living up to the potential the Lord created within them. Trapped by church traditions, smothered by concerns over status, and unwilling to test the resources of the all-powerful God they claim to serve, they wrestle with accepting and meeting the challenge of faith.

Due to poor self-esteem and a lack of trust that the Lord is who Scripture proclaims Him to be, many have merely accepted a comfortable, "churchy" lifestyle, choosing to remain ignorant of God's higher plane of Spirit-filled, resurrection-empowered life. However, that does not have to be you.

Today, consider and be brutally honest with yourself: Are you living up to your God-given potential? Are you availing yourself of the Lord's boundless resources? Do you have the courage to live completely, wholeheartedly in surrendered obedience to the will of God? If not, then you must learn the great lesson of walking by faith, not by sight. Open your heart to His fullness and trust His promises to be all-sufficient. Because that is what your soul is yearning to experience.

Jesus, I give my life to You wholeheartedly. Make me all You created me to be. Amen.

Wait for His Plan

I will extol You, O Lord, for You have lifted me
up, and have not let my enemies rejoice over me.

PSALM 30:1

David had just been anointed king over Israel when the Philistines attacked. The first thing he did was to go to God and inquire, "Shall I go up against the Philistines?" (2 Samuel 5:19). The Lord affirmed He would give David the victory and showed him what to do. Soon enough, Israel had defeated the Philistine onslaught.

In desperation, the Philistines attempted another raid. At this point, David could have looked at the situation in his human wisdom. His army had easily won the first victory, so if they repeated the same battle plan, they could probably win again, right? But David knew that was a losing strategy—making decisions apart from the Lord's guidance always invited defeat. After all, Joshua failed to seek God at Ai and lost terribly. So David immediately went back to the Lord and was told *not* to attack the enemy. Instead, God gave the young king a completely different plan.

Today, regardless of the battle you face, it's as crucial for you to wait on the Lord and His strategy as it was for David. God's timing and plan are always perfect. So commit yourself to following His lead because, certainly, He will never disappoint you.

Jesus, I await Your perfect plan. Thank You for defending
me. Amen.

Inner Room

*"Go into your inner room, close your door and pray
to your Father who is in secret, and your Father
who sees what is done in secret will reward you."*

MATTHEW 6:6

There will be times when no one will know the answer to your pleas but almighty God. No one will be able to comfort, strengthen, help, or encourage you like Jesus, and you won't know where to go. So it's crucial for you to have an inner room—a place set aside where you can spend time with the Lord and be renewed in His presence.

Yes, it's true that you can pray anywhere. But your inner room is where you go regularly to be quiet and secluded with God. It becomes your holy place where you fight your battles, wrestle with temptation, and deal with trials before the Father.

Find an "inner room," shut out the world, and pray. It doesn't have to be fancy; in fact, when I was in seminary, my prayer "room" was a place in the back corner of the living room marked out with a blanket. But over time, that place will become very meaningful to you because you interact with God there. It's just you, Him, and His Word. Surely, it will become that sacred place for which your heart yearns.

*Jesus, lead me to a special place where we can fellowship
daily. Amen.*

Escaping Temptation

God is faithful, who will not allow you to be
tempted beyond what you are able, but with the
temptation will provide the way of escape.

1 CORINTHIANS 10:13

The word *temptation* means something different for everyone. Some have a problem controlling their tongues, while others battle addictions to illicit substances or immoral behaviors. Whatever your struggle, understand that you're not alone. An actual war rages within every believer, and it's a spiritual conflict. The Enemy attacks our natural needs and desires, which are God-given and legitimate. For example, the Lord created us with the need to eat, but we can be tempted to consume food in a manner that injures our bodies. Anytime we go beyond the loving boundaries the Father has set, we tread on sinful ground.

But just as this war is spiritual, so is the way you defend yourself. The Holy Spirit indwells you and enables you to choose obedience over rebellion. So when you are tempted, turn to Him immediately, and ask Him to help you escape it. He will most likely identify thought patterns that need to change and may lead you to Scripture to liberate you, a godly friend to keep you accountable, or some other solution. The important thing is that He will guide you to true freedom, which is what you really need.

Jesus, thank You for setting me free from my sins. Show me the way, Lord. Amen.

Why Not?

Desire when it has conceived gives birth to sin,
and sin when it is fully grown brings forth death.
JAMES 1:15 ESV

D o you ever wonder why it is so important to resist temptation? After all, in Christ your sins are forgiven and wiped away completely. It is true that "if we confess our sins, He is faithful and righteous to forgive us our sins and to cleanse us from all unrighteousness" (1 John 1:9). However, engaging in sinful behavior still carries consequences that are not necessarily erased—some of which can be devastating to others as well. For example, you may receive forgiveness for adultery, but your relationship with your spouse will still be terribly damaged. In giving in to temptation, you may harm your future in ways that will be difficult to bear.

In a moment of temptation, never gloss over the destructive consequences of sin with naive justifications such as "This isn't so bad," or "It's not going to hurt anyone," or "I can quit whenever I want to." Instead, say no and seek the Lord immediately. Because when you do, God works through your response to build strength and instill His character into your life. And each time you're tested and overcome, you exercise your spiritual muscles and develop them for success in the future.

Jesus, please strengthen me against temptation and help me
always to say no. Amen.

Power for What?

May you be made strong with all the strength
which comes from his glorious power.

COLOSSIANS 1:11 GNT

Perhaps you read today's verse and are thrilled at the thought of having the strength that comes from God's glorious supremacy. After all, who doesn't want power? Yet understand that the Lord invests His might in a specific way—"so that you may be able to endure everything with patience" (Colossians 1:11 GNT). He doesn't empower you simply to fulfill your agenda. Rather, He fortifies you so that you will have the stamina necessary for your journey, regardless of the difficulties that arise.

Think about the progression. God gives you His strength so you might develop endurance as you face life's trials. The perseverance you cultivate helps you make spiritual progress, moving you forward in your prayer and devotional life, your service to Jesus and other people, and your worship. And the more you practice these disciplines as the world is shaking around you, the deeper your level of faith and fellowship with Christ becomes.

He gives you His power so you can grow exponentially stronger, closer to Him, and prepared for His blessings. So take Him up on it. Persevere by choosing to have faith in Him and become a vessel of His glorious might.

....

Jesus, thank You for giving me Your strength and training
me to endure. That's the path to life at its best. Amen.

Our Anchor of Hope

*This hope we have as an anchor of the
soul, a hope both sure and steadfast.*

HEBREWS 6:19

E arly Christians did not have the advantages we have today. For one, the New Testament was still in the process of being written. They had a large portion of the Old Testament but had to rely heavily on eyewitness testimonies of men like Peter, James, John, and Paul for the teachings of Jesus. Likewise, many died or were severely persecuted as a result of their Christian convictions. Yet they never lost their hope even when forced to worship in underground catacombs.

How did they maintain their faith? Archaeologists say one of the most common signs carved into the walls of those underground chambers was an anchor—the early Christian symbol of eternal hope in God through Jesus. In other words, they understood that in this tumultuous world, our life in Christ is absolutely secure, even when hurricanes of trouble assail us.

When you've prayed and trusted God, but there seems to be no end to your trials, remember who holds you. Jesus has neither forgotten you nor turned His back on you. The Lord has promised never to leave or forsake you. He has a plan for your life, and He will be the anchor that keeps you steady through every tempest.

*Jesus, thank You for being my hope and holding me steady in
the storms of life. Amen.*

Unshakable Faith

Faith is the assurance of things hoped for, the conviction of things not seen.

HEBREWS 11:1

Many people operate with a worldly understanding of faith. If they feel good about themselves, their jobs, families, and life in general, then they have a great deal of hope. However, if things aren't so positive and tend to worsen over time, their trust in God may fade. Of course, when all that we have today can be gone tomorrow, it's natural to have doubts. That's why we must not view things from the perspective of what we have in this world.

Instead, the faith the Father desires from us is based on the unchanging truth of Christ and the unshakable kingdom we're heirs to because of Him. Whatever you face today, there's hope because Jesus lives within you through the power of the Holy Spirit. And He promises to lead, guide, protect, and provide for you eternally.

So when your faith waivers and you begin to feel hopeless, realize it's because you've taken your eyes off Jesus and placed them onto your earthly circumstances. Fix your gaze back on Him immediately. When Christ is the center of your life, He gives you a profound peace that passes all understanding. After all, He's in control and works all things together for good.

Jesus, I will fix my eyes on You. Strengthen my faith. Amen.

His to Handle

*"Who is this uncircumcised Philistine, that he
should taunt the armies of the living God?"*

1 SAMUEL 17:26

When Goliath opposed the armies of Israel, everyone saw
the same towering figure and heard the same blasphemous
insults—but only one person made the right observation. Saul
and his men could only see the giant as too powerful for them to
handle. But David rightfully recognized that Goliath was really
challenging almighty God.

We all face Goliaths from time to time. Perhaps they are circumstances at work, relationships at home, or decisions too big for
us to handle. Like the soldiers of Israel, we're often overwhelmed
with our own sense of inadequacy. So we stand motionless. But we
must develop David's attitude, realizing that anything that comes
against us is actually God's to conquer.

As you contemplate today's challenges, don't make the mistake of measuring your potential success by your abilities. To do so
means insecurity. Instead, remember that God gains greater honor
through our availability than through our capability. He doesn't
expect you to work out the details of how everything will come
together. All He requires is that you show up and do what He wants
you to, trusting Him to hit the target.

*Jesus, thank You that all I face is actually Yours to handle.
Amen.*

Building Bridges

We are ambassadors for Christ, as though
God were making an appeal through us.

2 CORINTHIANS 5:20

Whether you realize it or not, once you accept Jesus as your Savior, you become His ambassador. God immediately empowers you through His indwelling Spirit to be an influential bridge builder to those around you who need to know Christ. You're surrounded by people who don't know about His amazing provision and are headed to hell because of it. His desire is for you to reach out to them. They may think they don't need Christ and want to be left alone. But realize that everyone wants to be loved, accepted, and freed from their sins. You can be the one to share all Christ has done for them and how much He cares.

Unfortunately, we often get distracted from this mission. We spend our lives as Christians pursuing our own happiness, prosperity, comfort, and authority. But that's just the overflow. Our true purpose is to represent Jesus to the lost and introduce them to Him. Just as Christ built the costly and everlasting bridge between us and the Father, we do the same between others and His awesome provision.

God has made you to be an extension of Jesus' life, love, power, and wisdom to those around you. See yourself as He does and be the best ambassador you can be.

Jesus, help me to reach others in Your name. Amen.

Following Jesus

"The Holy Spirit . . . will teach you all things, and
bring to your remembrance all that I said to you."
JOHN 14:26

Many of us have heard the expression "Follow Jesus" all of our lives. But what does it really mean? There are people who think they're pursuing Him when they agree to a morally Christian lifestyle. But if your idea of seeking after the Savior is merely going to church, listening to the Bible when the pastor reads it, giving money, and saying some prayers, you are missing the mark.

When Jesus was about to be crucified, He explained to the disciples that they would be able to follow Him just as closely after He was resurrected as they did when He walked the earth with them. How? Through the presence of His Spirit. The Holy Spirit would give them direction so that they wouldn't be left to do their own thing. The same applies to us. In following Jesus, we don't have to figure out *what* to do or *how* to carry out His will—He shows us.

Because Christ no longer physically walks the earth, we must develop a keen sensitivity to the promptings of the Holy Spirit. Once we learn how to listen to Him and obey faithfully, we need never doubt how Jesus wants us to follow Him.

Jesus, make me sensitive to Your Holy Spirit so I may always
follow You. Amen.

Strength to Be

*In Your hand is power and might; and it lies in Your
hand to make great and to strengthen everyone.*

1 CHRONICLES 29:12

David, the mighty warrior, skilled king, and gifted writer, knew the source of real strength. It begins and ends with God Himself. To David, the love and presence of the Lord were infinitely more valuable than the fame and fortune he had acquired and, indeed, all the treasures of earth. The once shepherd boy—the youngest of his father's household and, from a human perspective, the least promising—could look at his life and see the consistent hand of the sovereign God at work.

What else could account for his giant-slaying feat, his military victories, and his rise to leadership but the hand of the Lord? When David hid from Saul in dark, damp caves, shivering in cold desert nights, God sustained him. When David led men into battle against superior forces, the Lord gave him victory. Others could have been chosen; but David relied on God for his help, so the Lord honored him.

The same strength that God gave David can be yours today. You may not become a ruler, military leader, or psalm writer, but the Father will give you the strength you need for the tasks He assigns you. All you need to do, like David, is believe and receive.

Jesus, thank You for giving me strength. I rely completely on You. Amen.

229

God Can

*"If you abide in Me, and My words abide in you,
ask whatever you wish, and it will be done for you."*
JOHN 15:7

I can't, but Christ can." In this statement resides the secret to dealing with the challenges of life, whatever their cause or nature. You may not have all the resources to handle the difficulty before you today or all the answers to questions that rage in your heart. But God certainly does. In a sense, this should be very liberating. You don't have to engineer your own solutions. The key to your success is in Christ's wisdom and power. And you take hold of His awesome provision as you learn to abide in Him.

Abiding in Jesus simply means walking with Him, understanding that He is your life and worthy of your obedience and that He faithfully supplies your needs. As you daily submit to His Word, you count on Him to give you the power and guidance you require and the love you desperately want. Whether it's inspiration, endurance, strength, wisdom, love, joy, peace, patience, kindness, self-control, or whatever else you require, you can receive it from Christ, who always has plenty. You can't create these things yourself, which is perfectly okay—because Jesus can, and He's all you need. With God's help, all things are possible.

Jesus, thank You for always having exactly what I need and being more than enough. Amen.

AUGUST

Closed for Good

What he opens, no one can close; and
what he closes, no one can open.

REVELATION 3:7 NLT

T he contract you desperately need falls through. The avenue of financial blessing you were hoping for suddenly closes. The relationship that represented so much joy and possibility turns sour. *Slam. Slam. Slam.* Doors you thought God had opened wide become curtains of steel. What is the Lord doing? What is He up to? Why is He allowing you to face this reversal when all signs pointed to His approval of your hopes?

Despite your disappointment, remember this: God is sovereignly leading your steps on a path that will bring Him the glory and you the most benefit as you abandon yourself to His care. The next time your hopes are dashed, and the doors of your aspirations are slammed closed, remember that He has crucial reasons for shielding you that you may not yet see. He's not trying to disappoint you or cause you pain. Rather, He may be saving you from a disaster and is certainly preparing you for something far better. So rely on the all-sufficient wisdom of God, who alone knows the end from the beginning and which doors are ultimately best for you.

Jesus, this hurts terribly, but I will trust You. Open the
doors that are in the center of Your will and close all others.
Amen.

Bold Prayer

*We have confidence to enter the holy
place by the blood of Jesus.*

HEBREWS 10:19

Are your prayers weak and vague because you doubt that God will come through for you? If so, here are three significant truths that can revolutionize your prayer life.

One, you have complete freedom and access to God, not by your own merit but through the blood of Christ. You don't have to fear that the Lord won't find you worthy. You can approach the Father with confidence because Jesus has opened the way for you permanently through His sacrifice on the cross.

Two, you can confess God's Word. If you ever fear saying the wrong thing to the Father or asking for something inappropriate, simply pray Scripture and you can be sure you're headed in the right direction. The Lord always honors His Word.

And three, you don't have to figure out a plan; God does that for you. The Lord is strong enough to handle your trials, wise enough to know what you really need, and loving enough to minister to you in the best way possible. You don't need to tell Him what to do. Instead, rest in His faithful character and thank Him for His response.

*Jesus, I come before You with boldness. Thank You for
hearing and answering my prayer. Amen.*

235

Step-by-Step

My steps have held fast to Your paths.
My feet have not slipped.

PSALM 17:5

Are you wrestling with questions about the future? Do you wonder why God hasn't answered them? After all, He knows the end of your story before you're even born. So why does He disclose the path ahead only one step at a time?

Certainly, David had many of the same questions. The Lord appointed David king of Israel when he was merely a teenager, but He didn't divulge when or how David would take the throne. Along the way, David had amazing victories that won the love of Israel's people. However, David also spent several years avoiding King Saul, who sought to kill him out of jealousy. How do you think he would have responded if the Lord had earlier revealed the exhaustion and isolation he'd experience due to Saul's relentless persecution? By leading him step-by-step, the Lord navigated David through the triumphs without pride taking hold and the defeats without despair destroying him.

There are both good days and difficult ones on the path ahead of you, so the Father asks you to face life one day at a time with Him. He'll give you the grace and direction you need for the journey. Trust His wisdom about what to disclose. He'll tell you what you need to know right on time.

Jesus, I'll trust You one step at a time. Amen.

A Deliberate Decision

When I am afraid, I will put my trust in You.

PSALM 56:3

D o you realize that you can turn your worries into something positive? God repeatedly commands you not to fear—to make a deliberate decision whenever you experience apprehensions. So rather than allowing anxiety to take up residence in you, you view your worries as warning flags or triggers that directly drive you to the Father's throne of grace. In this way, your trepidations can serve to grow and strengthen your faith because you consciously make the choice to trust Him in them.

You see, prayer, infused with thanksgiving, is where the battle is fought and won against fear. When you go earnestly and boldly to the Lord regarding your concerns the moment they arise, you immediately focus on His power, wisdom, and sufficiency. And because He can handle anything that comes at you, fear's hold on you is weakened.

So when you are afraid, choose to trust in the Lord and commit yourself to Him in prayer and praise. Magnify the presence and power of God—think about what He has done in the past and what He's promised to do in the future. Not only will your anxieties flee, but the peace of God will certainly strengthen your heart.

....

Jesus, please remind me to turn to You as soon as fear arises so I can immediately express my trust in You. Amen.

Strengthen Others

Blessed are those who have regard for the weak;
the LORD delivers them in times of trouble.

PSALM 41:1 NIV

Today, understand that the strength the Lord is building in you is not merely for your personal assignments or ambitions; it's also for ministering to others who are wounded and troubled. You don't have to look far to find them—they sit next to you at the office, live in your neighborhood, and are with you at church. The Lord uses your trials to forge genuine wisdom, empathy, and compassion in you so you can lovingly extend comfort and support to others caught in similar challenges. He can work through your simple acts of kindness and words of encouragement to lift up a broken soul just as surely as He's used others to minister to you in your times of need.

Can you think of someone now who is hurting or at the point of exhaustion? Reach out to them with the strength and grace Christ has given you. Take time to pray, asking the Father how you can come to their aid. It doesn't take much—perhaps a note, phone call, visit, or lunch. God will show you what to do. The important thing is that you allow His power to flow through you to revive the fainthearted.

Jesus, show me who You want me to minister to and help me encourage them in Your name. Amen.

Denying Yourself

"If anyone wishes to come after Me, he must deny himself, and take up his cross and follow Me."

MATTHEW 16:24

Many believers today decide how they want to live by asking, "How can I get my needs met? How do I get folks to like and to accept me? How can I live what I believe is a full life?" Once they determine what they want, they go about trying to get it in the manner they deem best. However, to truly follow Jesus means that we change our question to, "Lord, how do *You* want me to invest this life that belongs to You?" It means we deny ourselves—we lay down our plans, goals, and ambitions and offer them as a sacrifice to the Savior. We choose to follow Him no matter where He leads and no matter what we must lay down.

If you want to serve God and be a blessing to others, it will mean denying yourself because you'll have to put others first, get under their load, and sacrificially help them in their time of need— just as Christ did. Are you willing? Don't spend the rest of your life wondering what God could have done through you had you been willing to obey Him. Deny yourself, take up your cross, and follow Jesus.

Jesus, make me a blessing to others by helping me serve them and put them first. Amen.

Surrender It to Him

Forsake your folly and live, and proceed
in the way of understanding.

PROVERBS 9:6

While it is comforting to know that our heavenly Father will never forsake us, it is challenging to accept that following Jesus as our Lord means we'll have to abandon some things we cherish—relationships, goals, material possessions, and sources of earthly security that God has required we leave behind for Him.

It is sometimes very painful to forsake that to which we've become attached. It is even more difficult when our attachment is not necessarily sinful but something our Lord compels us to give up for His own good reason. The great aim of the Holy Spirit is to help us surrender to Christ in every area of our lives. Then and only then can His power flow unhindered through us into the lives of others.

Is there any possession, habit, role, behavior, or relationship in your life to which Christ does not have complete access and control? Is there some area that you have reserved for yourself? Following Jesus requires that you abandon all to Him. Can you truthfully say to your Lord, "All that I am and all that I have is Yours"? I hope you can because that is true freedom.

....

Jesus, I surrender everything I am and all I have to You.
May You be glorified in me. Amen.

Unseen Strengthening

*The proof of your faith . . . may be found
to result in praise and glory and honor
at the revelation of Jesus Christ.*

1 PETER 1:7

When your faith is stretched to the limit and your dreams are shattered, everything in you may be telling you to give up. But don't—do not surrender. Choose to believe God despite everything around you. When you experience a situation for which answers are lacking and there seems to be no hope, you're facing a test of faith. However, be assured, there will never be a valley so deep or mountain so high that God is impeded from helping you. What's happening is that the Lord sees something in you worth developing, and He's removed evidence of His activity from your sight so your trust in Him will be exercised.

Each test of faith you endure is an opportunity for you to mature spiritually and believe God for greater things. Though it may be difficult for you to perceive the good in your trial, the Lord is getting you to the point where you can say, "Jesus Christ is sufficient." So be confident that you'll find Him absolutely faithful. Once He reveals what He's been doing in the unseen, you'll be able to share your testimony of His awesome provision with others with joy and authority.

*Jesus, I don't see You, but I will continue to trust You.
Amen.*

Repent and Refresh

*"Repent and return, so that your sins may be
wiped away, in order that times of refreshing
may come from the presence of the Lord."*

ACTS 3:19

I f God has put His finger on something in your life—convicting
you of some sin, relationship, or ungodly attitude—He will not
leave you alone until you deal with it. There's no way you can make
the Lord forget it by trying to convince Him that something else is
more important. His main concern is that you repent.

So examine your life: what about you is there that displeases
God? You know what it is because His Holy Spirit brings it to
mind. You may feel tempted to explain it away, but don't. In order
to continue having a living, vibrant, intimate relationship with
Jesus, you will have to address it. You cannot substitute anything
for obedience. You may think that more Bible study or service at
church will make the Lord forget about this rebellious area of your
life, but He doesn't work that way.

So don't make any more excuses. Confess your sin and repent.
Once you obey Him, you can stop worrying, fretting, and being
anxious. Yes, it may be painful at first, but God will help you
through it. He will cleanse you, and refreshing will surely follow.

*Jesus, I confess my sin. Teach me how to repent so I can be
pleasing to You. Amen.*

Count on Him

"LORD, there is no one besides You to help in the battle between the powerful and those who have no strength; so help us, O LORD our God, for we trust in You."

2 CHRONICLES 14:11

When King Asa saw the bloodthirsty million-man army of King Zerah advancing to destroy Judah, he quickly realized his weakness and turned to God for help. Had he relied on his soldiers' skill and fighting spirit, he would surely have failed. But he confessed his inadequacy and turned his attention to the Lord. And God gave him victory.

This must be our first response whenever we face difficulties as well: we must immediately turn to God to deliver us. Thankfully, the criterion to receive His assistance is simple: admit our helplessness.

So today, regardless of what you face, do not wait to call out to Him. It does you no good to focus on your deficiencies, as people so often do. That isn't humility; it's just wasted contemplation. Instead, center your attention on the Savior's adequacy to help you rise above your challenges and triumph. And remember that though others may fail you, He never will, for He is your loving, sovereign Lord. Then put your full trust in your Deliverer. He has helped you thus far, and He will not let you down.

....

Jesus, You are all I need. Deliver me, my Savior. I count on You. Amen.

In God's Hand

"It was not you who sent me here, but God."

GENESIS 45:8

If ever there was someone who had plenty of reasons for a foul attitude, it was Joseph. Almost everyone he knew betrayed him. His jealous brothers sold him into slavery. After he was traded to an Egyptian official, his master's wife falsely accused him of sexual harassment. A servant he helped and befriended in Pharaoh's prison quickly forgot Joseph's kindness after he was released. It wasn't until Joseph was thirty years old—about thirteen years after his brothers' betrayal—that he was elevated to one of Egypt's highest offices.

Had Joseph grown resentful over his circumstances, he wouldn't have been ready to assume the lofty position offered him by Pharaoh. A bitter person typically becomes isolated, withdrawn, and has little positive interaction with others. But I am convinced that the reason Joseph persevered and succeeded was his faith in God's sovereign hand in his difficulties. He said as much to his brothers in today's verse.

Because Joseph trusted the Lord's ability to bring good from the afflictions he experienced, God did astounding things through him. The same is true for you. So do not despair, and don't give in to bitterness. Keep obeying God—He will lift you up in due time.

Jesus, I am safe in Your hand, and I will trust Your plan. Amen.

Demonstration of Power

With great power the apostles were giving
testimony to the resurrection of the Lord Jesus.

ACTS 4:33

Has the truth of God's Word been accompanied by the demonstration of His power in your life? We tend to look for grand miracles in response to that question—such as the healing of an untreatable sickness—but the Lord exhibits His might in other ways as well. For example, He changes your habits, attitudes, and behaviors to conform you to your new identity in Christ. Believe it or not, ridding you of the habit of lying, gossip, or of abusive speech is just as extraordinary as healing you of a disease.

This is important because God's power is released in your life primarily for the purpose of making a statement to those who do not know Him. Have your unsaved friends and neighbors witnessed the Lord's sanctifying presence in your life, leading them to repentance and salvation? Your faithful witness concerning God's love for them is an open conduit for His mighty work—He operates in supernatural ways in them as you obey Him. So ask the Lord to use you as an extension of His life, an expression of His love, and an exhibition of His power to those around you. That is a request He loves to fulfill.

Jesus, conform me to Your likeness so that Your power in me may draw others to You. Amen.

Knowing the Truth

"You will know the truth, and the
truth will make you free."

JOHN 8:32

Many in the church today have come to accept the idea that we must hold the right views on every issue and we must spend every energy in defending them—as if our relationship with God is dependent on our intellectual agreement with Him. Although it is crucial to know the truth and to be accurate in our study and interpretation of the Bible, remember one very important thing: the truth is a person. Jesus said, "I am the way, and the truth, and the life" (John 14:6).

To know the facts or have correct beliefs is only a part of the story in knowing and serving Christ. The other part is becoming who He saved you to be. Jesus said, "If you continue in My word, then you are truly disciples of Mine" (John 8:31). A spiritual work must be done through the power of the Holy Spirit as you stay in His Word—He transforms you into His likeness from the inside out. That means you're like Him in every way—in character, mission, motivation, and love. Like Jesus, you're not focused on conquering in this world but are uniquely focused on helping others know God, so they may enjoy Him in eternity.

Jesus, teach me Your truth—in my mind, body, soul, and
spirit—so others may be set free as well. Amen.

How to Serve

"If anyone serves Me, he must follow Me."

JOHN 12:26

A life of ministry and a servant spirit are key ingredients for those who seek to follow Christ. But how do we serve others effectively in Jesus' name? Here are five qualities that are important in this pursuit:

First is *abandonment*, which speaks of your total dependence on God for everything in life and a total surrender of your hopes, abilities, and possessions to His use. Second is *abiding*. Because the Lord is your source of love, wisdom, and power, hold on to Him with everything in you to empower your service and make your ministry effective. Third is *awareness*. Be sensitive to those around you. Do you see the challenges others are experiencing and the underlying reasons for why they're struggling? Fourth is *availability*. Are you tied to your schedule, or are you flexible, ready to be the Lord's representative and answer to prayer when the need arises? This speaks of selflessness and a realization that people are more important than things. The fifth and final quality is *acceptance*. One of the keys to ministering to people is accepting them just the way they are, as Jesus would—because that's how God accepts you. So be great in His kingdom by learning to be a loving servant of all.

Jesus, help me to serve and honor You well so others can know You as Savior. Amen.

Advanced Planning

Many plans are in a man's heart, but
the counsel of the LORD will stand.

PROVERBS 19:21

As diligently as you may wish to plan, the future is a puzzle to all but God. Your supreme purpose, then, is to walk in harmony with the Savior by employing essential disciplines:

First, lay aside every encumbrance and sin. Willful disobedience and unproductive habits will hinder your spiritual growth. Ask the Father to help you rid yourself of these unnecessary weights.

Next, concentrate on endurance. Do not let disappointments or setbacks take you out of the race. Accept that they, too, are part of the course God has divinely planned for you.

Most of all, focus on Jesus. Turn away from all that distracts you from Him. Cast your burdens on Him and look in steadfast faith to Him. Seek His face daily through personal prayer and sustained time in His Word.

A trusting, faithful, unwavering devotion to Christ will lighten your load, equip you to handle the tough times, and guide you in His will every day of your life, regardless of what happens. And He will take you further than you could ever have imagined or planned on your own.

....

Jesus, my life is in Your hands. Lead me in Your perfect will.
Amen.

Return to Him

Let them turn to the LORD that he may
have mercy on them. Yes, turn to our
God, for he will forgive generously.

ISAIAH 55:7 NLT

Most Christians genuinely want to love God and please Him. However, we all feel distant and detached from Him at times. This can happen for any number of reasons. We get caught up in the hectic pace of work, school, family, or other meaningful obligations. Or perhaps we become ensnared by a sinful habit that's difficult to abandon, and our guilt is so overwhelming that we're ashamed to approach the throne of grace. But the result is that our times of communion with Christ have diminished.

Whatever the reason for your broken intimacy with God, there is good news. Jesus waits to embrace you with His unconditional, divine love. So pause, take a deep breath, and admit any misplaced priorities. Confess your sins, receive His infinite forgiveness, ask Christ to restore your soul, and agree with Him about the changes you need to make in your life. Then begin seeking the kingdom of God anew. It may take time for feelings of intimacy to return, but your fellowship with Jesus can again be sweet and fulfilling. Go to Him now. He is waiting for you with open arms.

Jesus, draw me back to the fullness of a wonderful
relationship with You. Amen.

Help in Trouble

*After you have suffered for a little while, the
God of all grace . . . will Himself perfect,
confirm, strengthen and establish you.*

1 PETER 5:10

The Bible is a riveting book of realism. It never denies or ignores our troubles; it simply reminds us of the transcendent truth of God's presence and power during our frequent bouts with difficulty. We may have many dangerous roads to traverse and obstacles to overcome, but with the Savior's enabling, we can endure. He keeps us strong when we are weak, gives us His peace when we're troubled, and directs us when the path ahead grows dim. And whatever our current lot, we can be sure that the suffering we now bear is not forever and that the Lord will ultimately lead us to a magnificent victory. His plan is so exceedingly good that words can't justly describe it.

So today, be confident that God will come to your aid. He will sustain you when you're at your breaking point. He will revive you when your body and spirit are exhausted and spent. And He will give you wisdom when you don't know what to do, and hope when all seems lost. So put your faith in the Lord and accept His help because He will see you through these difficult days perfectly.

*Jesus, thank You for being in this with me. I need You, my
Savior. Amen.*

Invest Today

Do not boast about tomorrow, for you do
not know what a day may bring forth.

PROVERBS 27:1

If you knew that today would be your last day, how would you live it? Tragically, many people have difficulty finding an answer to this question. Many say, "I wouldn't do anything different." Some would take the day off and spend it with family and friends. Others might use the time to rectify past wrongs. However, we must all take hold of the fact that yesterday has come and gone, tomorrow is not yet here, and all we have is now—today. What we do with the hours we're given is incredibly important.

What you do with today will be indelibly printed on the pages of eternity. So how can you live to the fullest if you're forgetting what's behind and not counting on tomorrow? You must have the right focus. So consider: What is the foundation of your hope? What holds your affection? What's most important to you? Missionary C. T. Studd sounds this warning: "Only one life, 'twill soon be past, only what's done for Christ will last." When you anticipate standing before Jesus, the way you should live your life becomes abundantly clear. So don't misspend your gift of time. Invest today in Him.

Jesus, I want to honor You with my life. Help me to live
fully for You today and every day. Amen.

Looking Within

*As believers in our Lord Jesus Christ, the Lord
of glory, you must never treat people in different
ways according to their outward appearance.*

JAMES 2:1 GNT

I t is human nature to prefer those who have and avoid those who
have not—to show more respect for people who are dressed to
impress and have resources, wealth, fame, and power than those
who have nothing. Yet it's plain from Scripture that God has a
different code by which His children should live. This is because
the Lord sees far more profoundly into people than we ever could.

Remember what we are told about Jesus: "He has no stately
form or majesty that we should look upon Him, nor appearance
that we should be attracted to Him" (Isaiah 53:2). Imagine missing
the Savior because He didn't look the way we thought He would!
We should never make judgments about what people are worth by
how they appear outwardly. We have no idea who is more faithful
to the Lord or who has the capacity to serve Him most sacrificially.

Therefore, we should treat everyone as the Lord's beloved. Seek
to look beyond what others wear and, with God's help, find the
treasure that may hide within them. You're certain to make many
wonderful discoveries.

*Jesus, help me to see people how You do and love them with
Your unconditional care. Amen.*

Unanswered Prayer

Wait for the LORD; be strong and let your
heart take courage; yes, wait for the LORD.

PSALM 27:14

There may come a time when you think the Lord has stopped answering your prayers. Your natural response may be to become discouraged and question God's love and involvement in your life. But don't. Very likely, you are on the verge of a dramatic discovery that will deepen, broaden, and strengthen your life in Christ.

When you find yourself in this place of uncertainty, observe the following cautions. First, don't confuse unanswered prayer with being unheard. God *always* pays attention to your pleas. Trust that He is working in the unseen rather than ignoring you. Second, when you fear the Lord isn't responding to you, you may be tempted to go elsewhere for information and guidance. Don't. Continue to wait for Him. Third, be honest with yourself. Humility and transparency are crucial for God to work effectively in and through you. Examine your life and make sure you are obeying everything He has instructed you to do. If not, go back to the last thing He said and submit to Him immediately.

In everything, trust that your heavenly Father hears you and that He will answer you at the right time. Be strong, take heart, and wait for Him to show you what to do.

Jesus, I wait for You. Lead me to do Your will. Amen.

Slow Down

"In quietness and trust is your strength."
ISAIAH 30:15

Years ago, I attended a weeklong photography class. We had hours of classroom work before we ever got to our first field trip. As you can imagine, I was anxious to get on with taking photos of the surrounding countryside. I still remember the frustration I felt when, in a very commanding voice, my instructor said, "When you arrive on location, leave your camera in the car for one hour. I want you to walk around, stop, look, and listen; or you will miss your best shots." I did what he said—and boy, am I glad. There's no telling how much I would've missed had I rushed out with camera in hand.

Of course, in our goal-oriented, high-achievement, fast-paced society, we hardly have time to think. But when we race through life, we fail to see so many blessings God has for us. We don't observe the beauty all around us, the importance of our relationships, and what Christ has done on our behalf. Even worse, however, we miss God's best for us because we're too hurried to wait on Him.

Don't make that mistake. Slow down. Stop, look, and listen. And observe all the awesome ways the Lord is working around you.

....

Jesus, help me to slow down so I can perceive all the
wonderful ways You're working around me. Amen.

The True Cost

"Sell all that you possess and . . . you shall have
treasure in heaven; and come, follow Me."

LUKE 18:22

The prosperous young man came to Jesus with the question that many of us subconsciously live by: "Good Teacher, what shall I do to inherit eternal life?" (Luke 18:18). He thought that he could do enough to buy his salvation. But his mistake wasn't about what he owned that he could give—it was about who owned him. It's the same error we make. Rather than realizing Jesus purchased and owns the totality of our lives on the cross, we think we can offer Him lesser tokens in exchange for eternal life.

Jesus told the rich young ruler to go and sell all he had; in doing so He was identifying what the man perceived to be the most important resource he had. Money held higher value in his life than God. He did not yet understand that all the wealth on earth and all the good things he could do would never be enough for the spiritual transaction.

Likewise, understand that Jesus isn't open to bartering about what your home in heaven is worth. He's already paid the great price. And He doesn't want your stuff. He wants you —your heart, mind, soul, and strength. So today, obey Him. And recognize that He is your true treasure.

Jesus, my entire life belongs to You. Thank You for saving
me. Amen.

Higher Purposes

"As the heavens are higher than the earth,
so are My ways higher than your ways."

ISAIAH 55:9

I f you find yourself confused about what to do and just cannot understand all the Lord is accomplishing through your circumstances, do not fret. Much of it is because He is the all-knowing, all-powerful God, and you are not.

Once you're saved, you are launched into the great adventure of learning about Him. You're indwelt by His infinite presence through the Holy Spirit, who teaches you to have the mind of Christ. You learn to think and act as He does. Yet do not imagine God will disclose everything—He won't because you can't handle it all. Sometimes that means that you will be left in a quandary about what to do. And that's okay because He is in control and teaching you to have faith. Instead, He patiently and lovingly unveils His path for you as you spend time with Him in the Word and in prayer. He helps you understand His will and all you need to know to step forward in obedience.

So when you don't understand what to do, sit at Jesus' feet and seek His wisdom. He will not only show you what to do but will reveal Himself and His purposes in ways that will change your life forever.

Jesus, I rely on Your higher thoughts. Show me what to do.
Amen.

Surrendered Ministry

Present yourselves to God as those alive from the dead, and your members as instruments of righteousness to God.

ROMANS 6:13

We cannot be effective in the ministry God calls us to if we aren't fully yielded to Him. The Lord does not invite us to serve Him so we can accomplish our plans in our own strength and receive recognition from others. Instead, Christ calls us to continue surrendering ourselves to Him continually—experience by experience, day by day, year by year. In this way, the Lord works through us to bring glory to Himself and real transformation to the lives of others.

This is often why God allows us to be broken as we serve Him. It is so we can remain in total submission and commitment to Him, mature spiritually, and minister to others powerfully as they face adversity. We can't grow in spiritual effectiveness without dependence on Him, and we can't engage in Spirit-led ministry without being willing to be His instrument of peace in others' conflicts, difficulties, and pain.

So when times of trial come, be willing to die to self, change, and grow. Surrender to Jesus completely. Because as He leads you to serve Him, you'll discover His awesome plans for you. And there's nothing more meaningful in which you can invest your life.

Jesus, I fully surrender my life to You. Work through me to minister to others. Amen.

257

Pruning Tools

*"Every branch that bears fruit, He prunes
it so that it may bear more fruit."*

JOHN 15:2

When we serve God faithfully, we may be shocked and confused when He allows adversity in our lives. After all, we are obedient to Him—shouldn't He reward us rather than allow us to experience pain? But realize that He doesn't allow challenges in your life for harm. Rather, He permits them because He sees the immense potential for fruitfulness in you, and He wants you to rely increasingly on Him. If He didn't prune you, you would eventually fail under the weight of your own success.

What can become especially disorienting, however, is *how* the Lord prunes you. God may work through hurtful remarks, false accusations, people manipulating situations for their own benefit, and great challenges that seem potentially devastating. But remember that you don't choose the tools God uses; He does. And the tool will most likely be sharp, painful, and unavoidable. This is because loss is always a part of the pruning process. However, don't get distracted by the method. Remember He is working for your good. Through it all, pray, "God, I'm Yours. No matter what happens, I will trust You." Because He will make you fruitful if you'll just endure.

....

*Jesus, I'm Yours. No matter what happens, I will trust You.
Remove whatever needs to go. Amen.*

Ready to Learn

*Joyful are those you discipline, LORD, those
you teach with your instructions.*

PSALM 94:12 NLT

When conditions are consistently favorable, growing spiritually is often put on the back burner. However, adversity serves as a great instructor—helping us discover more about the character and nature of God. We learn He is good, faithful, merciful, sovereign, generous, and compassionate. His love is unconditional, not distributed based on our performance. And if we'll allow adversity to drive us to the Lord's bosom, we'll find refuge and protection from the storm. So we should allow our struggles to propel us into deeper intimacy with the Savior. He will never disappoint, condemn, or fail us.

However, you will also discover a great deal about yourself during times of affliction. The dark times reveal your true character and spiritual maturity. Is there pride in you? Do you believe yourself wise in areas you shouldn't? Are you nursing grudges against others or even against God? Have you turned toward the Lord or away from Him? Such self-examination, if not overdone, is profitable. Adversity exposes the real you. It allows you to evaluate your value system and determine whether it aligns with God's or not. It also reveals to you if there's more you need to learn about Him and less you need to focus on yourself.

*Jesus, what do You wish to teach me through these
challenges? I am ready to learn. Amen.*

In God's Strength

*Those who wait for the LORD will gain new
strength . . . they will run and not get tired,
they will walk and not become weary.*

ISAIAH 40:31

I remember meeting the late missionary Bertha Smith at the air-port when she was a spry seventy-two-year-old. I'd gone to pick her up for a speaking engagement at our church, and I was amazed at how lively she was. At that time, she had the next five years of her life booked with meetings around the world.

At the end of the first long day at our mission conference, Ms. Smith was still going strong, so I asked her, "Don't you ever get worn out?" She replied, "I'm not operating in my strength. I am going in God's." That was it. No fluffy theology—just straight-forward faith. She said, "Here's what I do: I tell God what I have to do each day, and I let Him know I cannot accomplish it in my strength. Remember that Jesus said, 'You can do nothing apart from Me.' So I claim His power for each task, thank Him for it, and move on."

That may seem simple, but it works. In your weariness, weak-ness, tiredness, or frailty, God is more than willing to uphold and sustain you. He will fortify you with power from on high. So wait on His strength and count on Him.

Jesus, I will wait on You. Strengthen me, Lord. Amen.

Strength in Weariness

He gives strength to the weary, and to him
who lacks might He increases power.

ISAIAH 40:29

Are you weary today? Has there been a lot going on that's drained you of emotion, energy, motivation, creativity, and wherewithal? Most of the time, we can handle short doses of discomfort in our own strength. We can make it through a day or even a few weeks without perceiving a substantial need for God's help. But when there is a particularly painful and taxing loss or when challenges come to stay for a long time and refuse to relinquish their grip, our ability to cope is severely diminished. It is then that we can be especially open to God's support. In our exhaustion, we need to recall the vital truth that we can exchange our weakness for the Lord's inexhaustible strength.

Today, you may be tired, but you can keep going when the going gets rough by receiving God's strength. He can help you persevere and even thrive through the indwelling power of the Holy Spirit. It's okay that these difficulties have brought you to the end of your self-sufficiency—it's actually for your benefit that they have. Because now you're ready to experience the total adequacy of God for every situation. And when He is involved and empowering you, nothing will be impossible for you.

Jesus, thank You for giving me Your strength when I am weary. Amen.

Responding Well

In the day of prosperity be happy, but in
the day of adversity consider—God has
made the one as well as the other.

ECCLESIASTES 7:14

Whenever you find yourself in a season of adversity, here are some ways you'll be tempted to respond that you should avoid in order to endure triumphantly.

First, refuse to blame others for your situation. Your problems may have been instigated by others, but you're responsible for *your* reaction. Jesus calls you to extend forgiveness, and you will miss God's blessing if you play the blame game. *Second, don't feel sorry for yourself.* Self-pity is a form of unbelief because you're not trusting the Lord to bring good from your troubles. Resist it by confessing God's Word and reminding yourself often of His great love and purposes for you. *Finally, don't try to escape your problems.* You may be tempted to short-cut your challenges or find easy ways out of them, but don't. You will only make matters worse and may even deepen your suffering. Instead, develop your spiritual muscles by committing yourself to trusting God regardless of what happens.

Whatever adversity you wrestle with, you can be assured that you are never alone. Jesus is with you. So never give up. Instead, cling to Christ. He will help you advance, grow, and even conquer.

Jesus, help me to honor You in every situation, whether adversity or blessing. Amen.

Choose Forgiveness

*"If you forgive others for their transgressions,
your heavenly Father will also forgive you."*
MATTHEW 6:14

With every injury or mistreatment, you ultimately have two options: forgive the offender completely or refuse to let go, believing they owe you something to make up for what they've done. In the short term, keeping them accountable in your mind may seem to be the easier and more gratifying choice, especially when the individual is still in your life.

However, you probably know by now that when you harbor bitterness toward others, it will affect you profoundly. And time doesn't heal those injuries. On the contrary, left unhealed, your old wounds become infected and turn into a more serious emotional, spiritual, relational, and even physical illness. The poison of an unforgiving spirit can damage the entire person.

The only cure when resentment has taken root is forgiveness. Nothing else does the job of genuine healing. Of course, you may be afraid to pardon what's been done to you. After all, if you truly forgive those who hurt you, will anyone hold them accountable? But remember, you're not injuring them with your bitterness; you're only hurting yourself. So ask God to help you let go and forgive. And trust that the Lord will not only heal you as you obey Him but will also make all things right.

Jesus, I choose to forgive. Please set me free from bitterness. Amen.

Forgive Like Jesus

Be kind to one another, tender-hearted,
forgiving each other, just as God in
Christ also has forgiven you.

EPHESIANS 4:32

Is there someone you need to forgive? Perhaps God has been convicting you to let go of your hurt, but for some reason, you just can't. The pain runs so deep that you just don't know how to deal with it. If you've come to the point where you realize that you aren't capable of forgiving in your own strength, that's okay. As in everything else in the Christian life, when you can't, Jesus can. He enables you to let go of your bitterness based on what He did for you on the cross.

Think about it: Christ died a cruel death in your place, taking all your sin—past, present, and future—on Himself so you could have a relationship with God. Take a moment to think of the enormity of what He did for you. Every sin—absolutely forgiven. If He could pardon all that, He will certainly help you to let go of your resentment. Indeed, perhaps in thinking of the enormous grace you've been shown, you're already realizing you don't have the right to carry a grudge. So turn your pain over to Jesus and allow Him to help you. He will empower you to forgive others even as He forgave you.

Jesus, please help me to forgive as You would. Amen.

September

Tough Assignments

*"Just as I have been with Moses, I will be with
you; I will not fail you or forsake you."*
JOSHUA 1:5

At times, the Father will assign you tasks that will be daunting and even somewhat impossible. Joshua understood this well. At a pivotal point in the history of Israel, the Lord anointed Joshua to lead millions of Hebrews into Canaan, where many enemies awaited their approach. And he was required to do so without Moses.

You can imagine how Joshua felt without Moses' wise counsel and presence to guide and support him. Yet the Lord promised to be with Joshua every step of the way. And just as He had provided every triumph Moses experienced, He would give Joshua the victory as well.

Perhaps there are assignments from God or challenges before you that make you feel incredibly alone and overwhelmed. Yet He is with you as He was with Joshua and Moses. Jesus promised, "I am with you always, even to the end of the age" (Matthew 28:20). The Lord will never leave or forsake you, nor will He call you to accomplish something without providing for your needs. So do not fear. Go forward in this assignment with faith in His provision and joy in His coming victory.

*Jesus, I trust Your call and provision. I will obey and rely on
You every step of the way. Amen.*

Strength in the Word

Whatever was written in earlier times was written for our instruction, so that through perseverance and the encouragement of the Scriptures we might have hope.

ROMANS 15:4

The Word of God is replete with situations that mirror your experiences and offer you encouragement in them. For example, Joshua's conquest in the land of Canaan foreshadows how believers can possess a life of victory. In a literal sense, not many people will invade new territory, but we all have assignments the Lord has given us. We see the importance of believing God in them through the account of the twelve spies who went into Canaan (Numbers 13–14). Ten of the spies saw the giants who inhabited the land—not the abundant blessings that the Lord wanted to bestow on His people. Only Joshua and Caleb surveyed the land and returned with utter confidence that the Lord would do as He promised. They eventually led Israel to victory.

Trusting in God's sufficiency and power is necessary for the triumphant Christian life. Therefore, the Lord encouraged Joshua to meditate on the Scripture day and night and thus ensured his success (Joshua 1:8). You should too. Meditate on God's Word and think about how He's helped people in the past. You will certainly find encouragement for all you're facing today.

Jesus, speak to me through Your Word that I may obey You fully. Amen.

Into a Useful Vessel

*"Like the clay in the potter's hand,
so are you in My hand."*

JEREMIAH 18:6

Have you repeatedly found yourself facing familiar fights or being broken in the same areas? This may be so that your old nature can be chipped away and rough spots in your character can be sanded smooth. The process is often painful and difficult, but it is also good. If you truly want to be all the Father designed you to be, you must submit to Him during times of trial and allow Him to reveal why you're going through the challenging season and what He wants you to learn.

So face it with faith. God is at work in your life, shaping you into the person He knows you can be so that you might bring Him glory and be of maximum use in building His kingdom. Today, decide which you would rather be: a vessel of your own design, of fading value, based on your finite mind, limited creativity, and inadequate strength—or a vessel of God's creation, based on His infinite wisdom, love, and power, one of boundless use and eternal value. In choosing to be transformed by the Lord, you must inevitably yield to the challenges and allow Him to remake and renew you as He desires.

Jesus, I yield to You. Make me as You see fit. Amen.

Meditate unto Victory

*"Meditate on it day and night, so that you may
be careful to do according to all that is written
in it; for then you . . . will have success."*

JOSHUA 1:8

Meditation is the slow and deliberate consideration of Scripture—you really think about what it means, its significance in the lives of those in the past, and how the Father wants to apply it to your life today. When you dwell on specific verses that pertain to your challenges and agree with God, you absorb the truth that sets you free and enjoy the victory.

This is important because there are many battles you'll face in this life, and you need God's wisdom and might to fight them. Joshua experienced this when combating the impregnable walled city of Jericho (Joshua 6). Jericho fell, not because of Joshua's strategy or the Israelite's strength but because of God's power. Israel obeyed the Lord, and He made the walls fall.

The same is true for you with whatever obstacles you face today. Dwell on the Word and understand God's plan for you. Let go of the unbelief, deception, and fears that thwart your enjoyment of the life He promises to you. Allow Him to fight the battle. Embrace the truth and triumph.

Jesus, teach me Your plan. I humble myself before You and trust Your mighty hand to work. Amen.

A Sure Foundation

*God has already placed Jesus Christ
as the one and only foundation.*

1 CORINTHIANS 3:11 GNT

Upon what foundation is your life built? Is your confidence in your own wit and wisdom or strength and possessions? Or have you allowed God to be the basis on which you're established?

You'll only be able to stand the strains of life in proportion to the strength of the substance on which you rely. Therefore, it is essential for you to build your life on the Lord. Remember, He is the unshakable Sovereign of the universe, the God of love who is personally and sacrificially interested in you. He is just and wise and knows you inside and out. He is with you every moment, and His unlimited power is always available to you.

The problem is that if you don't really know Jesus, you will not believe Him. The real quality of your faith is evident when the bottom drops out and you don't have anyone to turn to but God. That's the crucible—the fire where your confidence in Him is tried to the breaking point, and you cannot wait for that moment to believe. You must learn now to walk in perfect trust in Him each day. So don't delay. Increase your faith foundation by knowing Him better today.

Jesus, You are my one true foundation and the basis of my life. Amen.

Overcoming Obstacles

*"O LORD our God, I pray, deliver us from his
hand that all the kingdoms of the earth may
know that You alone, O LORD, are God."*

2 KINGS 19:19

D o you realize that you can be in the absolute center of God's
will, doing exactly what He wants you to do, and have a
mountain of opposition? Does that mean that He is no longer
pleased with you or that you've failed Him in some way? No. Does
it mean that the Lord doesn't love you anymore? No. Does it mean
that He cannot handle the situation into which He's gotten you?
Absolutely not.

Rather, it means that God has allowed you a challenge by
which—if you respond correctly—you are going to deepen your
faith and become stronger in your relationship with Him. And the
Lord will be glorified as He removes the obstacles. The appearance
of hindrances, antagonism, adversaries, and barriers is never the
time to panic and become discouraged or throw in the towel and
give up. It is a time to fix your eyes on Jesus, trust Him, and confess your unwavering confidence that He is in control. Because it
is His responsibility to remove what stands in the way, not yours.
And when He does, everyone will recognize that He was the One
who triumphed.

*Jesus, thank You for overcoming all the obstacles on the path
of Your will. Amen.*

Where's Your Treasure?

"Store up for yourselves treasures in heaven,
where neither moth nor rust destroys."

MATTHEW 6:20

Throughout history, there have been people who have looked at the church as a place for achieving personal gain in possessions and power. Some would even point to abundance in those areas as proof of God's favor. But their mindset is based on a worldly understanding where the goal is building a man-centered empire on earth rather than the Christ-focused kingdom of heaven.

Yes, the Father will give you blessings that you can use here and now. And God always has your best interests at heart. But that does not mean your life will always be characterized by ease, comfort, wealth, or pleasure in this world.

On the contrary, because the Father knows you better than you know yourself, He does what it takes to mature you spiritually and work through you to accomplish His mission—what will truly fill your life with contentment, purpose, and significance. So the Lord's blessings may come in the form of adversity, difficulty, loss, or sorrow to refine your character and teach you. God alone knows what it takes to transform you and give you the ultimate blessing of a meaningful and eternally fruitful life. But you can be assured that the treasures He gives you are far better and will never fade away.

Jesus, I set my heart to serve You. You are my treasure.
Amen.

Confess Fully

How blessed is he whose transgression is forgiven.

PSALM 32:1

S aul deliberately disobeyed God, and even worse, he lied about it to the prophet Samuel. But the Lord will not be mocked, and soon enough Samuel delivered the dreaded message to Saul that God had rejected him as king. Was Saul sorry? Yes, but he never fully accepted blame for his actions and attempted to justify them, saying, "I have disobeyed your instructions and the LORD's command, for I was afraid of the people and did what they demanded" (1 Samuel 15:24 NLT).

However, look at the words of the king whom the Lord appointed to be ruler after Saul. David had sinned grievously as well, but he said, "My sin is ever before me. Against You, You only, I have sinned and done what is evil in Your sight" (Psalm 51:3–4). Can you see the difference between these two confessions? Saul refused to acknowledge the sin as his own. But David knew better. He fully acknowledged he'd done wrong and asked God for forgiveness.

That is the kind of repentance the Lord wants from you. He knows your heart and your weaknesses, and He wants you to admit them. Why? Because He loves you and wants you to experience the full relief, peace, and freedom that come from being completely forgiven.

Jesus, reveal any rebellion in my heart so I can admit my wrong and repent. Amen.

Focus on the Goal

Run in such a way that you may win.

1 CORINTHIANS 9:24

H as God placed a goal in your heart? The going may get rough, but never give up. Instead, move in the direction He shows you with swiftness and courage.

The apostle Paul certainly did. When the Lord called Paul to take the gospel to the Gentiles, he completed three successful missionary journeys despite persecution, adversaries, shipwrecks, imprisonments, and a host of problems. How did he do so? Paul explained by using the analogy of a runner—he fixed his gaze on the finish line and raced toward it with all his might. In other words, he did not allow the external challenges to distract him. He bypassed potential defeat by looking beyond his struggles to the goodness and sovereignty of God.

No one competes in the race of life without facing many trials and tribulations. But the key to living triumphantly regardless of your circumstances is to lean on the faithfulness of Christ while refusing to be caught up in the distractions of your surroundings. In the end, all the adversity Paul experienced served to mature him and strengthen his spiritual walk. Remember this principle when you are hard-pressed on every side—God will work it for your good if you persevere. So fix your eyes on Jesus and keep running.

Jesus, this is Your goal—I will follow You wholeheartedly to the finish line. Amen.

Faith and Goals

"LORD, God of my master Abraham,
make me successful today."

GENESIS 24:12 NIV

Genesis 24 tells a wonderful story of how faith and goals operate together. Abraham told his servant Eliezer to go into the land of his family to find the right wife for his son, Isaac. The servant knew exactly what he needed to do, but he also knew that he could not make the right choice in his own wisdom. So before he went any farther, Eliezer prayed for God to establish an action plan and grant him success. He then trusted the Lord for his mission. It wasn't very long before he arrived back home with Rebekah by his side.

The real satisfaction of Eliezer's adventure, and of yours as well, exists in seeing the Lord at work in the details of life—the different parts come together in a manner that cannot be explained by anything but His divine guidance. Do you desire to experience God's direction in this way? He wants to show you what to do. So don't allow another day to pass without seeking His plan for tomorrow and trusting Him to guide your feet along the path. It is never too late to enjoy the awesome leadership of the God who loves you and who has a perfect plan for you.

Jesus, I want to know Your plan and walk in it successfully.
Please guide me, my Savior. Amen.

God, Our Refuge

Trust in Him at all times, O people; pour out
your heart before Him; God is a refuge for us.

PSALM 62:8

There are certain trials that are so devastating that they take our breath away, no matter how well prepared we are spiritually. We feel unable to withstand them because they make it feel as if our world is crumbling beneath us. There's only one thing to do in those jolting moments, and that is take refuge in Jesus.

Throughout the Psalms, we repeatedly see that God desires to be our hiding place, fortress, shield, rock, and deliverer. He is the One to whom we can run when evil threatens to undo us. He is our place of protection when catastrophe strikes and we feel exceedingly vulnerable. And He is our unshakable shelter until the storms and destruction pass by. Whatever the perilous times, the Lord is our unfailing place of sanctuary in them.

However, it's always best to turn to Him quickly when trouble shakes your world. You see, debilitating emotions, particularly fear, grow exceedingly fast during such times, and the longer you nurture those feelings, the more powerful they become. But when you take refuge in Him, He comforts and cares for you, strengthens you, and gives you hope for the future. So run to Him and find the safety you long for.

Jesus, I need You. Be my unfailing refuge and deliverer.
Amen.

Get God's Wisdom

The fear of the LORD is the beginning of wisdom.

PROVERBS 9:10

Are you in a quandary about how to fix a problem? You don't have to wring your hands wondering, *What am I going to do?* Whenever you really want to know the truth about your circumstances or how to proceed, remember that no one will ever understand what is going on better than God. So the best, wisest thing you can ever do is seek His viewpoint concerning your situation.

Today's verse reminds you that demonstrating reverence toward the Lord is the beginning of gaining the wisdom you need. You fear Him by acknowledging His sovereign power and position as the Lord of your life. And you seek His insight into your challenges by meditating on Scripture—absorbing His viewpoint about the issues with which you're wrestling. Reflect on how God usually works in circumstances such as the one you're facing. Then apply His Word to your situation.

Of course, when the Lord reveals His direction, you may think, *That's not what most people do.* But if you want the wisdom and power of God, you must take the leap and trust Him by doing what He says. Because then He solves your troubles in the way only He can.

Jesus, I exalt You as Lord. Please show me what to do. Amen.

Your Ready Help

"The Helper will come—the Spirit,
who reveals the truth about God."

JOHN 15:26 GNT

Have you ever found yourself saying, "I don't need any help. If I want it done right, I'll do it myself." All of us at one time or another have thought those words or at least operated by that sentiment. However, such an attitude often puts us on a course to frustration and failure. This is because when it comes to the Christian life, we are to rely on God's power and wisdom rather than our own.

The Father knows you need help, and in His goodness and wisdom, He has given you a Helper without equal—the Holy Spirit. How does He assist you? He teaches you what you need to know (John 14:26). He comforts you with His presence (John 14:16–18). He guides you in your daily walk with Jesus (John 16:13). He prays for you in your weakness and strengthens you inwardly (Romans 8:26–27; Ephesians 3:16). He produces the character of Christ in you (Galatians 5:22–23). And He empowers you to witness and serve Him (Acts 1:8; 1 Corinthians 12:1–11).

Regardless of what you're facing today, you don't have to go it alone. The Helper is ready to lend you a supernatural hand. Call on Him and allow God to show you His best.

Jesus, thank You for Your Holy Spirit and all the ways You help me. Amen.

Endings and Beginnings

He who sits on the throne said, "Behold,
I am making all things new."

REVELATION 21:5

With God, there is never a finale. The end of one thing marks the beginning of something new. For example, the completion of every day is immediately replaced by the inauguration of the next. We cease from labor to rest. For the believer, the conclusion of life on earth is the start of life in heaven with our Lord.

So as Christians, our life has no real finality—just endings and beginnings that mark our journey. After all, we are going to live eternally, so there's never a consummation without a commencement that follows. Opportunities may come to their conclusion, but they always give way to fresh ones. And we really don't have to worry about tomorrow because Christ, who is our life, will walk with us all the way, making all things new. Do we really need more?

Many people drag their yesterdays into their todays—only to mar their beauty and miss the possibilities they hold. Didn't God give us night to separate one day from another? So leave yesterday where it belongs and make the most of the life the Lord has given you right now. He will certainly do something new right when you need it.

....

Jesus, thank You that when things come to an end it's
because You have a new beginning in mind. Amen.

Stop Fighting

*"May they experience such perfect unity that
the world will know that you sent me."*

JOHN 17:23 NLT

One of the greatest testimonies believers can have is unity in our faith. As Christians, we make up one church with one Lord and Savior. Sadly, one of the greatest hindrances to our witness is the division so often seen within the body of Christ.

For example, at Corinth, many believers had split into rival parties—some loyal followers of Paul, others of Peter and Apollos. We, too, may become enamored with a particular pastor or evangelist. What is especially destructive, however, is when Christian leaders publicly deride one another over cursory issues. Before long, their followers act hatefully toward one another as well. Regretfully, the Enemy uses such division to communicate to the watching world that the peace Christ came to bring is powerless.

Our deliverance from this dangerous behavior comes by remembering who was crucified for us. Yes, we are to respect godly leaders. However, our devotion, worship, and obedience belong only to the One who has purchased our salvation through His shed blood. We don't have to defend Jesus—He can do that Himself. We're just called to represent Him well. And others will know we are His not by our arguments but by our love.

*Jesus, help me always to be Your loving, unity-seeking
representative. Amen.*

Loving Light

*The Light shines in the darkness, and
the darkness did not comprehend it.*

JOHN 1:5

The idea that God sees the intimate details of your life in their entirety and shines a light on the dark parts may be disconcerting to you. The Lord has an unobstructed view of your sins, ugly thoughts, and wounds. That thought can be embarrassing and scary.

But remember, you've been thoroughly and eternally forgiven through Christ's sacrificial death. His soul-penetrating gaze is not to condemn or shame you; instead, it is to identify what continues to injure you, how you defeat yourself, and the ways you remain in bondage.

If you've ever wondered, *What's wrong with me?* or *Why does this keep happening—what am I doing wrong?* the Lord knows and wants to help you. Others may reject you, but He will never abandon you. You are not alone in this world. God sees you, and He cares for you profoundly. He watches over every intimate detail of your existence, so He can minister to your most pressing needs and deepest hurts. So allow Him to shine a light on the things you'd prefer be left in the dark. He will speak to your spirit, calm your fears, bring understanding to areas of confusion, and set you free from all that holds you back.

Jesus, thank You that the light You shed on my life sets me free. Amen.

He Sees You

*"You are the God who sees me," for she said,
"I have now seen the One who sees me."*

GENESIS 16:13 NIV

I n this world with so many voices, sometimes we can feel like no one sees us—not really. We may have people who love us, but do they really understand the sacrifices we make or what makes us tick? At times, the answer to that may be a sad and lonely no.

No doubt this is how Hagar felt. She had been given to her master Sarai's husband, Abram, to bear their child. When she got pregnant, Sarai got jealous and angry—treating Hagar terribly. So the slave girl fled, without anywhere or anyone to go to—a human speck in the vast wilderness. If anyone felt like a nothing, it was Hagar.

But the Lord spoke to Hagar and promised that her offspring would be blessed. She described the encounter by exclaiming, "You are the God who sees me." Her tears did not escape the all-seeing eye of the Father, and neither do yours. He knows your situation, sacrifices, regrets, shame, loneliness, and pain. He realizes how hard you try, and He proclaims that what you do out of love for Him is important. So do not despair and don't give up. You matter profoundly to Him. Get up, trust Him, and keep going.

Jesus, I am so grateful that my life matters to You. Amen.

Plots and Prayers

"Your God whom you constantly
serve will Himself deliver you."

DANIEL 6:16

A plot was afoot. Daniel was in the good graces of King Darius and was about to be promoted over the whole kingdom. So the group of commissioners devised a scheme to get rid of him. The problem was that they could find no ground for accusation against Daniel because he was a godly man. So they set a trap for him. They convinced Darius to make a law that forbade prayer to anyone except the king for thirty days, with the penalty of violating the decree being death by lions. Of course, Daniel refused to pray to anyone but Yahweh and was immediately thrown in the lions' den because of it.

Taking a stand in faith will sometimes entail negative consequences, at least from an earthly perspective. Unbelievers can be angered by a Christian's godly life or how God blesses those who serve Him. If you've ever been harassed by others because you represent Jesus, then you understand a little of what Daniel experienced. But just as God shut the mouths of the lions, He can silence your detractors as well. So keep praying and trusting Him. He will deliver you and turn their plots into a vessel for His glory, just as He did with Daniel.

Jesus, my life is in Your hands. Help me to represent You
well. Amen.

Your Teacher

*It is God who is at work in you, both to will
and to work for His good pleasure.*

PHILIPPIANS 2:13

We can try so hard to succeed at the Christian life and become so focused on our efforts to grow spiritually that we lose sight of God's role. We try to be like Jesus, but the more we work at it, the more frustrated we become. But the Lord didn't save us to let us flounder in uncertainty and anxiety. He doesn't leave us alone to plot our own course to spiritual maturity. Instead, the Savior who redeems us is also the Teacher who shows us how to follow and serve Him.

From the moment you trust Jesus to save you, He begins the work of *sanctification*—the lifelong process of developing Christlikeness in you. Through the supernatural power and presence of the Holy Spirit, He convicts you of sin, frees you of bondage, heals your hurts, and teaches you to walk according to His ways.

God never gives up on you, and He won't stop transforming you—so don't give up on yourself. When you feel like you have no faith left, and you just don't know what to do, remember that He promises to work in you for His good pleasure. So trust Jesus to teach you in the way you learn best.

Jesus, thank You for teaching me how to be Yours. Amen.

Confronting Habits

Walk by the Spirit, and you will not
carry out the desire of the flesh.

GALATIANS 5:16

As you grow in Christ, you've probably discovered some negative behavioral tendencies that seem to surface repeatedly. For example, perhaps you talk harshly about particular people or respond angrily to certain types of situations. Maybe you turn to a bad habit when stressful situations arise. Like the apostle Paul, you may want to do the right thing and honor God, but invariably, you give in to those destructive practices (Romans 7:14–24). It's exceedingly frustrating because you feel so out of control. And what makes matters even worse is the nagging fear that the Lord will forsake you because of your all-too-frequent failures.

First, be assured that the Father would never abandon you and that there's hope in your struggle. Second, realize that the key is not to try harder but to yield to the ministry of the Holy Spirit. You see, this problem is beyond your strength and wisdom but well within Christ's ability from which to free you. You must listen to Him in prayer and through His Word and agree with what He shows you. This voluntary surrender to the enabling presence of the Spirit of God will put you on the path to freedom from your worst habits.

Jesus, I surrender. May Your Holy Spirit teach me the truth
that will free me. Amen.

In the Ups and Downs

*"By supplication I will lead them; I will make
them walk by streams of waters, on a straight
path in which they will not stumble."*

JEREMIAH 31:9

If we were to make topographical maps of our spiritual walks, they might look like a range of mountains jutting heavenward with many spiritual peaks and dropping just as sharply into spiritual valleys. That is because the Father navigates us through seasons of both blessing and trouble so we will trust Him in the journey. However, maintaining a consistent walk with Jesus Christ through all the ups and downs is one of the most difficult challenges we face.

Think about it. What is the primary culprit that disturbs your confidence in God? Isn't it your changing circumstances—the external situations of life that rise and fall? In a sense, they influence our relationship with the Lord and how we view Him—often too much. However, as believers, we have the unchanging, steady, indwelling presence of Jesus Christ. He can handle anything that arises on our path. And if we will remain in a daily, deliberate walk with God, He will stabilize us on our journey, regardless of what happens. So stay close to Him and trust Him to sustain, strengthen, and guide you whether the ground rises or falls before you.

Jesus, steady my trust in You in both the mountains and the valleys. Amen.

Stop Running

O Lord, You know it all. You have enclosed me
behind and before, and laid Your hand upon me.

PSALM 139:4–5

At times, the lessons of life will appear too much for us to handle. The Lord calls us to an impossible task, permits our dreams to be shattered, pinpoints something important in our lives that we need to relinquish, or allows such profound loss that it leaves us reeling.

At that point, perhaps our instinct is to run away from God—resisting His claim on our lives and escaping what He requires of us. We just cannot face it all. Our hearts are too weak, our fears too real, our suffering too profound. We don't want to yield to Him—to release our will to His. We say, "Lord, I know what You want me to do, but I can't. There has to be a better way." But how do we run from the presence of the infinite God, who is everywhere at all times—constantly beckoning us to return to His arms?

You cannot—and that's on purpose. Friend, Jesus does not leave you alone, because He loves you. He knows this situation is difficult for you, and He wants to help you. So don't be scared of facing Him. There is strength, healing, and hope with Him. So stop running. Go to Him and live.

Jesus, I'll stop running. Thank You for helping me. Amen.

The Right Person

"The eyes of the LORD move to and fro
throughout the earth that He may strongly
support those whose heart is completely His."

2 CHRONICLES 16:9

Too often, I've heard people making the erroneous assumption that the Lord only wants to work through people endowed with great natural talent. But that is scripturally unfounded. Throughout the Bible and history, seemingly insignificant individuals are often used in a remarkable way by God. The prophet Amos was a sheepherder. Many of the disciples were fishermen. William Carey, the missionary, was a cobbler. They were ordinary in themselves, but they served the extraordinary God.

The spiritual equation for being useful to God is:

Humility + Inadequacy + Willingness = Usability

The Lord is looking for people who are willing to trust Him so He can glorify Himself through them. So if you've decided God cannot use you because you don't have the right connections, looks, resources, skills, or knowledge—please reconsider. He can work through you to accomplish His wonderful purposes. Place yourself in Christ's capable hands. You'll see the awesome ways He can work through you.

Jesus, I am willing. Work through me, Lord, and glorify Yourself. Amen.

Broken to Build

We had the sentence of death within ourselves
so that we would not trust in ourselves,
but in God who raises the dead.

2 CORINTHIANS 1:9

Today you may be wondering why God allows you to face challenges that are so tough and trying to your soul. Sometimes it may feel as if the very life is drained from you. However, understand that the Lord's purpose is to break your will—not your spirit. His purpose is not to destroy you but to build you powerfully—bringing you to a position of maximum wholeness, maturity, and usefulness in His kingdom.

However, this means you must yield complete lordship of your life to Him. And you may have a very difficult time giving up control—most of us do. But God uses the brokenness you feel in adversity to bring you to the point where you have nothing to say except, "Lord Jesus, what would You have me do?"

God makes no mistakes in this process of maturing and transforming you. He knows precisely what areas to target in your life. Yes, it may be painful. But He is efficient, wasting nothing. He recognizes what circumstances will be effective and what tools to use. He also realizes how much pressure you can take as He perfects and strengthens you—for your good and His glory.

Jesus, You are my life. Help me to endure and serve You well. Amen.

Freedom Through His Mercy

"I do not condemn you either. Go,
but do not sin again."

JOHN 8:11 GNT

When the Pharisees departed, Jesus looked with compassion at the woman lying at His feet. She had been caught in adultery, and it was obvious He was a man of God. How exposed and embarrassed she must have felt in His presence—that is, until the Savior forgave her.

She marveled at how He had rescued her and restored her dignity. Adultery was an act that the law declared punishable by stoning to death. But Jesus did not condemn the woman. Instead, He exposed her accusers by saying that the one without sin could cast the first stone. As each man dropped the rocks in his hands, she realized she owed her life to Christ.

Perhaps there is something in your life you wish you could erase. Just the thought of it brings feelings of condemnation and sorrow. Yet just as Jesus set the woman free, He liberates you as well. If there's something you have done, know that when you repent, bringing it to God in prayer and seeking His mercy, He is faithful to forgive you. And He loves you so much, He will never bring the matter up again.

Jesus, I confess my sins and repent. Thank You for forgiving me. Amen.

Power in Your Witness

My message and my preaching were not
in persuasive words of wisdom, but in
demonstration of the Spirit and of power.

1 CORINTHIANS 2:4

D o you ever have difficulty deciding what to say when you share your faith? There are so many approaches to evangelism that it can be confusing. What questions should we ask? Which Scripture verses are best to use? However, Paul clearly teaches us that sharing the good news of salvation has nothing to do with clever or eloquent presentations.

Paul's chief concern was not to obscure the simple truth of the gospel with cunning speechmaking, which would only draw attention to his own skills. Rather, he wanted the emphasis to be on Christ. This is because success in evangelism isn't based on formulas or methods but on the powerful message of Jesus' death, burial, and resurrection, which alone can save.

So when you witness to others about your faith, don't worry about what you will say. Instead, just be faithful to tell others about Jesus. Then, depend on the Holy Spirit to convict others concerning the cross of Christ and to draw people to Himself. Because the hearer's faith does "not rest on the wisdom of men"—or your delivery for that matter—"but on the power of God" (1 Corinthians 2:5).

Jesus, please draw people to Yourself as I testify about all
You've done for me. Amen.

293

Beware the Consequences

Joyful are those who obey his laws and search for him with all their hearts. They do not compromise with evil, and they walk only in his paths.

PSALM 119:2–3 NLT

If ever someone had it all, it was Solomon. Unfortunately, although he had everything going for him—great riches, unsurpassed wisdom, and abundant authority—he failed terribly in his role as monarch of Israel and lost the kingdom (1 Kings 11:11–13). What went wrong?

What eventually poisoned Solomon's heart toward the Lord were his marriages to women who served other deities, which God had strictly forbidden. Little by little, "his wives turned his heart away after other gods; and his heart was not wholly devoted to the LORD" (1 Kings 11:4). You see, there are *always* consequences when we ignore God and embrace sin. Scripture portrays doing so as *compromise*—as serving two masters and dividing our loyalty. However, we're called to live completely under the lordship of Christ because that's always the unfailing path to ultimate success.

The cure to compromise is to repent from sin and wholeheartedly pursue Jesus. Begin now—because compromise always exacts a terrible price—it can completely wreck your life as it did Solomon's. Yet you'll never lose when you genuinely commit to and obey God.

Jesus, please reveal any area of compromise in me so I can serve You alone. Amen.

Surrender All

Love the LORD your God with all your heart and
with all your soul and with all your might.

DEUTERONOMY 6:5

O ften we have no problem defining something, but describing how to accomplish it is another matter. Take *surrender*, for example. How would you explain all it signifies? Well, in the Christian life, it really means the complete transfer of the undivided possession, control, and use of your total being—spirit, soul, and body—to the Lord Jesus Christ, to whom you rightfully belong by right of creation and redemption.

First, it must be a *deliberate* act on your part. Just as an engaged couple state their commitment to each other by taking marital vows, you need to be intentional in your singular and wholehearted devotion to Jesus. Second, it must be *voluntary*. No one can force you to serve God or act as your proxy. It must be a personal choice. Third, it is *final*. In the Lord's eyes, when you commit to Him, the transaction is complete once and for all. And because growth always plays a part, surrender is a *progression*. It is a continuing act whereby you turn ever more over to Him as you mature.

So today, consider: Has your commitment to Jesus deepened over the time you've known Him? Have you surrendered all to Him?

....

Jesus, I surrender all to You deliberately, voluntarily, finally,
and progressively. Amen.

Peace That Conquers

*"These things I have spoken to you, so
that in Me you may have peace."*

JOHN 16:33

E urope trembled as Hitler's menacing armies annexed Austria
and set their sights on Czechoslovakia. Attempting to appease
the dreaded dictator, England's prime minister Neville Chamberlain
traveled to Germany and, on September 29, 1938, signed the
infamous Munich Agreement. Upon his return, Chamberlain triumphantly announced, "I believe it is peace for our time." Less
than a year later, Germany had conquered Czechoslovakia and
invaded Poland, and World War II had begun.

Was Jesus' talk of peace like Chamberlain's optimistic boast?
After all, war, violence, hatred, and persecution still exist. Yet when
Jesus promised that He would leave us His peace, He did not ignore
the reality of conflict in our lives. That's why He immediately followed by explaining, "In the world you have tribulation, but take
courage; I have overcome the world" (John 16:33). You *will* face
adversity—indeed, you may be enduring some today. But when
overwhelming circumstances arise that threaten to shake your tranquility, Christ promises that He will be your wise and victorious
defender. He is more than able to triumph over whatever you could
possibly face.

*Jesus, thank You for being my defender and my peace in
every situation. Amen.*

Watch Your Words

Rejoice in the Lord always; again I will say, rejoice!

PHILIPPIANS 4:4

When you face challenges, how you react emotionally is very important, but how you respond *verbally* is just as crucial. Words are like containers that carry our ideas. When we make statements, they affect us as well as the people with whom we are speaking. Therefore, we must be very careful in what we express when we come to a challenge because negative attitudes and responses can be devastating. "There's nothing I can do about it" or "I just can't go on" weakens your faith and is a terrible testimony. But a good confession of God's awesome wisdom and strength has a powerful effect on us.

When the apostle Paul was in prison and facing possible death, he understood this. So instead of complaining, he said he had not lost his peace with God in the midst of his difficult situation but had learned the secret of contentment. What was it? "I can do all things through Him who strengthens me" (Philippians 4:13). He rejoiced in the Lord his God and was a tremendous witness.

You can be too. Speak faith over your circumstances and exalt Christ regardless of what happens. It will not only make a difference in your own heart, but it will also bless everyone around you.

Jesus, please help me to remain positive and worshipful—honoring You in all I say and do. Amen.

297

OCTOBER

Purpose in Pain

He takes no pleasure in causing us grief or pain.

LAMENTATIONS 3:33 GNT

It is never God's goal to break your spirit or to cause you pain. Rather, your heavenly Father, the sovereign King of creation, always has a positive, crucial, eternal purpose when He allows bad things to happen, and it extends not only to your life but to the lives of the many people you influence and help.

It is true that the Lord works all details together for the good of those who love Him. So whatever you may experience and however broken you may feel because of the trials that assail you, always remember that the Father has a blessing in store for you. Never give in to the thought that this is the end or that there's a limit to God's ability to redeem even the worst, most pain-filled experiences in your life and turn them into something worthwhile. Instead, accept that He knows your pain, He is powerful, He loves you unconditionally, and He is at work in the unseen for you.

You may not be at fault for what has happened to you, but you are accountable for your response to it. So always ask yourself, *How can I honor God in this adversity? How can I grow closer to Him from this?*

> *Jesus, this is difficult, but I know You work for my good and Your glory. Amen.*

Purge the Pride

Pride goes before destruction, and a
haughty spirit before stumbling.
PROVERBS 16:18

A re you the type of person who expects people to treat you in a particular way because of who you are? Do you look down on anyone? Your first reaction may be, "Of course not." But really think about it. You may demonstrate your self-perceived superiority in any number of ways. It could be that you see your opinion as always important enough to express or better than that of others. Maybe you like to stay in control by telling others exactly how things should be done. Perhaps there are times you catch yourself treating people in a service capacity as inferior.

If any of this is true for you, understand that God hates this kind of arrogance. To Him, it is self-idolatry—it is the subtle worship of oneself. This means that Christ is not at the center of your life, and that's a real problem. Indeed, when people struggle with egotism, they often try to use the Lord rather than serve Him—and that never ends well. So if you perceive any selfish ambition or vain conceit within yourself, purge it. Humble yourself before God, confess Him as your Lord, and ask Him to help you love and appreciate others. Pride always precedes a fall, but with humility, there is honor.

Jesus, please purge all pride from my heart. I humble myself
before You. Amen.

Pride and Blessings

*The pride of man will be humbled and
the loftiness of men will be abased.*

ISAIAH 2:17

God will not bless pride. Just because there are arrogant people who are skillful at manipulating their circumstances does not mean the Lord favors them. On the contrary, "God is opposed to the proud" (1 Peter 5:5), and He will bring them to account soon enough. However, it is crucial for you to realize that just because someone has cleverly crafted their image and makes it seem as though everything's perfect in their world doesn't actually make it so. Most often, those who are arrogant and narcissistic are truly miserable individuals—always seeking control, endlessly trying to prove their worth, and forever envying others.

Jesus has better for the one who belongs to Him. God's answer to our hunger for recognition, position, and power is to humble ourselves and allow Him to give our lives true significance, worth, and meaning. It is in Him we have abundant life. May the Father grant each of us the wisdom to identify pride in our lives so that we may confess and repent. Because it is as we humble ourselves before Him—giving Him control, accepting the identity He gives us, and seeing others as better than ourselves—that He truly blesses us and lifts us up.

*Jesus, I know true blessings come through humility. I submit
to You and obey. Amen.*

Emergency Exits

The Lord knows how to rescue the
godly from temptation.

2 PETER 2:9

I n most major stores and public buildings, emergency exits are clearly marked so if there is a fire or other emergency, people know how to get out of harm's way. The same is true in the Christian life—God has provided avenues for your escape when you're tempted to sin. Sometimes they come in the form of interruptions—something or someone distracts you long enough to break the lure's hold on you. At times, they appear as roadblocks—the internet goes down or your credit card doesn't work.

However, there are also exit signs that are different for each person. This is because there are diverse thoughts and stimuli that personally trigger us to disobey God. Paul admonished, "Take captive every thought to make it obedient to Christ" (2 Corinthians 10:5 NIV). He knew well that temptation begins in our minds, so if we can use God's Word to counter the pattern of thinking that set us on the path to sin, we will triumph.

The point is, the Lord "will provide the way of escape" (1 Corinthians 10:13), but you must be open to taking it. So look for the exit signs and trust Him to help you break free when you're enticed to sin against Him.

Jesus, help me to always take Your divine exits so I can flee temptation. Amen.

Your Kind Defender

*"Take My yoke upon you and learn from
Me, for I am gentle and humble in heart,
and you will find rest for your souls."*

MATTHEW 11:29

I f you ever worry that God is an unappeasable taskmaster who
is just waiting to smite you, immediately replace that thought
with the truth. Jesus is gentle and loving toward you. Yes, the Lord
will discipline you at times for your good, but He does so as a caring Father, not as a vengeful enemy. He is kind toward you. God
knows that you need His tenderness, especially when your heart is
broken or you're under attack.

Recall when the Lord spoke to Elijah in a gentle whisper. The
prophet was scared and exhausted. So God demonstrated the power
with which He would protect him—through a whirlwind and
earthquake that rent the mountains. But He also spoke to Elijah
through a peaceful breeze. His quiet voice reminded the prophet
of His care.

Jesus is tender toward you as a shepherd is to his sheep. This
does not mean He is weak, ineffective, or a pushover. He is still the
mighty Warrior—the almighty King of kings who will ultimately
triumph over every foe. Rather, it signifies He'll always treat you in
a loving way. So go to Him and find rest for your soul.

*Jesus, thank You for being so tender, loving, and kind
toward me. Amen.*

Wait on Him

*Our soul waits for the LORD; He
is our help and our shield.*

PSALM 33:20

There are times when you'll go to the Lord in prayer, ask Him about some concern, and feel assurance that He will answer your request. But then you'll experience a long period of silence. To make matters worse, during that time, God may give you little indication of what He's doing, and it may appear as if nothing is going on. You may wonder, *Did I hear Him right?*

What are you to do when the Lord creates those gaps in your life? One of the most basic lessons you must learn is to let God be God. He will work in the unseen and in ways you cannot imagine. You must leave the "how" and the "when" in His hands and acknowledge they are His responsibility. Do not try to interfere or manipulate your circumstances—you'll only make a mess. He will show you when and if He wants you to act.

Remember, the Lord always reserves His best for those who are willing to wait on Him in faith—even when they can see nothing happening. So consider: do you want God's best? If so, have confidence in Him, stay close to Him, and wait. Because those who trust in Him are never disappointed.

....

*Jesus, I will wait on You. Strengthen my faith so I can
always honor You. Amen.*

Soar in the Spirit

Having begun by the Spirit, are you
now being perfected by the flesh?
GALATIANS 3:3

I n today's verse, Paul gives us an excellent question for self-evaluation. If he were present today, the apostle might phrase his comment this way: "I know you say that your salvation is based completely on your faith in Christ's atoning death on the cross, but it seems to me that you're placing a lot of emphasis on what you do or don't do—and not so much on *who* you are or *who* you belong to."

You see, when we accept Jesus as our Savior, He takes our dead spirit and gives us a new living one. This is not something we can achieve on our own—He must do it in us. But sometimes we mistakenly revert to our fleshly nature. We're like the caterpillar that undergoes metamorphosis and becomes a butterfly. However, instead of flying, it continues to crawl on the ground, completely unaware of the gift and power now available to it.

Your old nature is powerless to attain all God has for you, so why would you strive so unproductively in your flesh? Don't do it. Instead, make sure you're walking by the Spirit. Allow the Lord to change you from the inside out because He will certainly teach you to soar.

Jesus, teach me to walk in the Spirit and experience all You
have for me. Amen.

Do What He Says

"I will do as You say and let down the nets."

LUKE 5:5

As a seasoned fisherman, Peter's professional opinion was that what Christ was telling him to do wouldn't work. Most of the fishing done in the Sea of Galilee was done at night in shallow water, not during the day in the deep, as the Teacher was insisting. But it was Jesus asking, so he complied.

Maybe you're facing a similar situation. The Lord instructs you to proceed in a way that, in your experience, makes no sense. But it is the all-wise, all-powerful Sovereign of creation who is leading you, and trusting Him means looking beyond what you can see to what He knows—and He knows everything. So the absolute best thing you can do is obey God and leave the consequences to Him. Peter did, and he drew in such an overabundance of fish that his nets began to break.

Throughout your life, some of the Lord's directions to you will seem overwhelming, illogical, and even impossible. But when the Almighty tells you to do something, you should do it simply based on who's instructing you—trusting He will see you through. So set out into deep water and let down your nets. Do what God says. Because you don't want to miss out on all He desires to do for you.

....

Jesus, I will do what You say and trust You. Amen.

Produce What Lasts

*The world is passing away . . . but the one
who does the will of God lives forever.*

1 JOHN 2:17

This world is passing away, but there are eternal blessings when you serve Jesus. So it is crucial for you to make the commitment: "Lord, I choose to obey You—enabled by the Holy Spirit, for the sake of Your purposes." This is a significant pledge because to submit to Christ signifies that you are transferring the authority of your life from your kingdom to His. His will becomes your lifestyle—the way in which you respond to the circumstances you face. And you do so with the understanding that whatever is invested here will fade away, but when your treasure is in heaven, it lasts forever.

So when you make decisions, ask yourself: "Does the choice I'm making honor the pledge I made to obey the Lord?" There's no way for you to do God's will if you have reserved the right to direct your own path. So every day, wait on the Lord in prayer. There are things that He will require of you in service to His heavenly kingdom that you won't know how to accomplish and will not have the resources to achieve. But He does. So get your direction from Him, and He will enable you to produce "fruit that endures" (John 15:16 GNT).

*Jesus, help me to serve You and produce fruit that lasts.
Amen.*

Believe Him

"Whoever says to this mountain, 'Be taken up and cast into the sea,' and does not doubt in his heart, but believes that what he says is going to happen, it will be granted him."

MARK 11:23

There is a spiritual principle that will cause positive, powerful changes in your life if you'll apply it diligently. Through it, your prayer life, conversations with other people, and how God works through you will be transformed. The principle? *Believe God; do not doubt what He says.*

In today's verse, Jesus spoke about moving mountains—obstacles in your life that no bulldozer or dynamite could possibly budge. However, these mountains are opportunities for your faith. So consider how you respond to them. Perhaps when you face such challenges, you tell God what you want Him to do, discuss it with friends, or go to counselors for advice. You do all you know to do, but the mountain still stands. In fact, it seems to become larger, more overwhelming, and increasingly immovable as time passes. The problem is that you've tried to move it in your strength.

As the Lord instructs in Psalm 46:10, "Cease striving and know that I am God." Resist the temptation to conclude that He isn't in the mountain-moving business any longer. Instead, choose to trust that if He says He will help you, He absolutely will. Stop doubting and believe Him.

Jesus, I praise You for moving this mountain. Amen.

Faith Without Doubt

*Ask in faith without any doubting, for
the one who doubts is like the surf of the
sea, driven and tossed by the wind.*

JAMES 1:6

Are there times when you struggle to maintain your faith in God—especially as time passes or troubles increase? James warned against allowing your confidence in God to be shaken by your circumstances. So what can you do to strengthen your faith so that the storms of life don't rend it asunder?

First, fix your attention on Jesus. If you're focused on your circumstances and the impossibilities before you, you will face defeat. But the omnipotent Creator of the universe will always lead you to victory. *Second, keep your mind on the Word.* Throughout Scripture is the repeated testimony that the Lord is faithful to His promises and always defends His people successfully. Therefore, continue reading the Bible so God can remind you of His help, renew your mind, and transform your life. *Finally, regardless of how you feel or what you see, make a choice to trust God.* When you know the Lord's direction, just do it—don't look back, and do not look anxiously about you. Instead, have faith that when He says, "I will strengthen you, surely I will help you, surely I will uphold you with My righteous right hand," He means it (Isaiah 41:10).

Jesus, please forgive me for wavering. Help me to stand strong in faith. Amen.

Seek Him with Wonder

I consider Your heavens, the work of Your fingers,
the moon and the stars, which You have ordained.

PSALM 8:3

Have you ever noticed that the people who have the beautiful quality of godliness often fear and honor God to a profound degree? They genuinely seem to know and love Him in ways that are so personal and intimate. They have a sense of awe—a reverence for the Lord that supersedes everything else in their lives. Perhaps you would like that characteristic yourself, but where do you begin when your subject of study is God Himself? How do you even approach such an awe-inspiring endeavor?

Of course, it begins as you search His Word on your knees in prayer. However, it also requires a sense of sheer wonder at who He is. Think about it—you're approaching the glorious, eternal throne of the One who created the heavens and the earth. Imagine all He's seen—how He crafted each organism, plant, person, mountain, and planet with His wise, omnipotent hand. Consider how He's aware of the smallest particle while at the same time controlling the vast workings of the universe. He is completely astounding!

So if you genuinely want to know God, seek Him with an open, inquisitive heart. He will surely reveal Himself to you and "tell you great and mighty things, which you do not know" (Jeremiah 33:3).

Jesus, I want to know You profoundly. Please reveal Yourself
to me. Amen.

Prepared for Action

Prepare your minds for action, keep sober in
spirit, fix your hope completely on the grace to be
brought to you at the revelation of Jesus Christ.

1 PETER 1:13

W hen tough times arise, one of the first places affected is your thinking. You can become confused, overwhelmed, preoccupied, or even foggy when challenges assail you. Therefore, it is crucial to be on the right track mentally when you are about to undergo persecution or difficult times.

So how do you prepare your mind for action? You must decide that you won't allow anger, unforgiveness, jealousy, fear, or doubt to plague you. When you face situations beyond your control, these negative attitudes can paralyze and even defeat you completely. On the other hand, if you respond with the right mental attitude—viewing your circumstances from God's perspective and understanding who you are in Christ (chosen and protected by Him, born again to a living hope, and empowered by the indwelling Holy Spirit to do His will)—then you can walk victoriously through your difficulties, knowing they will not last forever.

So as you prepare for rough times, focus on your attitude and how you will respond in faith. Because when you think as God does, based on your identity in Christ, nothing will be able to shake your confidence.

....

Jesus, help me prepare my mind so I can honor You no
matter what happens. Amen.

Ever-Present Help

*The nearness of God is my good; I have
made the Lord GOD my refuge.*

PSALM 73:28

One of the foundational beliefs that you can always cling to is that God is ever-present—everywhere, at all times. No matter how many adversaries or troubles seem to encompass you, the Lord is even more immediate, real, and available to help you.

Elijah understood this, which is why he continued to have confidence even though he was surrounded by 850 prophets of Baal and Asherah. You can imagine the scene on Mt. Carmel—the one faithful servant of God stood alone in faith against the army of pagan diviners. Yet Elijah realized that they were no real challenge to him because they were counting on false deities, made by human hands from wood and stone. But Elijah's defense was the unshakable, unconquerable God of Israel. And once the Almighty demonstrated His unchallengeable power, all the people acknowledged, "The LORD, He is God" (1 Kings 18:39).

Do you feel likewise surrounded by challenges today? The Lord encompasses you with His presence. So even though you can see your troubles, and God is unseen, you have no reason to fear. You can face your difficulties with faith and confidence in your Redeemer, for He is your "refuge and strength, a very present help in trouble" (Psalm 46:1).

Jesus, thank You for always being my ever-present help. Amen.

Your Inheritance

*Did not God choose the poor of this world
to be rich in faith and heirs of the kingdom
which He promised to those who love Him?*

JAMES 2:5

Most of us have probably dreamed about what our lives would be like if we were to inherit massive fortunes. But how should our thinking and living change when we understand that we are the heirs of a kingdom beside which even the wealthiest earthly estates pale?

The amazing truth is that the Lord has named you a beneficiary of His marvelous inheritance. Romans 8:16–17 proclaims, "The Spirit Himself testifies with our spirit that we are children of God, and if children, heirs also, heirs of God and fellow heirs with Christ." What does the Lord own? Everything—it all belongs to Him. As Creator of heaven and earth and all that is in them, the Lord is the sole proprietor of the universe, and it is in His hands to provide all that you need.

Therefore, consider, do you live life like a pauper—always fearing the deficits or dreaming of what others have? Then stop. You have an inheritance that never fades because you are the heavenly Father's indisputable heir. So praise Him and rejoice that in Christ you already have everything you truly need.

Jesus, thank You for making me Your coheir and providing what I need. Amen.

Contentment

*Not that I speak from want, for I have learned
to be content in whatever circumstances I am.*

PHILIPPIANS 4:11

D o you ever struggle with contentment? Perhaps you live in good conditions with enough to eat and clothes to wear. But something is still off—there's something missing. We can learn a great deal from the apostle Paul, who was in prison, without many necessities or personal freedoms, but was still able to remain hopeful and contented.

Paul was not a foolhardy optimist who denied reality. He had endured a great deal of physical hardship, rejection, and persecution. Indeed, he had even been unjustly jailed for his faith in Jesus. Yet he could still say, "I have learned this secret, so that anywhere, at any time, I am content . . . whether I have too much or too little" (Philippians 4:12 GNT). How did Paul endure? By depending on Christ's strength for everything.

Paul did not operate in a spirit of fear or disappointment. He knew that he would receive God's best for him by abiding in Him daily and trusting Him to furnish whatever he needed. You can too. The dissatisfaction you feel in your soul is due to your focus. So learn from Paul and fix your eyes on Jesus. All you need or want is in Him.

*Jesus, help me to find all I could ever need or want in You.
Amen.*

Peace in the Storm

*The peace of God, which surpasses all
comprehension, will guard your hearts
and your minds in Christ Jesus.*

PHILIPPIANS 4:7

Some people believe that when they reach a certain age or level of spiritual maturity that the tempests of life will subside or at least diminish in intensity. However, the truth is that we'll face trials until we see Jesus face-to-face in heaven. Thankfully, when the Lord doesn't choose to end the storms that assail us from without, He is faithful to calm them from raging within. We can have His peace in the midst of the whirlwind.

Jesus assured us that He has overcome anything we can face. So how do we take hold of the peace He offers us? "Be anxious for nothing, but in everything by prayer and supplication with thanksgiving let your requests be made known to God" (Philippians 4:6).

In other words, choose to trust the Lord. Give everything that concerns you over to Him—the One who can handle it. And give thanks that He will see you through your darkest hour. He is in absolute, eternal, unshakable control, and you are His beloved, encompassed in His care. That will give you greater tranquility than anything on this earth can offer.

*Jesus, You are my peace. Thank You for always helping me.
Amen.*

Recovery Time

*The LORD is near to the brokenhearted and
saves those who are crushed in spirit.*

PSALM 34:18

When we go through trials that are especially difficult, we may experience a time where all we can do is process what has occurred. During such a season, some people throw themselves into their work or hobbies, others become hermits, and many work out their feelings as they talk with loved ones. In such instances, we may wonder if we've let God down because we're not serving His kingdom as we usually do. Our reasoning is that we are not living up to our own expectations, so we're probably failing Him as well.

Yet remember that Jesus loves you unconditionally and compassionately. Just like physical operations require recovery, so does spiritual surgery. You need time to heal. So don't be afraid that He's disappointed in you. That would mean His love is based on your performance, and it isn't. Of course, He doesn't condone sinful behavior—it grieves Him, and He'll prompt you to turn back to His path. Rather, the point is that you can be free from guilt as you take time to process and apply the spiritual lessons He's taught you. And when the recuperative time is over and you get going again, He'll be right by your side, empowering you to face the future with courage.

Jesus, thank You for being my Great Physician and helping me recover. Amen.

317

Your Friend

*"I have called you friends, for all things that I have
heard from My Father I have made known to you."*
JOHN 15:15

Hours before His death on the cross, Jesus revealed the startling new intimacy of our bond with Him—He calls us *friends*. This is one of the most precious, unforgettable, comforting, and reassuring truths to be found anywhere in God's Word. Though we serve the Lord, we are not captive slaves. Though He is our God, He is not distant and unapproachable to us. The Almighty does not look at us through the lens of wrath but the heart of love. He is our friend.

And as your great friend, Jesus accepts you the way you are, but He also helps you grow into all you can be. He is always available to you and wants you to be completely honest with Him at all times. He's experienced every kind of test you'll ever face and has consistently overcome—and He's eager to help you prevail as well. He doesn't overlook your deficiencies or sins; rather, as the true lover of your soul, He does what's best for you. He sticks closer than a brother and lays down His life for you. Therefore, recognize the great gift you've been given through a relationship with Him, and treat Him as your friend in return.

Jesus, thank You for being my best and closest friend. Amen.

Intervention

*"Blessed be the LORD God of Israel, who sent
you . . . and blessed be you, who have kept
me this day from . . . avenging myself."*

1 SAMUEL 25:32–33

David was angry. He and his men had protected the shepherds and flocks of a wealthy man named Nabal and had treated them very well. However, when David's men asked for sustenance, Nabal—who was known to be "harsh and evil in his dealings" (1 Samuel 25:3)—refused to return the favor. Indeed, he was so insulting that when David heard about it, he immediately commanded his men, "Each of you gird on his sword" (1 Samuel 25:13).

However, the Lord worked through Nabal's wise and godly wife, Abigail, to stop David from killing him—an act that would have had terrible implications when he took the throne of Israel. It's a good reminder of how God, in His goodness, will intervene and keep us from wrongdoing as well. Someone hurts our feelings, and we get mad and immediately want to retaliate. But somehow the Lord stops us and reminds us of the painful consequences we could face.

Your Savior is willing to go the extra mile to keep you from trouble. So whenever you're tempted to do something that you know is opposed to God's will, turn to the Lord and ask Him to stop you, help you, and intervene on your behalf.

....

Jesus, thank You for delivering me from evil. Amen.

OCTOBER 21

Refinement

Gold . . . is tested by fire; and so your faith,
which is much more precious than gold,
must also be tested, so that it may endure.

1 PETER 1:7 GNT

The refining of precious metals—especially silver and gold—begins at low temperatures. This is because certain impurities respond quickly to heat, and as they rise to the surface, they can be skimmed away. The heat is then increased, and other contaminants then ascend to the top of the cauldron of molten metal and are removed. Only under extremely intense temperatures will the most stubborn of pollutants separate from the metal and emerge at the top where they can be extracted.

The process is the same in our lives. God purifies our lives by degrees—He refines us layer by layer. If the Father moved immediately to the most profound strongholds of sin in us, we couldn't stand it. We'd be so overwhelmed that not only would our wills be broken, but our spirits would be shattered as well.

This is often why the trials seem to intensify as you mature in your faith. However, do not despair or fear. God has not rejected you. On the contrary, He has seen the vein of pure gold-level faith in you and works through the fire of adversity to make sure it shines forth from you for His glory.

Jesus, thank You for refining me slowly, layer by layer, in Your wisdom. Amen.

It's All True

"These are true words of God."

REVELATION 19:9

How often, after reading a biblical account where the Lord moves mightily in the nation of Israel or the early church, have you caught yourself thinking, *I would never doubt God if I had an experience like that!* The whole narrative of the Bible is packed with illustrations of His unfathomable power. From Genesis to Revelation—from creation to His final judgment and ultimate rule over all the earth—we are confronted with the truth that the Lord is God and that He faithfully redeems His people.

It is devastating, therefore, when we erroneously treat the Bible as a book of tales and myths rather than the inspired Word of God. What we read in Scripture is not a creative story or even a lopsided narrative of events. It is the absolute truth—the real, trustworthy, historical, verified, eyewitness account of the Lord's working in the world and in the lives of His people.

Once we accept Scripture as true and get a glimpse of God's majesty, we will be awestruck with wonder. Our response will be like those around the throne crying, "Hallelujah! For the Lord our God, the Almighty, reigns" (Revelation 19:6). Do you want to experience the power of God in your life? Stop focusing on your circumstances and believe the One who is on the throne.

Jesus, I believe You! You reign over all! Amen.

What's Your Motivation?

Fear the LORD your God, serve him only.

DEUTERONOMY 6:13 NIV

A re you truly committed to Jesus? If so, what motivates your devotion to Him? Are you trying to get as much for yourself as you can? Or do you truly love and respect Him for who He is? This is important to understand because there will be seasons when submitting to Him will be very difficult. At such times, when your faith is stretched and you're not sure if you should follow the Lord's direction, consider this question: *Would you rather obey God and allow Him to bless you, or disobey Him and spend the rest of your life wondering what He would have done in and through you if you had trusted Him?*

That's a sobering question, isn't it? There are many Christians who find themselves looking back to a time in their lives when they stood on the threshold of decision and, because of an unbroken will or a weakness of the flesh, chose to serve self instead of God. They were weak because their motives were wrong. And they were left helplessly wondering what the Lord would have done through them if only they had submitted to His authority.

Don't make their mistake. Make sure your devotion to Jesus is based on a sure foundation.

Jesus, I love You and respect Your authority. Help me to always honor You. Amen.

Take the Step

"Repent and turn away from all your
transgressions, so that iniquity may not
become a stumbling block to you."

EZEKIEL 18:30

I s there an unresolved issue that keeps surfacing when you spend time with God? Is there an unyielded desire, hidden sin, or some relationship that needs to be mended or severed? Let go of that hindrance—it isn't serving you. It's only holding you back from discovering the joy, significance, and freedom you truly long for.

It may be painful to take this step of obedience because of the dependency you've formed. You may even realize that your sin is standing in the way of your usefulness to the Lord, but you can't bring yourself to stop because you're afraid. But understand that on the other side of your decision, God's grace dresses your wounds, and He gives you liberty, contentment, and a greater revelation of what He can accomplish through you.

So your challenge is to look at the thing that holds you in bondage in the light of eternity and weigh its value. When compared to the immensity of the Lord's unlimited resources of love, mercy, power, wisdom, strength, and the rest, it will become apparent how truly worthless the earthly snare that imprisons you really is—and how abundantly worthwhile it is to take that step of obedience toward God. So do it and be free.

Jesus, I repent. Lead me in liberty. Amen.

Persevere in Prayer

*Devote yourselves to prayer, keeping alert
in it with an attitude of thanksgiving.*

COLOSSIANS 4:2

What does it mean to devote yourself to prayer? The Greek wording indicates that we are to *persevere, stay at it*, and *refuse to give up*. In other words, we should not stop too soon, but keep on interceding.

Of course, this is difficult because most of us are quite impatient with God. We make a request and expect an instant reply from Him. If we don't get it, we quit, thinking, *The Lord must be angry with me* or *I guess it's just not His will*. However, Jesus teaches we "ought to pray and not to lose heart" (Luke 18:1). This is because we engage in a spiritual battle as we do business with God. We join the Lord in His war with the forces of darkness. So we can expect to be harassed because the Enemy wants to keep us off our knees.

But I believe many of us would see the Lord do a great deal more in our lives if we would just persevere in prayer. It's not just some words we send up and expect an instant message in return. It's a battle we engage in the heavenly places, where we're able to see the kingdom of God always prevails.

....

*Jesus, thank You for the gift of prayer. Please help me to
continue interceding until You provide the victory. Amen.*

A Living Testimony

Worship Christ as Lord of your life. And
if someone asks about your hope as a
believer, always be ready to explain it.

1 PETER 3:15 NLT

O ne of the great problems of this age is that so many of God's people act one way at church and another during the rest of the week. So their testimony has no impact or power in the world, which needs to witness it most.

So today, consider: Do the lost people you interact with know that you're a believer without your having to tell them? You shouldn't have to say, "I'm a Christian, so don't tell any dirty jokes around me." Instead, your life should be so possessed by Jesus that your very presence says it. Because there is something powerful and convicting about a truly Spirit-filled believer that people cannot help but notice the difference. They see and hear it as they interact with you. And they want what you have, so they ask you about your hope. That's when you can say, "Let me tell you how the Lord Jesus has worked in my life."

The Christian life is not an act—it's a union with God so intimate that Jesus freely lives through you. So walk with Him in such a way no one doubts who you truly belong to.

Jesus, please be so powerfully present in me that others will
want to know You. Amen.

Thought Blueprints

Be transformed by the renewing of your mind,
so that you may prove what the will of God is.

ROMANS 12:2

L ong before hammers, saws, and bulldozers arrive at a building site, the contractor has an architectural blueprint of
the finished building. Pipes, beams, walls, windows, and doors
are installed according to the detailed rendering. Our growth as
Christians is strikingly similar. Of course, God has a specific plan
for maturing us. But what we may not realize is that our visible
behavior is inevitably a product of the mental blueprint we're following. In other words, what we do is an expression of our internal
mindset—every act begins with a thought.

That is why Jesus said, "It is from within, out of a person's
heart, that evil thoughts come—sexual immorality, theft, murder"
(Mark 7:21 NIV). Real change, therefore, must proceed from the
inside out. We must replace our internal blueprint.

This means that we need to become aware of the thought
patterns that have become deeply entrenched in our psychological
and emotional grid systems, because they cannot be trusted. This
can only occur as the Holy Spirit reveals them to us through the
daily intake of God's supernatural change agent—divine truth.
Thankfully, Christ makes it possible for our minds to be transformed so we can live by His blueprint of life.

....

Jesus, please transform my mind so I can live by Your
blueprint. Amen.

Have You Forgiven?

*"Forgive us our sins, as we have
forgiven those who sin against us."*

MATTHEW 6:12 NLT

Is there anyone you truly despise? Before you lightly or quickly answer no, honestly examine your heart by asking yourself:

1. Do I have any memories of past injustices that I just can't shake?
2. Is there anyone who has hurt me so terribly that I am unable to wish them well?
3. Has anyone injured me to the point that I want them to suffer as much or more than I have?

Has anything surfaced as you ask these questions? Whose name comes immediately to mind? Whose face do you picture? Often, we suppress memories of the past wrongs done to us, incorrectly thinking that if we can just forget them, they'll go away. But the truth is, the emotional trauma remains. So if recollections of past maltreatment haunt you, you must deal with and resolve them by choosing to forgive. Do not try to claim a "right" to hold on to your grudge. As a believer in Jesus who has been thoroughly and graciously pardoned, that is never an option. Instead, show you've grown in the likeness of your Savior by forgiving others as He has you.

....

*Jesus, I know who I need to forgive. Help me to honor You
and let go of the hurt. Amen.*

Loved and Worthy

See how great a love the Father has bestowed on
us, that we would be called children of God.

1 JOHN 3:1

People derive their value from all sorts of things—social status, occupation, power, position, authority, intellectual prowess, family, popularity, beauty, fitness, possessions, achievements, and even living in the "right" neighborhood. And we may judge them for it, especially if their focus is different from our own. But if we're honest, we'd admit that we all struggle with our sense of worth.

The Father, however, wants our concept of self to be completely grounded in His love. He created us, accepts us, makes us family, and finds us worthy in Christ. But getting to that point of understanding can be difficult. The more we cling to whatever we're trusting instead of acknowledging the worth that He gives us, the more challenging life can become. At times, the Lord must painfully remove the other things we rely on so we can experience His best. Why are we so afraid to let go? Because we don't want to lose control. We are afraid that God doesn't care enough about us to meet our needs, fulfill our desires, or give us contentment. In other words, our trust issues are due to a lack of understanding about His love.

Jesus, I need a better understanding of Your perfect,
unconditional love. Teach me, Lord. Amen.

The True Enemy

*Be on the alert. Your adversary, the
devil, prowls around like a roaring
lion, seeking someone to devour.*

1 PETER 5:8

D o you realize that you have an enemy? Yes, there are people
in the world who may not like you, but there's one who is far
more dangerous than they could ever be. Of course, Satan would
never come out and tell you he's your biggest threat. But Scripture
is clear that the Enemy and his forces relentlessly persecute believers. Their goal is to keep us from knowing and serving Jesus as our
Savior and Lord.

The trouble is that the Enemy comes as an angel of light—a sly
counterfeit of God's truth. He has four objectives: to come between
you and Jesus, to make you doubt Scripture, to tempt you to sin,
and to destroy your usefulness to the kingdom of God. Far too
many believers are deceived by his tactics, opening themselves up
for attack by engaging in activities that seem harmless outwardly
but provide a destructive alternate to meeting your needs God's
way. Don't fall for it. The adversary is smart, subtle, and strategic,
and he will use things that are "good" to distract you from God's
best. So watch out for him, and make sure you're staying in step
with the Lord.

*Jesus, reveal and remove any stronghold the Enemy's using to
separate me from You. Amen.*

You Have the Advantage

*"I have given you authority over
all the power of the enemy."*

LUKE 10:19 NLT

D o you ever fear serving Jesus because you don't want to rile up the spiritual opposition? If so, there's good news for you. Although the Enemy wants to undermine God's plan in your life, his power is limited—he's not omnipresent or omnipotent, and he certainly doesn't know all God does. For this reason, he prefers to defeat you by tempting you with what will undermine your effectiveness in the kingdom and deceptively causing you to be afraid of what will happen if you refuse to go along with the crowd.

This is why Jesus spoke to the disciples about the authority they had over the Enemy and the need to avoid the mindset of this world as they carried out His mission. As believers, one of the most important principles we must learn is that Christ's victory on the cross has absolutely broken Satan's power over us. We don't have to shrink back in fear but can stand triumphantly against the Enemy as long as the source of our strength is Jesus. So go forward in whatever He has called you to do and do not be afraid. Obey God and leave all the consequences to Him because He unfalteringly leads you to victory.

*Jesus, You are wiser and stronger than any enemy—I will
trust in You. Amen.*

NOVEMBER

People and God's Purposes

If someone says, "I love God," and hates
his brother, he is a liar; for the one who
does not love his brother whom he has seen,
cannot love God whom he has not seen.

1 JOHN 4:20

Perhaps you've discovered that one of the greatest enemies of joy in your life is conflict with others. Relationship problems in your work, family, church, or community can contribute significantly to your sense of discontentment and despondency. Dealing with difficult people is challenging enough, and managing your negative thoughts about them can be even harder.

Maybe you're stuck being around them, you've had as much as you can take, and you really don't know what to do. But God promises to give you the wisdom and strength you need to deal with them with grace. And the most important step is realizing He allowed those people to be in your life for His purposes. So instead of allowing their actions to become the focus of your thinking, ask the Lord what He is teaching you or providing for you through them.

When the inappropriate, ugly words and deeds of others drive you to turn toward the Lord, they can actually be the unwitting agents of your spiritual growth. So make the choice to turn toward God because that's the way you lay the groundwork for triumph.

Jesus, help me to forgive others and to honor You. Amen.

Shelter in Him

You are my hiding place; You preserve me from
trouble; You surround me with songs of deliverance.

PSALM 32:7

Today, regardless of what challenge or enemy assails you, take refuge in the Lord. Ask Him to be your protection and defense. Commit yourself to His safekeeping, knowing that He is faithful and only allows the trials that will ultimately serve for your good.

Pursued intensely by the jealous King Saul, David found comfort, peace, and joy by taking shelter in God. The Lord was David's support and hiding place. Did Saul's actions always make sense to David? Not by a long shot. And much of what Saul did was truly heartbreaking. But through it all, the Lord taught David to trust Him completely and prepared him for greater service.

The same can be true for you. Praying specifically about your problem and staying in the Word of God are the most practical ways you can find shelter in adversity. Through those times of communion, He teaches you how to entrust yourself completely to Him. Will He deliver you from all that troubles you? Eventually, perhaps He will. No trial lasts longer than is useful in His economy. But the important thing is that you keep honoring Him and doing as He instructs. God will exalt you as you make Him your refuge.

Jesus, You are my refuge and hiding place. Thank You for
protecting me. Amen.

Fresh Encounter

*Be renewed in the spirit of your mind, and
put on the new self, which in the likeness of
God has been created in righteousness.*

EPHESIANS 4:23–24

I f you want joy and success in the Christian life, it's vital that
you have fresh encounters with the Lord. You must have those
experiences with the Savior that renew your soul, give you strength,
and propagate hope. Face it, your personal relationship with Jesus
can grow stale, become an unsatisfying routine, be mired in tradition, and lack spiritual vitality. The tyranny of the urgent can
thwart your intimacy with Christ. So you need to encounter Him
in all His glory and get back on track.

If you need a fresh touch from God, the most important step
you can take is to spend uninterrupted, focused, quality time
with Him. Give Him your full attention, heart, soul, mind, and
strength—without any agenda other than knowing Him. Admit
you haven't sensed His presence as you once did. Be completely
honest and don't try to rationalize anything He identifies as need-
ing repentance. Commit to taking whatever steps He instructs. And
have full confidence that He will accept you and reveal Himself to
you. After all, He longs for you to call on Him, and He always
wants to give you what your soul needs to be restored.

*Jesus, I need You. Help me to have a fresh encounter with
You. Amen.*

Accountability

*Confess your sins to one another, and pray for one
another so that you may be healed. The effective
prayer of a righteous man can accomplish much.*

JAMES 5:16

M ost people don't like to admit their shortcomings and struggles to others. We like it even less when other people tell us what to do. Yet throughout Scripture, we learn that we are accountable both to God and others—we're responsible to one another for our actions and spiritual growth. So consider: Is there anyone in your life who has been given permission to counsel you, challenge you, and rebuke you when necessary? Do you have even one friendship that involves transparency, confession, prayer, spiritual support, and mutual encouragement? If not, it's in your best interest to find one.

Accountability to others is a wise check and balance for your life. Through it, God provides a measure of protection, allowing others to discuss areas of weakness that could result in eventual ruin and hold you in check. You are prepared for the day you stand before the Lord to give an account of your life.

So if you don't have an accountability partner, find one. Be honest and vulnerable about your limitations, failings, and faults. Pray together and support each other spiritually. Because God blesses this kind of mutual edification abundantly.

*Jesus, please help me to find a wise and godly accountability
partner, and help me to be that person to someone else. Amen.*

Considering Criticism

He is on the path of life who heeds instruction,
but he who ignores reproof goes astray.

PROVERBS 10:17

Have you been criticized lately? The ugly, disparaging words of others can be very painful indeed. But whether or not the reprimand was deserved, you can grow spiritually with the right response. When you disregard censure outright, you limit your capacity for spiritual, emotional, and mental growth. You may fail to examine a blind spot in your life or to address a deficiency that is in desperate need of improvement. This is because, like the red indicator lights on an automobile dashboard, criticism warns us of potential problems that, if uncorrected, can wreck our relationships and plans. But when you take others' reproofs to God and ask if there is any truth in them, He can work through their words—even the ugly ones—for your betterment.

So when others rebuke you, don't build up a wall and say, "This is the way I am—like it or not." And don't attack those who reprimand you. Instead, say, "Thank you very much." Demonstrate a teachable spirit and accept the criticism for what it is. Then confront your weaknesses and examine your heart with God's help. He can transform you if you're open to dealing with unpleasant aspects of your personality and behavior.

Jesus, help me always to receive others' words with Your wisdom. Amen.

Procrastination

To one who knows the right thing to do
and does not do it, to him it is sin.

JAMES 4:17

D o you ever put off until tomorrow what you should be doing today? Perhaps there's something God's called you to do, someone you need to contact, or an important task that you're dreading. Somehow, you just never seem to get around to it—and the days keep passing. Maybe you're procrastinating because parts of the task are uncomfortable or cause you anxiety. Or it could be that you feel inadequate and are running out the clock over your fear of failure or criticism. Whatever the case, you continually feel the pressure of the task looming over you.

Thankfully, there's a solution for procrastination. The root cause of your hesitancy is due to how you feel about yourself, and you can deal with it by remembering that you are a child of the living God, empowered to serve Him through the wisdom and power of His indwelling Spirit. You have all you need to achieve every goal the Lord has set before you. Therefore, you don't have to fear. Through Christ, you can do this. So stop wrestling with your anxieties and get the job done. And begin living your life with the joy and assurance of God's unlimited resources.

Jesus, I know what I must do—help me to complete the task well. Amen.

The Word of Warfare

*The weapons of our warfare are not of the flesh, but
divinely powerful for the destruction of fortresses.*

2 CORINTHIANS 10:4

Every morning when you wake up, whether you realize it or not, you are at war. Many believers acknowledge this but don't take it as seriously as they should. When we talk about spiritual warfare, however, we must remember that daily we face a real and personal battle with spiritual forces that are trying to defeat us. Failure to recognize this has resulted in painful losses for even the most dedicated Christians. Just when they think they have an area of sinfulness conquered, it rises back up to overpower them again.

Perhaps you've experienced this and wonder, *If Scripture is as mighty as God has promised, then why am I still facing defeat?* The problem isn't that the Word is lacking in power—it's that we do not always understand how to clothe ourselves in it to fight effectively. It's not merely something we can quote when we feel vulnerable—though that's always a great thing to do. Rather, it's both a defensive and offensive weapon that must become an active and daily part of each area of our lives. And if you wield it correctly, it will not only protect you but will put your every enemy on the run.

*Jesus, show me how to use Your Word as an effective weapon
of spiritual warfare. Amen.*

340

Warring Kingdoms

He rescued us from the domain of darkness, and
transferred us to the kingdom of His beloved Son.

COLOSSIANS 1:13

S ince Satan's fall, there have been two supernatural realms at war: the kingdom of God and the dominion of darkness. This means we were born into conflict—caught in the middle of the struggle for power between these two domains. Even though we may not be able to see it, it's real and will continue to rage until Christ finally returns as the reigning King of kings and Lord of lords.

You may not recognize this conflict in your own life, but it's certainly present throughout Scripture and has permeated every area of society. Indeed, watching the news and observing the evil and suffering present throughout the world is almost enough to make us question whether the Enemy is winning. However, do not fear. God will always be victorious.

With this in mind, how should you live? You must prepare yourself for the spiritual battle—standing strong in the Lord and the power of His might. You do so by strapping on the full armor of God (Ephesians 6:10–18) but also by understanding that obedience to the Lord is imperative. Therefore, cast off anything the Enemy can use against you to his advantage and march in lockstep with the Savior.

Jesus, help me in all ways to serve You and Your kingdom.
Amen.

Cut Straight

Be diligent to present yourself approved to God
as a workman who does not need to be ashamed,
accurately handling the word of truth.

2 TIMOTHY 2:15

I f you want to have a sound, strong faith, you must be grounded in Scripture. This doesn't happen automatically just by reading. Instead, you must be diligent to understand the Word of God through study, prayer, reflection, and meditation.

The phrase that Paul used in today's verse, "accurately handling," means to cut a straight line such as a plowman would through a field. That is, when we read the Word of God, there's a straight line from the truth to our lives. We aren't turning or twisting it to suit us. Many people handle the Bible backward. They decide how they want to live and then pick verses out of context that appear to support their decisions. But that doesn't work. Instead, we must examine the full counsel of Scripture—not just a couple of passages in isolation—and base our lives on what it says.

Most people want to hear what makes them feel better about themselves. But the Bible is about transformation—through instruction, encouragement, and, when necessary, conviction. So be ready at all times to agree with the Word—even when it hurts. That's how you'll both strengthen and purify your faith.

Jesus, help me to apply Your truth to my life diligently and accurately. Amen.

Complete

In Him you have been made complete, and
He is the head over all rule and authority.

COLOSSIANS 2:10

On a scale of one to ten, how complete would you say your life is? What person, occupation, possession, or achievement would make your life more meaningful and fulfilling? Those may be difficult and complicated questions considering your current circumstances or how others have judged you. However, take comfort in the fact that once you place your trust in Christ as Savior, you become "complete in Him." The word *complete* in the original Greek means "full"—as when there's no room for anything more. You are without lack—not missing anything required for wholeness or acceptance.

Think about it. Jesus—who is "the fullness of Deity" (Colossians 2:9)—is the Sovereign of the universe and the sum of all holiness and perfection, without blemish or want. And He dwells in you and supplies all your needs. In Him is all the wisdom, strength, provision, direction, love, joy, peace, patience, kindness, gentleness, self-control, faithfulness, counsel, and comfort you will ever require. Therefore, when you have Christ, you have absolutely everything. Nothing of eternal worth is absent from you.

So really, it doesn't matter what others have said you need or what society says will make your life better. Christ is your life, and He is far more than enough.

Jesus, thank You so much that I lack absolutely nothing in You. Amen.

Step of Faith

The righteousness of God is revealed from
faith to faith; as it is written, "But the
righteous man shall live by faith."

ROMANS 1:17

T ake the step of faith. Whatever it is that God has shown you to do, stop allowing fear and indecision to hinder you. Just go forward, trusting that He knows what He is doing even if you're not sure. This does not rely on your skill, knowledge, or capability—so don't use those as excuses anymore. The Lord has directed you in this manner so you can see how abundantly sufficient He is for everything in life.

This is the way by which you experience God more and advance in the Christian life. Your conduct, behavior, and lifestyle—every area of your personhood—should reveal a continuously unfolding, progressing, increasing expression of trust in Jesus. Can others look at you and recognize that you are growing in your likeness to Christ and faith in Him?

You've lived your life trusting your limited senses, but now it is time to rely fully on God's unlimited wisdom, strength, knowledge, and love. So prepare yourself by reading Scripture, praying, and remembering how He has helped you in the past. Then do what you know He desires of you. He will do whatever is necessary to lead you to triumph as you obey Him.

Jesus, I will obey You. Lead me, Lord. Amen.

Active Waiting

My soul, wait in silence for God only,
for my hope is from Him.

PSALM 62:5

When you wait on the Lord for some request or opportunity, it may feel like you are wasting time. Indeed, it may feel as if your whole life is on hold. Like David, you may find yourself crying out, "How long, O LORD? Will You forget me forever?" (Psalm 13:1). But just as God had not abandoned David, He has not deserted you either. The Lord did a great deal of important work in David's life and character during the waiting times, and He does so in you as well.

Therefore, understand that your life is not on pause. On the contrary, you must actively position yourself for God's continuing instruction. To wait on the Lord requires strength and courage—it is not a time to be passive, irresponsible, or slothful. Rather, you must choose minute-by-minute to be obedient to the Father and His schedule regardless of how long your request takes. Do not become impatient or rush into a solution of your own making— you'll only hinder God's plan and prolong the delay. Instead, trust the Lord's awesome timing and allow Him to do His essential work in you and your circumstances. He will certainly do beyond all you imagine.

Jesus, You are my hope. I'll seek You with everything in me and wait on You. Amen.

Speak Faith

Let no unwholesome word proceed from your mouth,
but only such a word as is good for edification . . .
so that it will give grace to those who hear.
EPHESIANS 4:29

We always need to be careful about what we say because our words have an extraordinary effect on us and others. What we verbalize we also hear—and it affects us physically, mentally, emotionally, and spiritually. Choose to speak negativity all day long, and your day will be a lot worse than if you decide to be positive. So consider: Do the words you're expressing enhance or contribute to whatever it is you want to achieve?

You may say, "But you don't understand. My life is difficult. Complaining is how I release my feelings." However, you must remember that your words communicate your beliefs. If you're always speaking defeat, that's where you'll remain. This is why David prayed, "Set a guard, O LORD, over my mouth" (Psalm 141:3). He knew "death and life are in the power of the tongue" (Proverbs 18:21). Instead, when you face heartaches and burdens, try making a good confession of faith. When you get into a difficult spot, say, "Lord, thank You for Your promises because I know You're going to see me through this and bring good from it." It will make all the difference in your circumstances.

Jesus, set a guard on my mouth and help me always to speak
faith. Amen.

Every Part

Having loved His own who were in the world, He loved them to the end.

JOHN 13:1

It was before Passover, and Jesus knew His time had come. The mission was almost over. Soon, He would leave behind the suffering of His limited human body and return to His rightful place at the right hand of His beloved Father. He would again be clothed with the glory and honor due Him.

But this was a bittersweet moment because Jesus truly loved His people. Even though Judas had already betrayed Him, his treachery did not dissuade Christ from serving them. Jesus knew "the Father had given all things into His hands" (John 13:3); the victory was His, so He wanted to give the disciples an unforgettable picture of how intimately God Himself ministers to us. Like the lowliest servant of the household, the Lord of lords knelt, "poured water into the basin, and began to wash the disciples' feet" (John 13:5).

Don't miss this beautiful picture, because this is how much God loves you—even the smallest, uncomfortable grains of dust and sand on your feet are of concern to Him. There is nothing too lowly for Him to touch; He wants you completely clean. So don't hide anything, even the things that are most shameful. Let Him minister to you.

Jesus, thank You for cleansing even the most shameful parts of me. You are truly my Savior. Amen.

An Ephraim Attitude

"God has made me fruitful in the land of my affliction."
GENESIS 41:52

Joseph spent thirteen long years in Egyptian servitude and imprisonment before becoming its second most powerful leader. Yet he named his second son Ephraim, which means "twice fruitful." Why? The name reminded Joseph that the Lord had woven his sufferings into a beautifully designed plan. Joseph became the godly man he was created to be *because of* his sufferings, not in spite of them.

Joseph chose to trust the Lord's sovereign plan for his life. Speaking to his brothers who had betrayed and sold him into slavery, he emphatically stated, "You meant evil against me, but God meant it for good" (Genesis 50:20). He not only forgave them but gave the Lord glory for His transformative purposes.

We all have scars that remind us of the wounds we've suffered because of our own harmful behavior or from the destructive words and actions of others. Many times, we try to forget about them, ignore them, or suppress them. These strategies are seldom effective. Instead, recognize that the Father will work through your pain to strengthen you and develop your character if you let Him. So don't deny your suffering or become bitter because of it. Like Joseph, embrace it as the Lord's tool to build you up.

Jesus, give me a heart like Joseph, one that sees Your good purposes even in adversity. Amen.

Trust His Goodness

In You they trusted and were not disappointed.

PSALM 22:5

Often, our failure to trust Jesus is based on a lack of confidence in the goodness of God. We want something and cannot imagine why He won't give it to us. We pray and pray, but for whatever reason the situation remains the same. So when He asks us to step out in faith, we're hesitant.

But remember, the Father promises to supply all your needs in the manner that is most beneficial to you. And He assures you that if you make His kingdom a priority, you won't need to fret over the necessities of life (Matthew 6:24–34). However, when you doubt God's kindness to meet the fundamental demands of your existence—physically, spiritually, financially, emotionally—you are apt to seek your satisfaction through pursuits that will never really fulfill you and will ultimately tear you down.

So today, don't doubt. Remember that God is *always* good to His people—there's never a moment when He fails to work for your best interest, even if that entails discipline. So obey Jesus, not merely because it is your duty but because goodness, mercy, love, and wisdom undergird all His commands. Do what He says and trust Him for all things because those who depend on Him are never disappointed.

*Jesus, help me to trust Your good purposes in every situation.
Amen.*

Get Wisdom

The beginning of wisdom is this: Get wisdom.
Though it cost all you have, get understanding.
PROVERBS 4:7 NIV

Throughout Scripture, the process of acquiring wisdom is often seen as a journey—its purpose is to lead you on the correct path. As you pursue it, it guides you to greater insight and more understanding about God's character and ways. This is because fear—or reverence—for the Lord is the beginning of wisdom. You can only begin the expedition to find it by acknowledging that God is the Creator and Source of it and that He comprehends more about it than you ever will.

Thankfully, if you ask the Lord what He thinks about the different situations that concern you, He will tell you. His goal is that you'll stay on course with Him; therefore, whenever you ask for His guidance, you can trust that He will answer you. However, you need to be listening to Him to distinguish the right way to go.

When God looks at your circumstances, He always knows exactly what you should do. And He doesn't want you to live a merely "good" life; He wants you to experience the very best existence possible. So listen to Him because the wisdom He'll teach you "is better than jewels, and nothing desirable can equal it" (Proverbs 8:11 CSB).

Jesus, please lead me on this journey and teach me to be wise. Amen.

Press Forward

*Forgetting what lies behind and reaching forward
to what lies ahead, I press on toward the goal.*

PHILIPPIANS 3:13–14

D o you think about your past—the mistakes you've made, the wrongs done to you, or the good things you were able to accomplish? It may seem harmless, but focusing on days gone by can hinder your faith.

The apostle Paul understood this well. He could have gotten caught up in the fact that he had persecuted the church and sent many believers to their deaths. The guilt could have eaten him alive. Instead, he chose to embrace Christ's forgiveness. Then there were the people who had cursed, beaten, and betrayed him. Paul could have been bitter toward them. Instead, he chose to extend the grace that Jesus had shown him. Paul also could have gotten stuck on the glory days—when he was an up-and-coming leader among the Pharisees, on the path to wealth and notoriety. Instead, he counted it rubbish compared to knowing Jesus.

Paul understood that when our gaze is too fixed on the mistakes, injustices, and even the victories, we aren't going to make the progress God wants. So he pressed forward and made Christ his focus because that's the path to life at its best. Therefore, today, put the past behind you, where it belongs, and watch Christ transform your future in ways you can't imagine.

Jesus, I press on, look forward, and seek You. Amen.

Encourage Them

Encourage each other daily . . . so that none
of you is hardened by sin's deception.

HEBREWS 3:13 csb

Discouragement is one of the most destructive weapons in the Enemy's arsenal, so as believers, we need to be aware of how important it is to encourage one another. Disheartened Christians on the verge of losing their hope and focus because of their struggles can be strengthened through the caring words and actions of their brothers and sisters in Christ.

One of the wonderful examples in Scripture of this is how the Lord used Barnabas in the life of John Mark. Mark had deserted Paul and Barnabas during their first missionary journey, so Paul refused to travel with him again. But Barnabas, seeing his cousin Mark's potential, gave him another chance and nurtured him. And it made all the difference. Eventually, Mark not only became an important leader in the early church but also wrote the Gospel of Mark. Even Paul wanted Mark by his side as he faced imminent death.

It's human nature to reject those who fail us. However, God's purpose is always redemption. So when a fellow believer falls, don't kick them when they're down. Instead, be like Barnabas and help them up. Encourage them, trusting that the Lord still has good and important plans for their lives.

Jesus, show me who I can encourage with Your love and
truth today. Amen.

In Everything

God causes all things to work together for
good to those who love God, to those who
are called according to His purpose.

ROMANS 8:28

D o you believe God is in everything that happens to you? This may be a difficult question considering the suffering you may be experiencing. However, it's something that every sincere believer should think about deeply. After all, we won't be able to understand or explain everything that happens to us. We know that God loves us and that He's never the initiator of evil. But even while the Lord may not *cause* what is happening to us, He is still in it with us. And as omnipotent, omniscient God, He also makes the final decision concerning what can touch our lives and helps us overcome.

As a believer, however, you're assured that the Lord is working through every detail in your life. Because you cannot see His big picture, you may misunderstand some of the circumstances you experience. But all the while, He is orchestrating and guiding your life in the manner befitting a loving Father.

So do not fear or despair. Instead, continue to listen to God and believe His Word. He will certainly take the most disastrous challenges and the most hopeless situations and, in His wise and supernatural way, turn them for your ultimate good.

Jesus, thank You that I can always trust You regardless of what happens. Amen.

In His Name

O LORD, our Lord, how majestic is
Your name in all the earth.

PSALM 8:1

Harriet Tubman. Sir Winston Churchill. Mohandas Gandhi. Albert Einstein. Billy Graham. At the mere mention of them, your mind may jump to who they were and what they were able to accomplish. That is because a person's name reflects far more than mere identity—it suggests character, personality, and the sum of a person's being.

This is why it's an excellent idea to get to know the names by which God is called in Scripture—it can enhance your worship and prayer time with Him. For example, He is *Yahweh Yireh*—your great and mighty provider. He is the One who perceives your needs and faithfully supplies what will fulfill them. He is *Elohim*—the One who is infinite in power and absolutely faithful to keep His promises to you. He is *El Shaddai*—the Most High over all, almighty God, who is always victorious. He is also *El Roi*—the God who sees you; *Yahweh Rohi*—your shepherd who guides you; *Yahweh Rapha*—the One who heals you; and *Yahweh Shalom*—your peace.

So get to know the Lord's titles and character—in doing so, you will get to know Him. He is truly majestic and wonderful in every way.

Jesus, Your name is above every other name. Teach me who You are. Amen.

Profound Praise

They praised the LORD because the foundation
of the house of the LORD was laid.
EZRA 3:11

Throughout history, God has patiently taught His people in the ways of praise. Many times, their worship came as a result of His deliverance from some trial. For example, Ezra recounts the restoration of the Jewish people to their homeland following the Babylonian captivity. Once they returned to Jerusalem, they found very little left of the temple. This was their only true place of worship, and it lay in ruins. However, they set up an altar and began to sacrifice again amid the rubble. And when they'd cleared away the fallen stones and laid the foundation of the temple, they praised God anew.

Judah had lost everything, spending nearly seventy years in Babylon. Yet instead of bitterness, Ezra recorded their deep desire to reestablish a place of worship and praise to the Lord. Their time in bondage renewed their recognition of their profound need for God. Stripped of every other security, they saw their true hope was in Him. Likewise, the Father may at times use your stiffest trials to teach you to trust and worship Him—that He is all you really need. And it's in those times of sacrificial praise that you'll find strength in God's presence that absolutely nothing can shake.

Jesus, when You're all I have, I see that You're truly all I need. Amen.

Counting Your Blessings

*I will give thanks to the LORD with all my
heart; I will tell of all Your wonders.*

PSALM 9:1

A t times, is it a challenge for you to name your blessings? Is it
difficult to see any good in your life? Perhaps you're enduring a particularly demanding season with financial, relational, or
physical problems that have robbed you of joy. If so, then consider
this: when you have Jesus, you have the greatest blessing possible
that will never be taken away.

That may sound like a spiritually simplistic or naive statement,
but it is profound in ways that are crucial for you to grasp. Indeed,
your recognition of who Jesus is can transform your existence. In
Christ, you have the guarantee of eternal life, which begins even
now as you know Him (John 17:3). He shapes your character, nour-
ishes your soul, and energizes your spirit, giving you a new identity,
wisdom, love, strength, joy, peace, comfort, hope, and patience. In
Christ you have a true and unwavering friend for every season—He
understands your disappointments, rejoices in your triumphs, and
stands with you in your trials. You can confide in Him, weep before
Him, and celebrate with Him.

Therefore, whenever you consider your blessings, begin with all
you have in Jesus. Because then you'll always have plenty to count.

*Jesus, You are truly my greatest blessing. Thank You for all
You are to me. Amen.*

Choose to Praise

*Even if I am being poured out as a drink
offering . . . I rejoice and share my joy with you all.*

PHILIPPIANS 2:17

The journey had not gone as Paul and Silas had anticipated. God had called them to the city of Philippi, and people had responded to the gospel. But then the situation went awry quickly—they were falsely accused, stripped, severely beaten, thrown into prison, and restrained in stocks.

You can imagine that the duo—bloodied and badly bruised—could have given in to despair. But instead, they began to sing hymns and worship God. And the Lord responded to their act of faith by sending an earthquake that broke the chains that held Paul and Silas tight. The jailer, certain that they had escaped and fearful that he might lose his life, instead found them sitting composed in their cells. So compelling was their witness that the incredulous jailer invited them to his house, where he and his family accepted Christ.

Paul and Silas probably hadn't felt like singing. Their circumstances were awful, and their prospects were grim. But they did something that every believer can do that will make an amazing difference—they chose to praise God. You can too. And when you do, you can be certain that the Lord hears and does miraculous things on your behalf as well.

Jesus, like Paul and Silas, I praise You in all situations. Amen.

Yes, Everything

*Give thanks for everything to God the Father
in the name of our Lord Jesus Christ.*

EPHESIANS 5:20 NLT

As we read the word *everything* in today's verse, it may trouble us. Does God really mean we're to give thanks in all things, or can we make a few exceptions? But understand that the man who wrote this passage was a man who knew what it meant to be hungry, betrayed, imprisoned, beaten, shipwrecked, persecuted, and left for dead. He suffered all kinds of difficulties and heartaches. Yet the apostle Paul declared we are to give thanks in *everything*. That includes the good things that we enjoy—the health, friends, promotions, and blessings. But it also involves the painful things—sickness, disappointment, criticism, mistreatment, trials, temptations, and the loss of loved ones.

Why are we to give thanks? Because when we express our gratefulness, we acknowledge the sovereignty and wisdom of God. He's in control of everything we face and can take whatever we experience and transform it for our good and His glory. You may not understand how or why; you're simply to trust that He can. Because in every difficulty there's an opportunity to learn essential spiritual lessons that will strengthen your relationship with Jesus, transform your character, and fit you for service. So stay close to God, have faith, and praise Him for all of it.

Jesus, I will thank You even when I don't understand. Amen.

Focused on God

*I shall joyfully sing of Your lovingkindness in
the morning, for You have been my stronghold.*

PSALM 59:16

Driven from his home and everything he knew, David—who had been anointed by God to be the future king of Israel—ran for his life. Humanly, it made no sense. He was pursued by King Saul, who should have been his mentor but instead had gone mad with envy and rage. So for years, rather than learning the intricacies of the throne, David lived the forsaken life of a fugitive. Everyone he loved or who helped him was in danger, and some were even killed. The only people who followed him were "in trouble or in debt or . . . were just discontented" (1 Samuel 22:2 NLT).

So how could David wake up in the morning with praise in his heart? As a boy in the sheep fields, he wrote and sang songs of worship and praise to God. And as he fled, those hymns—which today comprise much of the book of Psalms—rose within him as a constant reminder of the Lord's closeness, protection, and deliverance. Had David fixated on his circumstances, he would have become hopelessly discouraged. But instead he focused on God's love and promises and received the encouragement he needed to persevere and honor the Lord in all he did.

*Jesus, help me to focus on You and praise You in every
situation. Amen.*

Abundant Life

*"I came that they may have life,
and have it abundantly."*

JOHN 10:10

What is the abundant life? Many Christians believe that you experience it when your days are trouble-free and when blessings flow. But Jesus sees it differently. His goal is to live within you—for you to exchange your life for His. It's not merely going to church, reading your Bible, giving money, and witnessing. Rather, you trade your old self, your dead spirit, your will, and your rights for His Spirit, His resurrection, His mission, and His victory. In other words, Christ in you is the abundant life.

This may seem counterintuitive because when most of us were saved, we thirsted after God's presence. So we joined churches and were given lists of rules to live by. But the harder we tried to earn our way to the Lord, the more parched we became for Him.

Yet Jesus says, "He who believes in Me . . . 'From his innermost being will flow rivers of living water'" (John 7:38). Think about that. A river cuts its own way through and makes a significant difference in all it touches. This is instructive because you are the channel through which Jesus flows. So ultimately, the key to the abundant life is yieldedness. If you allow Him, Christ will course His life through you, and your thirst for His presence will be lavishly, overflowingly supplied.

Jesus, be my abundant life. Flow through me, Lord. Amen.

Sabbath Rest

There remains a Sabbath rest for the people of God.
For the one who has entered His rest has himself
also rested from his works, as God did from His.

HEBREWS 4:9–10

The seventh day—the Sabbath—was the day God rested from His work of forming the heavens and the earth and enjoyed His masterpiece. But when you read the creation account, there's no mention of nightfall on that seventh day. Every other day of creation recorded a morning and evening—a beginning and end—but not the Sabbath. Why? The rabbis taught that this is because the Lord's rest had no conclusion—it lasts eternally.

This Sabbath rest is what God desires for each of us. Yes, in heaven we will rest from our labors. But even on earth, the Father doesn't want us to be people of continual worry and striving, unable to recognize His peaceful, joyful, and all-sufficient presence in our midst. Yes, we still must pray, plan, work, and obey God. After all, Ephesians 2:10 instructs, "We are His workmanship, created in Christ Jesus for good works, which God prepared beforehand so that we would walk in them." Yet behind all our endeavors is the wonderful awareness of the Lord's adequacy. And He wants us to rest in the knowledge that He has it all figured out, even when we don't.

Jesus, thank You that I can always rest in You. Amen.

He'll Finish It

"Truly I have spoken; truly I will bring it to pass. I have planned it, surely I will do it."

ISAIAH 46:11

God is committed to getting the job done. Understand this today, especially if you're waiting on some precious promise to be fulfilled or there's some task He's called you to carry out. Jesus said He glorified the Father in heaven by "finishing the work [He] gave me to do" (John 17:4 NIV). Completion is important to Him. And when the Lord decides to do something, you can be assured that He will accomplish it.

However, do not presume that He will act in the manner you expect or that His finished work will look like you've pictured it in your mind. He works in a strategic manner to carry out His purposes. There were many towns Jesus didn't visit, plenty of people He didn't teach or heal. Instead, He carried out the Father's specific plan. Does this mean He left things undone? Absolutely not. As He said, *"All things* which are written about Me in the Law of Moses and the Prophets and the Psalms *must be fulfilled"* (Luke 24:44, emphasis added). However, sometimes His priorities and timing are different from ours. He knows what's most important and what will make the greatest impact. So trust Him to do as He's promised perfectly.

··

Jesus, thank You for keeping all Your promises. Amen.

Keep at It

*Let us not lose heart in doing good, for in due
time we will reap if we do not grow weary.*

GALATIANS 6:9

There will be times when serving God and even life in general will feel like a long slog—tiring, mundane, and seemingly unproductive. We'll hear about the Lord's miracle-working power, His rewards, the abundant life He has for us, and how He shines His glory through our obedience to Him. But we won't feel it. We'll look for some evidence of a breakthrough on the horizon, but we just won't see it.

In such times, you will be tempted to give up, but don't. Remain committed and keep going because that's how you'll reach all God has for you. The Lord may be working through your devoted service in ways that are unseen at present, but soon enough He will bring forth a harvest. So stay at it. Fight the urge to become apathetic and lethargic or to procrastinate. Each day, pray, "Lord, I'm available to do Your will in Your way today. Work through me." And when you don't see a reason to keep going, fix your eyes on Jesus—because He is always worthy of your devotion and will not fail to reward your faithful service to Him.

Jesus, I'm weary, but I trust You. Thank You that nothing done in obedience to You is ever in vain. Amen.

DECEMBER

Forgiven Again

Who will set me free from the body of this death?
Thanks be to God through Jesus Christ our Lord!
ROMANS 7:24–25

O ne of the wonderful blessings of knowing Jesus as Savior is living in the goodness of His grace. Even when you mess up and commit the sin you never wanted to engage in again, He is there with open arms to forgive you. So the moment you realize you've done wrong, turn to Him immediately. Do not delay because unnecessary guilt and fear will build in your heart and hinder your fellowship with Him, and He does not want you to bear a load that He has already taken on Himself. Remember, there is no limit to His grace; all of your sins—past, present, and future—are covered by His blood.

Once you have confessed and repented from your sin, then it is time to learn from your mistakes and walk in God's ways. He wants you to be completely free from that sinful stronghold, so His plan for you may involve several steps to restoration. Accept how He leads you. Don't get discouraged or stubbornly try to move forward without His direction. Instead, let the Lord turn your personal failures into triumphs, for yourself and as a living testimony to others of His victorious love and power.

....

Jesus, thank You for forgiving me, restoring me, and
teaching me to walk in Your freedom. Amen.

Good News

*"Go into all the world and preach
the gospel to all creation."*

MARK 16:15

The Greek word for gospel—*euangelion*—means "good news." Its central theme—Christ's death, burial, and resurrection—is a distinctly positive message of hope and triumph. God redeems us, restores our relationship with Him, gives us a brand-new nature, and provides us with an eternal home in heaven. What a blessing! It may make you wonder why so many people are resistant to the gospel.

Most often, it's fear. Before we can appreciate the awe-inspiring benefits of the good news of salvation through Christ, we must first face the bad news about ourselves. Most people measure themselves morally against the behavior of others—typically with those whose conduct is worse. So often, we hear people say, "I'm a pretty good person." And certainly, unbelievers can do some noble things—such as help sick neighbors and give financially to worthy causes. In general, they lead what our culture would deem a "good life."

The problem from God's perspective is that they are spiritually dead and alienated from Him. They don't realize that this means separation from Him and horrifying suffering in eternity. So we must gently help others face their spiritual condition and the truly good news of Christ's redemption. If we love them, we'll tell them.

Jesus, help me to faithfully tell others the truly good news. Amen.

The Personal Word

*The word of God is alive and active. Sharper
than any double-edged sword, it penetrates
even to dividing soul and spirit . . . it judges
the thoughts and attitudes of the heart.*

HEBREWS 4:12 NIV

God will do His greatest work in you as you meditate on His
Word. He will transform you during those times when you
open Scripture and allow Him to speak to you individually about
who you are and what He desires for you. You will miss out significantly if you solely depend on someone else to feed you from the
Word of God. Certainly, the Lord uses Bible preachers and teachers
to help you, but there's nothing like the blessing of personal discovery as the Holy Spirit teaches you during your private times of
communion alone with Him.

Of course, one of the reasons we avoid reading the Bible is that
it can be very convicting. The Lord sees who we are and works
through His Word to sift out our rationalizations and lay our hearts
bare. Though this may sound unpleasant, there's really nothing as
uplifting and freeing. This is because the Father helps us to see our
lives from His point of view—including the incredible hope and
potential He has built into each of us. And once we see our lives
through His eyes, we'll never want anything less.

*Jesus, teach me to meet with You personally through Your
Word. Amen.*

After God's Heart

*"I have found David the son of Jesse, a man
after My heart, who will do all My will."*

ACTS 13:22

Can you think of any higher goal in life than to be a person after God's heart? Although David was far from perfect, this is what he was commended for. I believe this was because of four characteristics David demonstrated, which we would be wise to emulate.

The first quality that set David apart was that he prioritized his personal fellowship with God. If you need evidence of this, look to the Psalms. David made it a habit to commune with the Lord and mediate on His Word. *Second, David exhibited a strong desire to obey God.* Regardless of what the Lord called him to do, he did so with reverence and devotion. Twice he could have killed Saul but refrained out of respect for the Almighty. *Third, David had the courage to put his faith in God.* There's no more striking example of this than when he faced Goliath. *Fourth, David demonstrated a servant's spirit.* Even when Saul tried to kill him, David continued to serve faithfully.

By following David's godly example, you can be a person after God's own heart as well. Certainly, there's no higher calling than that.

....

Jesus, help me to be a person after Your heart. Amen.

Leave Him the Choice

The LORD loves justice and does
not forsake His godly ones.
PSALM 37:28

A bram and Lot had a problem. The land they had migrated to was unable to sustain the great number of livestock they'd acquired, and heated quarrels had broken out between their hired hands. So Abram stepped in with a solution: "Let there be no strife between you and me . . . Please separate from me; if to the left, then I will go to the right; or if to the right, then I will go to the left" (Genesis 13:8–9).

The situation could have been a terrible mess. Abram could've said, "I'm your elder and the one with the promise from God. I'll tell you what to do." But instead, he approached his nephew Lot with humility, as a peacemaker. And because he honored the Lord, God rewarded him with the best of the land.

We can learn a lot from Abram. Too often, we fight for our rights, not realizing how our methods damage our relationships. But as missionary Jim Elliot wrote, "God always gives His best to those who leave the choice with Him." Therefore, regardless of the situation, always ask the Lord what He wants. You don't have to fight for what you deserve; just let Him decide what to do and He will honor you.

Jesus, help me to be a humble peacemaker and honor You in every situation. Amen.

Battle Plan

*"We are powerless before this great multitude . . . nor
do we know what to do, but our eyes are on You."*

2 CHRONICLES 20:12

It was a time of national emergency. The enormous armies of the Moabites, Ammonites, and Meunites were about to march on King Jehoshaphat and the nation of Judah, and they had no way to defend themselves. Most leaders would have called their advisers or mustered the army, but Jehoshaphat employed a different strategy. He looked to God. He didn't falter, complain, or waste time in pessimistic thinking. Instead, he immediately called the people together for a time of prayer with fasting.

Notice the attributes of God that Jehoshaphat named in his prayer: "O LORD . . . are You not God in the heavens? . . . Power and might are in Your hand so that no one can stand against You" (2 Chronicles 20:6). The king recognized God's ultimate power and authority, and therefore he was not afraid of what mere men might do. And because of his earnest faith, the Lord gave Judah the victory.

There will be times when the problems against you are far greater than you can handle, and you just won't know what to do. Don't fret. Instead, follow Jehoshaphat's example and seek the Lord in faith. Because that's the battle plan that always leads to victory.

*Jesus, regardless of what happens, I will keep my eyes on You.
Amen.*

God Loves You

*"As the Father has loved Me, I have
also loved you; abide in My love."*

JOHN 15:9

D o you realize how profoundly God loves you? If not, you may
feel discouraged and unfulfilled in your walk with Him. I
can say this by experience. When I was in my mid-forties, I was a
very frustrated Christian. I'd been a believer for more than thirty
years, and yet something was missing from my fellowship with the
Lord. But I didn't know what it was. I knew God. I prayed daily,
read Scripture regularly, and served Him. But I didn't have the
divine joy promised in Scripture.

However, a transformation began as I grasped the love the
Lord has for me. God loves me. As simple as that may seem, I'd
never truly understood its profound significance. He cares for me
personally. God revealed His powerful, bountiful, intimate, unconditional love to a very grateful Charles Stanley, and He's become
more real, joyful, satisfying, and glorious to me every day since.

That is what I pray for you. So please, take a pen or pen-
cil and finish the sentence by writing in your name. God loves
_____. Think about that statement. Close your eyes
and say it to yourself several times each day. And accept it as true.
God loves you. Personally. Completely. And He will never stop.
Praise His wonderful name.

Jesus, thank You for really loving me. Amen.

Make It Personal

*There is nothing in all creation that will ever
be able to separate us from the love of God
which is ours through Christ Jesus our Lord.*

ROMANS 8:39 GNT

Consider the profound, personal nature of how the Lord cares for you. *God* loves you. The most magnificent person in the universe delights in you. The Godhead—Father, Son, and Holy Spirit—cherishes you. Immeasurably and eternally, the Sovereign of the universe has set His affection on you. You are the apple of His eye, the crown of His creation.

God *loves* you. This is not mere sentiment. His infinite goodness is directed to you in myriad ways—through how He created, saved, indwells, guides, and protects you. He listens to your petitions, gives you new mercies every morning, sustains you each day, and watches over you every night. And nothing in all creation can stop Him.

God loves *you*. He cares for you uniquely as an individual. No one knows you like He does. He knows your dreams, desires, and potential and wants to see you succeed. He calls you by name and speaks to you through His Word in the most intimate way.

"God loves *me*." Begin and end each day with this affirmation. Rehearse it in your soul. And may you come to know in the most personal way how true it is.

Jesus, keep me mindful of Your love always. Amen.

Stand Free

It was for freedom that Christ set us free; therefore keep standing firm and do not be subject again to a yoke of slavery.

GALATIANS 5:1

There are forces all around you working to undermine the freedom Jesus died to give you. Whispers of condemnation, feelings of fear and insecurity, graceless messages from well-meaning believers, constant criticism from those you love. Day after day your spiritual liberty and God-given identity are assailed from all sides.

It was this very threat that moved the apostle Paul to write today's verse. He knew from watching the Christians in Galatia that a believer's freedom must be constantly guarded and defended. For just as the truth can liberate us, so the lies of the Enemy can send us right back to the bondage and defeat we once knew.

So today consider: Are you standing firm in the freedom Christ provided at the cross? Are you taking hold of His Word daily? Are you asserting who you are in Him? If not, take a few minutes to review the strongholds and areas of weakness that the Lord has identified and desires to overcome in you. He wants to liberate you. Ask Him for specific Scripture verses that you can memorize and meditate on. Then stand firm in your faith by clinging to the truth that sets you free.

Jesus, help me to experience the fullness of Your truth and freedom. Amen.

Be Generous

He who is generous will be blessed.

PROVERBS 22:9

Are you completely focused on meeting your own needs, or have you experienced the joy of giving and ministering to others? Since it is God's nature to be generous, He wants those of us who follow Him to be generous as well. After all, the world tells us, "Get all you can. Look out for yourself because no one else will." So when we unselfishly share our time, love, talents, resources, and wisdom with others, it makes a statement about our faith in Him and what we value. We align ourselves with the purpose and character of God, who is tenderly concerned for those who suffer lack.

Of course, you may think, *I don't have much money to spare.* But generosity is not about the amount of wealth you possess—it's the Spirit that indwells you. It is a mark of your character—a heart that's available to serve the Lord in whatever way He chooses.

So today, look for ways that you can extend God's generosity to others. Ask Him for opportunities to give of yourself, your time, and your resources for His glory. He will certainly answer that prayer and show you the wonderful fulfillment and blessing of seeing Him work through you in the lives of others.

....

Jesus, help me always to be generous and represent You well. Amen.

Do Not Fear

"Do not fear, for I am with you . . . I will
strengthen you, surely I will help you."
ISAIAH 41:10

A re you anxious? Do you struggle with fear? When you're filled with apprehension, it can be difficult to see God as loving and gracious. Indeed, you may picture Him as angry and the trials He allows as never-ending and bigger than they actually are. But understand, this is a distorted view of the Lord, who "does not willingly bring affliction or grief to anyone" (Lamentations 3:33 NIV). And a fixation on your fears will always stifle your relationship with Him and hinder your potential.

So if you're constantly questioning when the other shoe will drop, realize you need to deal with the anxiety in your life. God specifically commands you not to be frightened, so you have a choice in the matter—your emotions do not need to rule you.

What can you do? Admit you're anxious and ask the Holy Spirit to help you identify the source of your insecurity. The Lord will show you what's really going on and will point you to the truth you need to overcome it. Depend on Him and realize that when He is helping you, there's never a reason to be afraid.

Jesus, please reveal the source of my fears and teach me the truth so I can be free from them. Amen.

Freed from Fear

The LORD is for me; I will not fear.

PSALM 118:6

Yesterday our topic was anxiety, and perhaps you were able to identify some fears that have taken hold in your life. The Lord's supernatural power will free you from apprehension when you abide by two essential principles—*focus* and *have faith*.

First, focus. You must concentrate on what God's Word says. When all your attention is on your situation, it always looks worse. But when you meditate on Scripture, your mind is fixed on all the Lord can do on your behalf, and your perspective changes. You see how almighty, wise, and loving He is and how He delivered others in situations similar to yours.

Second, have faith. Once your focus is right, you're positioned for your trust in the Lord to be strengthened. Remember, faith is when you believe "that God exists and rewards those who seek him" (Hebrews 11:6 GNT). Those are the two requirements: 1) accept as true that He is real, and 2) have confidence that He will answer you in a positive way.

With a clear focus on God's Word and with faith in His unfailing presence and power in your life, all your fears can and will be defeated. Count on it. Turn to Him and be free.

....

Jesus, I will focus on and have faith in You. Free me from my fears. Amen.

Enduring Temptation

He is able to come to the aid of
those who are tempted.

HEBREWS 2:18

Perhaps you've noticed that the greatest temptations seem to arise when you're under a lot of pressure. This is the Enemy's usual mode of operation because he knows this is when you're weakest. For example, after His baptism, Jesus fasted forty days and nights before beginning His ministry. It was at that point, when Christ was especially drained, that the devil began tempting Him to take shortcuts rather than relying on the plan and faithfulness of the Father.

This is the same way the Enemy will lure you to forsake God. Perhaps you are especially tired, hungry, overwhelmed, lonely, or emotional because of the burdens you bear and the things you must get done. You need rest, relief, and help. So the Enemy will offer you alternatives that will not satisfy but will only make matters worse. Don't fall for it.

God has not forgotten you in this stressful time. On the contrary, He wants to be your energy, strength, resource, and shield. And because Jesus experienced and understands your human needs, He knows exactly what you need to persevere triumphantly. So endure by committing yourself to Him. Focus on doing the will of the Father, and praise Him for helping you. Because then no temptation will overtake you.

Jesus, thank You for protecting me from temptation. Amen.

The Source

*"Rivers of living water shall flow from the
inmost being of anyone who believes in me."*

JOHN 7:38 TLB

A n artesian well sits in a pasture along a picturesque rural
road. Flowing from a small pipe, the water has provided cool
refreshment for man and beast for decades. Its stream, issuing from
deep within the earth, has never diminished or varied—even in
times of severe drought.

Wouldn't it be wonderful to be that steady and consistent
in how we live as believers? Unfortunately, our moods are often
governed by our circumstances. A good day at church, home, or
work can be invigorating. A flat tire in the rain or a particularly
ugly comment can be debilitating, leaving us deflated. That type
of emotional variability takes its toll spiritually and leaves non-
believers wondering about the reliability of our faith.

Like the artesian well, if we wish to remain steady regardless
of the season or circumstances, the supply is the key. And there's
no source so unlimitedly abundant, unchangingly reliable, unwaveringly trustworthy, and unshakably steadfast as Jesus, who is the
same yesterday, today, and forever. This is why it's so important
that we stay connected to Christ. When He guides and empowers
us through His indwelling Spirit, we can consistently produce love,
joy, peace, patience, kindness, goodness, faithfulness, gentleness,
and self-control regardless of the situation.

Jesus, You are my Source. Flow through me, my Savior. Amen.

The Gift Jesus Wants

*"He who has My commandments and
keeps them is the one who loves Me."*

JOHN 14:21

As you prepare for Christmas and purchase gifts for family and friends, you may spend some time considering what your loved ones would like to have. After all, you want them to enjoy the presents you buy them. But have you ever wondered what you could get God that would please Him? How can you show your love for Him? What does He want?

Some people believe that what God desires is for us to go to church, read His Word, share our faith, serve in various capacities, and give generously. And it's true—the Lord often calls us to these things. But what Jesus really desires is for our simple obedience to His commands. So we best show our devotion for Christ by walking in the will of God as revealed in His Word. We become His servants and represent Him well to others. And everything in our lives comes under His authority and is open to His guidance and transformation because our goal is to glorify Him.

There is no greater gift you give Jesus than to obey Him with all your heart, mind, spirit, soul, and strength. So submit to His clear and simple truth and express your love in the way that means most to Him.

Jesus, I love You, so I will obey You wholeheartedly. Amen.

He Is Your Adequacy

"The Lord is with you, O valiant warrior."
JUDGES 6:12

Gideon was in hiding, desperately trying to conceal his meager portion of grain from the Midianites who had invaded and were oppressing the Israelites. So when the angel of the Lord approached him and announced that God had chosen him to free Israel from their grasp, he was skeptical, scared, and fully aware of his personal inadequacy. Surely, God should pick someone else. "O Lord, how shall I deliver Israel? Behold, my family is the least in Manasseh, and I am the youngest in my father's house" (Judges 6:15). In other words, he was the least important member of a family of nobodies.

Have you ever felt this way—like you just don't measure up? As if there is nothing in you that's worthy for the Lord to use? Then realize God successfully worked through inadequate Gideon to do just as He promised—deliver Israel. And the Father says the same to you as He did to him, "Surely I will be with you" (Judges 6:16). The Lord doesn't choose you for what you can do but for what He can accomplish through you. He isn't interested in your self-evaluations; instead, He wants your submission and obedience. So today, don't make excuses. Obey Him like Gideon did and expect Him to succeed through you.

....

Jesus, You are my adequacy. I will obey whatever You say.
Amen.

Joy in Others

I thank my God in all my remembrance of
you, always offering prayer with joy.

PHILIPPIANS 1:3–4

Have you ever noticed that the letter Paul wrote to the Philippian church from the confines of his jail cell is remarkably upbeat? Although Paul mentioned his imprisonment, he didn't allow his chains to spoil his attitude. What's the reason for Paul's unshakable joy despite his terrible circumstances? Of course, it's his personal fellowship with the Savior. But it's also due to the wonderful relationships he'd developed with the believers in Philippi, which he gave God thanks for with gladness.

Throughout his ministry, Paul found abundant joy in serving others and watching them advance spiritually. We can too. Especially as we mature in the faith, we can experience a great deal of fulfillment when we allow God to minister to others through us. Watching them grow strong in the Lord can take on special meaning for us and give us significant joy because we know that we're building the eternal kingdom of God.

Do you want to grow in your own faith and increase your joy? Put the interests of others above your own and seek ways to help them mature in Christ. After all, Jesus "did not come to be served, but to serve" (Matthew 20:28). You're never more like Him than when you're ministering to others.

Jesus, thank You for working through me to draw others to Yourself. Amen.

Change Your Mind

*"The things that proceed out of the mouth come
from the heart, and those defile the man."*

MATTHEW 15:18

Most people don't realize how essential it is that they control their thoughts. They'll say, "I don't think about the sinful things that would compromise my relationship with God." However, they completely miss how much their ugly, critical, and bitter thoughts and feelings toward themselves and others impact their lives. We all view ourselves in light of what we believe to be true. So even if we subconsciously live by a negative belief system concerning who we are, then we will not experience all the joy and blessings Jesus has for us.

Therefore, my challenge to you is to refuse any negative or disparaging thought that arises about yourself or others. If your inner voice says you are unworthy or inadequate, look in the mirror and tell yourself, "I am a child of God, and He loves me just the way I am—end of discussion!" If some wrong comes to mind, reply, "I forgive them in the power and love of Jesus!" Change the way you think by replacing your undesirable, unconstructive thought patterns with God's Word. Because that is the way He will transform your life and make you more like Jesus. And that's certainly a subject worth thinking about.

*Jesus, identify my negative thoughts and replace them with
Your Word. Amen.*

Lay It Down

"I lay down My life."
JOHN 10:15

P erhaps you've heard about people who risked their lives to save others. At crucial moments, they disregarded their own safety and future to give someone else a chance at life. Their sacrifices appear to be extraordinary.

Yet this is the love Jesus demonstrated when He came to earth to die for your sins. For a time, He gave up the honor and glory that are due Him as a member of the Godhead to become a human being (Philippians 2:6–8). He did so for your sake, both to purchase forgiveness for your transgressions and to understand what it is like to be you. His goal was to break the power of the one thing that separates you from the love of God—sin.

You see, sin blocks God's love from flowing in your life. Before you receive Jesus as your Savior, your offenses completely prevent a relationship with the Lord. But after Christ redeems you, sin prevents intimacy with the Father. This is not because He rejects you but because you refuse to let Him be God in those broken areas in your life. But it's time to stop pushing away the One who sacrificed His life for you. Lay down your life and find freedom.

Jesus, help me to love and trust You more in every area. Amen.

Grateful Joy

You have been my help, and in the
shadow of Your wings I sing for joy.
PSALM 63:7

There are people whose circumstances give them good reason to complain and yet their attitude is surprisingly joyful. What is the key to their wonderful outlook? Gratefulness.

I remember seeing this principle in action one morning many years ago. I woke up discouraged, so I spent some time in God's Word. However, my mood was still heavy, so I decided to go to work even though it was still very early. Along the way, I went to a small drive-thru and ordered a biscuit. The elderly man who greeted me at the window was amazingly cheerful. His smile and bright countenance were infectious. As he handed me my food, I asked him why he was so happy so early in the morning. He said, "At my age, I don't take any day for granted. So I've made it a habit to always thank God for the gift of another day." I drove away encouraged, and I've never forgotten his positive words.

The person who keeps a grateful heart despite their circumstances has learned the secret of joy. So when you're gloomy, think of all the blessings the Lord has given you and praise Him. Because when you're thankful, gladness will certainly follow.

....

Jesus, help me to be the kind of person who always gives You
thanks. Amen.

Let God Choose

The LORD God is a sun and shield . . .
No good thing does He withhold from
those who walk uprightly.

PSALM 84:11

W hat is it that you long for with your entire being? Do you lay awake at night wondering how you can make it happen? Are you so caught up in pursuing it that you've failed to ask the Lord what He thinks about it all?

The wisest thing you can do is let God choose for you. This means putting the matter before Him in prayer and being honest with Him about your feelings but leaving the decision in His hands. After all, would the Lord give you anything less than what's best? Of course not. So isn't it better to let Him decide what's right for you—especially since He knows what will happen in the future?

You may be stressed out because you just don't know how to make your dreams come true. But God knows what you were created for and what will truly bring joy to your heart. So place your life into the hands of your omniscient, omnipotent, omnipresent Father, who will give you nothing less than His absolute finest. Because when you allow Him to supply your needs and desires, you'll find the peace that passes understanding and the contentment that satisfies your soul.

Jesus, thank You for always choosing what is best for me.
Amen.

Herald Him

"It is he who will go as a forerunner . . . to
make ready a people prepared for the Lord."
LUKE 1:17

Heaven had been silent for almost four hundred years. The word of the Lord had not been heard since the days of Malachi, and many generations had passed without a word. That was, until the angel Gabriel spoke to Zechariah about the upcoming birth of his son, John. God was about to send salvation through His Son, Jesus. To prepare, He made sure that there would be a person—John—who would herald Christ's arrival and help people understand the gift He was giving.

So how did John prepare the people for the Lord? He proclaimed a single, radical message: "Repent, for the kingdom of heaven is at hand" (Matthew 3:2). John helped people to understand they were sinful, but he also told them the good news that the forgiveness of their sins had come through Jesus.

We can learn from John because God now looks to us to testify that Christ has come. We can help people understand that their greatest sins, deepest wounds, and most profound hopes are answered in Jesus. So don't miss an opportunity to be like John. When you find someone seeking answers, point them to "the Lamb of God who takes away the sin of the world!" (John 1:29).

Jesus, help me to faithfully witness to those who are seeking
You. Amen.

God-Given Joy

God gives wisdom, knowledge, and
joy to those who please him.
ECCLESIASTES 2:26 NLT

A re you longing for genuine joy today? Then spend some time in dedicated, unbroken fellowship with Jesus. Be quiet. Be still. Listen to Him. And let the Lord speak to you through His Word. Joy is a fruit of the Spirit, and for it to be produced in you is a living, dynamic process whereby you're actively connected to Him. It is planted, nurtured, cultivated, and blooms as you walk with Him. This is why old memories and worldly pleasures may bring us some temporary, fleeting happiness but not abiding joy.

Of course, there may have been times when you've fellowshipped with the Lord but didn't notice any change—anxieties and burdens continued to weigh on you. If you sincerely ask God why this is, He will show you. He is in the life-transforming business, and your time with Him today lays the groundwork for His future work in your life. He may direct you to remove some spiritual "weeds" that are sapping your joy or to add what will nourish it. He knows what your soul requires to be replenished and will give you all you need to have ever-increasing joy. So spend time with Him, heed what He says, and expect Him to produce a harvest of joy in you.

Jesus, give me the joy that comes exclusively from You.
Amen.

No Mistake

When the fullness of the time came,
God sent forth His Son.
GALATIANS 4:4

It was no accident that night in Bethlehem when Mary and Joseph knocked on the innkeeper's door and heard the response, "No room." Born in a cave and laid in a manger—that's no way to enter the world. That is, unless you're a lamb. And, of course, Jesus Christ is the ultimate Lamb of God, who came to take away the sin of the world.

This is instructive to you today in your own challenges. The Lord makes no mistakes. There are details in your life that may make no sense to you right now. But if you'll seek the Lord's wisdom in it, you will see He is doing something extraordinary in your life.

Remember, Jesus' role as our Savior was foreshadowed for hundreds of years through the offerings of lambs made at the temple. Then, at the cross, He made the final sacrifice for the forgiveness of our sins, so we can have a relationship with the Father. Every detail of His life fits together to reveal God's beautiful orchestration of our redemption. So do not despair about the aspects of your life you don't understand. God knows what He's doing. And when the time comes, you'll rejoice at how specifically and perfectly He's provided for you all along.

....

Jesus, I trust You in all that You're doing. Amen.

With You

"They shall call His name Immanuel,"
which translated means, "God with us."
MATTHEW 1:23

Since creation, God has demonstrated a passionate desire to be with His people. He instructed Moses to build a tabernacle in the wilderness where His holy presence would dwell. Later, He commanded Solomon to construct a temple in Jerusalem where, again, His presence would abide in His people's midst. The Father's urge to be with us—in our lives, minds, hearts, and emotions— was fulfilled in the birth, life, death, and resurrection of Christ. Through Jesus, God was with us as never before—eating, speaking, healing, and teaching.

Today, God is with us in an even more intimate way, indwelling each believer through the abiding presence of the Holy Spirit. The Spirit imparts the very life of Christ to our souls, infusing our ordinary lives with the never-ending presence of God. The Father, in sending His Son and His Spirit, has accomplished His dearest plan—to dwell with us so that we can enjoy a relationship with Him for all eternity.

God is with you today. He is with you tomorrow. He is with you forever because *with you* is where He longs to be. You are not alone. Embrace the immeasurable gift of His everlasting presence this Christmas.

Jesus, thank You for being with me. I am overflowing with gratefulness to You. Amen.

Time to Rest

O God, restore us and cause Your face to
shine upon us, and we will be saved.

PSALM 80:3

E lijah was bone tired—body, mind, and soul. Fresh from clashing with the 850 false prophets on Mount Carmel, the prophet found himself on the run from the evil queen Jezebel, who was determined to have him killed. He fled ninety miles on foot to Beersheba. Finally, he was so completely drained that he despaired of life, sat down under a juniper tree, and said, "It is enough" (1 Kings 19:4).

Perhaps you understand Elijah. Maybe now that Christmas has come and gone with all its activities, visitors, gifts, cleaning, and complications, you find yourself completely exhausted and ready to declare, "Enough!" just as he did. Few conditions deplete our faith and joy more rapidly and completely than weariness. Thankfully, the Lord understands our limits and restores our souls.

Sometimes we need to follow Elijah's example, taking a step back from the situation and letting the Lord refresh us. We may need a physical break like a day away from work or from our burdens. But stopping from all our activities and taking time to simply be with the Lord can help clear our minds, give us perspective on our circumstances, and provide the energy to keep going in the days ahead. So sit down, rest, and be strengthened in the Lord.

Jesus, thank You for being my rest and restoration. Amen.

Sifted for Service

"Satan has asked to sift you like wheat. But I have prayed for you that your faith may not fail. And you, when you have turned back, strengthen your brothers."

LUKE 22:31–32 CSB

If you hope to serve God, expect to be sifted. This is a process much like winnowing wheat, which is thrown up into the air so the wind can carry off the chaff and separate it from the valuable grain. Peter experienced this kind of threshing the night of Christ's arrest when he denied Jesus three times. Although he'd previously promised to stay with Jesus even unto death, in those terrible moments after Christ's arrest, he realized how weak his faith really was.

The guilt and sorrow must have been terrible. He knew what it meant to fail at the worst possible moment and be so fearful as to even deny God. But because Jesus restored him, he also knew the joy and humble gratefulness that results from the Lord accepting us despite our failings. And that made him well prepared to minister to others.

This is the hope we have in Christ—even when we let Him down, He never gives up on us. So whenever the wind blows your world apart, let Him restore you. Because through that process, He's sure to make your life a blessing for others.

Jesus, make me into Your wise, faithful, obedient, and compassionate servant. Amen.

Check Your Spirit

Let us press on to maturity.

HEBREWS 6:1

Like physical growth, you can detect spiritual growth by looking back at where you've been and seeing where you are now. So if you ever want to check your progress, here are some things to look for.

Increasing awareness of sin. As you mature in your faith, you'll develop a keener sense of sin in your life—a sharper awareness of when your actions are not aligned with God's will. The closer you are to the Lord, the more cognizant you'll be of how you fall short of His holiness.

Intensification of spiritual battles. When you begin to wrestle with issues of obedience in everyday life, spiritual attacks may come from surprising places—even from people you thought supported you. You will learn how important it is to put on the spiritual armor of Ephesians 6.

Amplified desire to serve. The more you take hold of God's unconditional love, the more you'll want to share it with others.

Decreased desire to be critical. The more you are aware of your struggles and God's overwhelming grace for you, the less inclined you are to be harsh with others.

Don't take your spiritual maturity for granted. Make sure you continue to grow closer to Christ day by day and year by year.

Jesus, help me to make sure I'm growing more mature in You each day. Amen.

Keep Dreaming

I will hope continually, and will
praise You yet more.

PSALM 71:14

Keep dreaming. Trust God for the future and seek His goals for your life. A person who isn't motivated or inspired—who doesn't keep aspiring for more—is not going to enjoy life for very long. Of course, you may think, *At this point, I don't see anything to dream about.* Why? I understand that sometimes setbacks and limitations can be disheartening. But you still have life and potential in you. And what it comes down to is a matter of attitude—you've got to have hope and something to work toward.

So stop wondering why other people get along better than you do. Quit being mired in the past and what you can't accomplish. Consider the things you *can* do. Start thinking about what's possible. You're a child of God! You're indwelt by the Holy Spirit! The wisdom and power of the Lord are available to you! Don't live in the past, thinking about what you can't do. Don't write yourself off.

Give God the privilege of laying out your future. Trust the Lord to work in your life in the way He desires. And don't underestimate Him or yourself. You can do anything God calls you to do. So keep dreaming and expect Him to do great things.

Jesus, plant Your wonderful dreams in my heart and make them grow. Amen.

Rewarding Work

*We must all appear before the judgment
seat of Christ, so that each one may be
recompensed . . . according to what he has done.*

2 CORINTHIANS 5:10

All believers will be rewarded for their service to God on earth when they appear before Christ. That includes you. The key is not the scope of your work—where or to what assignment the Lord calls you is never the issue. Rather, what matters is your motivation. Are you serving out of love for God—to obey and please Him—or for some other purpose?

Colossians 3:23–24 admonishes, "Whatever you do, do your work heartily, as for the Lord rather than for men, knowing that from the Lord you will receive the reward of the inheritance. It is the Lord Christ whom you serve." If you're trying to gain wealth, prominence, or even salvation for yourself, or if you're attempting to please others, then your efforts are misplaced. But if your heart is bent toward God, and more than anything you want to hear Him say, "Well done, my good and faithful servant" (Matthew 25:21 NLT), then you're on the right track.

Remember, the rewards you get here on earth are temporary, but those you receive in heaven are eternal. So invest your life wisely by dedicating it to His use.

Jesus, teach me how to invest my life so I may honor You always. Amen.

Forevermore

*You will make known to me the path of
life; in Your presence is fullness of joy.*

PSALM 16:11

T oday, rejoice that God faces the coming days with you for-
evermore. He will move heaven and earth to show you His
will. When others accuse you wrongly or treat you shamefully, He
will vindicate you. When you sink in the mires of trouble, He will
set your feet on a rock. When people reject you, He will sustain you
with His everlasting love. When you fail, you can ask His forgiveness. When you grow weary, you can seek His strength. And when
every other source of security and provision fails, He "will supply
all your needs according to His riches in glory in Christ Jesus"
(Philippians 4:19).

So stay close to Him and put Him first in every area. There's
no life higher or better—with more complete fulfillment, contentment, and significance—save the one you'll receive when you arrive
at your eternal home in glory. And when you reach your destination
in heaven, you'll see His loving face and hear the wonderful words
that you've longed for: "Well done, My good and faithful servant."
Surely, that thought alone makes this journey of faith with Him
absolutely worthwhile. So trust Him for the coming year and praise
His holy name.

*Jesus, I exalt You! Thank You for always being with me
every step of the way. Amen.*